PATTERNS OF THE FUTURE

Understanding the Next Wave of Global Change

Markku Wilenius
University of Turku, Finland

Foreword by **Tarja Halonen**
Former President of Finland

NEW JERSEY • LONDON • SINGAPORE • BEIJING • SHANGHAI • HONG KONG • TAIPEI • CHENNAI • TOKYO

Published by

World Scientific Publishing Europe Ltd.
57 Shelton Street, Covent Garden, London WC2H 9HE
Head office: 5 Toh Tuck Link, Singapore 596224
USA office: 27 Warren Street, Suite 401-402, Hackensack, NJ 07601

Library of Congress Cataloging-in-Publication Data
Names: Wilenius, Markku, author.
Title: Patterns of the future : understanding the next wave of global change /
Markku Wilenius (University of Turku, Finland).
Description: New Jersey : World Scientific, [2017]
Identifiers: LCCN 2016049018| ISBN 9781786342874 (hc : alk. paper) |
ISBN 9781786342881 (pbk : alk. paper)
Subjects: LCSH: Social prediction. | Social prediction--Finland.
Classification: LCC HM901 .W549 2017 | DDC 303.49--dc23
LC record available at https://lccn.loc.gov/2016049018

British Library Cataloguing-in-Publication Data
A catalogue record for this book is available from the British Library.

Copyright © 2017 by World Scientific Publishing Europe Ltd.

All rights reserved. This book, or parts thereof, may not be reproduced in any form or by any means, electronic or mechanical, including photocopying, recording or any information storage and retrieval system now known or to be invented, without written permission from the Publisher.

For photocopying of material in this volume, please pay a copying fee through the Copyright Clearance Center, Inc., 222 Rosewood Drive, Danvers, MA 01923, USA. In this case permission to photocopy is not required from the publisher.

Desk Editors: Kalpana Bharanikumar/Mary Simpson

Typeset by Stallion Press
Email: enquiries@stallionpress.com

PATTERNS OF THE FUTURE

Understanding the Next Wave of Global Change

We are the consciousness of the world.
Awareness creates global reality.

–PENTTI MALASKA

CONTENTS

FOREWORD

The sustainable development goals adopted by the UN in the fall of 2015 and the connected Paris Climate Agreement are major accomplishments that many of us have worked very hard to reach. The 17 sustainable development goals encompass 169 more detailed sub-goals. Reaching the above-mentioned agreements was the single most important endeavor by the previous UN Secretary-General, Ban Ki-Moon and his staff. A new kind of working culture, or rather, simply culture, needs to be created in order to implement the goals in practice. Executing on the goals is indeed the most important task of the new Secretary-General, António Guterres and his advisers.

In order to succeed, genuine commitment and participation is required of the member nation governments. Even that by itself is insufficient: the desired results also call for citizen action and participation by the business community. Immediate action is needed in order to put the planet on the right path. I believe people are already aware how urgently we need to halt the global climate change, but reaching the rest of the goals doesn't allow for procrastination either. We are the last generation that can prevent a catastrophe — but we have the power to do it.

Each of the 17 sustainable development goals are important, but they are also interconnected. That is why it is equally important that we grasp not only the individual goals, but also the big picture. The major contrast to previous global agreements is precisely that we are now concerned with the environment, social equality and with the economy in the aggregate, as well as how they relate to each other.

Markku Wilenius explains clearly how deep and wide the change needs to be. He is very familiar with the developments in the past decades since the famous Club of Rome report, *Limits of Growth.* He has also collaborated with numerous hard-working sustainable development experts around the globe. Understanding history helps in analyzing the present and in constructing the future. It is very useful to become familiar with the Kondratiev wave theory. Markku Wilenius's text is not difficult for a novice and wakes new thoughts in even experienced minds.

Thanks to the work of scientists, we know much more today about the state of the world and about the ways to affect it than we ever did before. However, constructing a future that is sustainable requires each one of us.

H.E. Tarja Halonen
The former President of Finland

ABOUT THE AUTHOR

Markku Wilenius has worked over 20 years with futures studies, most of that time for Finland Futures Research Centre. He is Professor of Futures Studies for Turku School of Economics at University of Turku. He is also UNESCO Chair in Learning Society and Futures of Education. In 2015, he co-founded the Turku Complex Systems Institute at the University of Turku. In recent years, his research interests include understanding socio-economic long-term waves, the future of financial and forest industries, climate and energy politics and the future of non-hierarchical organizations. His latest project is the future of cities and communities. He is the President of two foundations. He has also worked for a number of years at Allianz, the world's largest private insurer, leading their strategic research and development. He is a member of the Club of Rome and has led the Finnish expert delegation in the Johannesburg Sustainable Development Summit. He has published several books and hundreds of articles on futures-related topics. Wilenius has lectured in all continents and given several interviews for international media. He lives with his wife and two sons in Helsinki.

ACKNOWLEDGMENTS

I wish to convey my gratitude to those in Finland and elsewhere in the world who have inspired me through the years to study the next era. Pentti Malaska, who has passed on, was my greatest inspiration. He was professor at Turku School of Economics and an international pioneer in Futures Studies. My colleagues at the Finland Futures Research Centre (founded by Malaska) have been priceless discussion partners. I'm especially grateful to Sofi Kurki, who has already participated in many of my research projects that have laid the foundation for this book, and with whom I made several research trips to Silicon Valley. During the many years I worked at the financial behemoth Allianz in Munich, I became acutely aware of the powerful idea of long economic cycles. I had the support of an international team helping me understand the next phase of globalization.

As chairperson for a few foundations that fund technology research, I've had an excellent vantage point that has helped me better understand the advancement in new technologies and innovation. I have gained perspective on the long industrial traditions in Finland through my family company, Ahlström. My partnership in Fibertus Oy has helped me appreciate the challenges in ambitious startup companies. Dozens of speaking engagements in Finland and elsewhere have forced me to adjust my views and allowed opportunities for discourse with all kinds of interesting people. My students at Turku School of Economics, studying in our international masters program for futures studies, are a constant source of inspiration.

I'm thankful for my colleagues and to my wide network in Finland and elsewhere in the world — many have become close friends. Attempting to list every person who has inspired me in the recent years would produce a list far too long. My projects in various sectors have allowed me to become acquainted with a wide group of outstanding personalities who are working in their own fields to create the society of tomorrow. I'm fortunate to have my family and a circle of friends with whom to toss around ideas while traveling, sailing, jogging, working out at the gym and enjoying fine beverages in restaurants.

I would like to thank Commissioning Editor Dr. Jane Sayers of World Scientific Publishing, United Kingdom for her marvelous and at times intensive support in the course of working on this manuscript. In-house editor Mary Simpson, also from World Scientific, has also helped me a lot on the way. Also, Ms. Kalpana Bharanikumar helped me patiently through the arduous book editing phase. I also extend my thanks to the Finnish publishing house Otava for publishing the earlier Finnish version; to Eva Reenpää and Irja Hämäläinen from Otava; and to my own colleagues Anne Arvonen and Krista Heinonen, who all helped me along the way. My second cousin Merit Kuusniemi did a great job translating the majority of the book. Laura Pouru, my multifunctional chief of staff, and Nicolas Balcolm Raleigh helped me greatly in polishing the manuscript. Christopher Ryan Jones carefully checked the English language, for which I thank him dearly. I am grateful for Brigitte Chernohorsky for her great comments.

Finally, I would like to thank my family. My wife, Aamu, has had to see her husband absorbed in writing this book on far too many weekends. I thank my father, Reijo, for our many fruitful conversations over the years. The energetic look in the eyes of my now-deceased mother has illuminated my path during tough times. Fammu, my paternal grandmother, left us this admonishing observation: “God doesn’t provide for the lazy.” I thank my sons for inspiring me; this book is mostly about their world, after all.

Markku Wilenius
Helsinki, the Daughter of the Baltic Sea
September 23, 2016

INTRODUCTION

Capitalism, the cornerstone of our industrialized society, is at a crossroads. It seems to be working in fits and starts. Everybody is yearning for innovation-driven and sustainable growth, but very few succeed in finding it. Simultaneously, environmental concerns, especially climate change, appear to erode the value created in the economy. Coal mines and oil companies have become destroyers of the environment from being creators of value. It is becoming ever more evident that the longer we wait to make changes, the more expensive the changes will become.

There are other reasons for the fitful economy besides environmental pressures. The market economy has always been founded on the principle that capitalist profits are reinvested in production. Growth in the industrial era was based on this. This cycle is showing signs of slowing down. The financialization of the economy means that profits remain with the owners — investments in production are lacking. There is stark statistical evidence, in fact. More than half of the profits of the S&P 500 companies are being used for stock buy backs.[1] It goes without saying that investing in R&D suffers as a result. Profits are not going to the employees either. United States household income has not grown in real terms from 1990 to 2014, although the gross domestic product (GDP) grew by 78% in the same time frame.[2]

Economic vitality is dependent on new information created from investing in new things. This in turn, makes it possible to find new opportunities. This is not a linear, but rather, an evolutionary process. Markets, technology, scientific progress, invention of applications, and in the end, investments, are created in interactive loops. In this interaction, the role of the public sector is at least as important as that of the private sector.

Marina Mazzucato, Professor at the University of Sussex, has systematically concluded in her research that while in the throes of austerity policies following the financial crisis, the public sector has not only lost its role as a flagbearer for R&D, but also its active role in R&D. She supports her claim with the fact that, contrary to popular belief, massive public investment has been behind the Apple and Google success stories. Public investment has in fact been completely indispensable for their global success.[3]

At the same time, the private sector share of investing in basic research has diminished. It is evident that the two activities — Research and Development — have to be in balance in order to create the right kind of ecosystem for innovation.[4] The shift in the wrong direction is a result of the shareholder thinking that has taken hold in the past few decades. It has led to short-term profit seeking and construction of new kinds of ownership models and structures to encourage that. The victory march of short-term capitalism culminated in the financial crisis, lessons of which have not been completely learned, it would seem.

We must acknowledge that short-termism is not some internal, natural phenomenon of the market economy. Short-termism can be mitigated in many ways: through fiscal and legislative measures that support industrial investment, and through setting of long-term political goals upon which to build governmental research and innovation policies. It is precisely the role of government to guide innovation.

However, our fundamental problem is our inability to learn from history. Professor Carlota Perez at the London School of Economics has studied the long cycles of the economy at length. She notes that without sufficient analysis of history, it is impossible to understand the dynamics of future progress, let alone predict it.[5] A systemic approach is required: that is the only way to understand the path of global capitalism from crisis to growth and back again to the bottom of the wave. Various feedback mechanisms in markets, technology and their applications, politics, science and investments create a combined structure. The change of one factor, such as the role of government as an investor, causes an inevitable shift in the dynamics of the structure.

Innovations don't come about by accident any more than the future does. They result from various intentions. The fifth wave of industrial society development ended with the financial crisis (see Figure 1) and we are now in the beginning of the sixth (see Chapter 3). The central question of the sixth wave is whether we can generate enough and very diverse innovations. That means new technologies and new business models, in other words, solutions that are based on more intelligent production, consumption, and distribution models.

Above all, the environmental stress caused by economic growth must be minimized so that the growth adds to our resources, rather than exhausting them. This pertains to the well-being of both the environment and humankind. The present growth model is unsustainable and causes more long-term harm than benefit. The economic structures must change to produce equal progress, not unemployment, inequality, climate change, and destruction of the biosphere, as is the case presently.[6]

Just as innovations do not come about by accident, the same goes for the future in general. As the famous economist Joseph Schumpeter noted decades ago when he created the theory of evolutionary economics, creative destruction is based on forces that tend to guide the economy towards disequilibrium and thus, any change is always path dependent. Paradigm shifts, where a technology or business model permeates the society and the economy, come in waves created by the dynamism of history.

We are in the midst of such a paradigm shift. New technologies, business models and new cultures arise from the creative destruction that originated in the distant past, but was crystallized in the financial crisis that started in 2008. How can we fix the above-mentioned fundamental flaw of the market economy which had led to short-termism, increased inequality and stagnated growth? How do we decarbonize our energy and production systems? How do we create conditions for cleaner and more productive technology? Where do we find patient capital that is needed to develop the budding innovations?

But above all, I seek to understand how the future can already be seen around us. How do we understand the future in light of historic developments? What are the signals from the future, and how should we interpret them?

We live in exciting times and shifting eras. This is why I wrote this book. Now is precisely the moment to see the forest for the trees and understand the whole that we are a part of. Moreover, this book is written for all those asking themselves two simple questions: What will the future bring, and what direction will society go from here? And perhaps also: How did we get to this point?

The basic goal of this book is to bring to the forefront the factors that significantly affect future development. But because many coming events have roots in the past, our aim is to understand the past just as much as we aim to understand the future. The message of this book brings together years of work in many different areas of research, education and developmental projects in Finland, Europe, Silicon Valley and elsewhere. It seems that the time is ripe for presenting it.

I have a method, a tool, with which to understand the past, the present and the future. This method helps to understand how societies repeat their cycles, and how, at the same time, they reinvent themselves. But most of all, the method helps us find an answer to what comes next, even if the answer isn't always perfect.

This is the basic premise: Contrary to common belief, societies do not advance at a steady pace. They also don't advance by leaps or just randomly. Rather, they function like the seasons: Spring follows winter and so forth. The basic rhythm of societal advancement is cyclic, just like in nature. The economic cycles are, however, significantly longer than nature's annual cycle: 40–60 years.

But in addition to being cyclical, societies also evolve. In each cycle, they resemble something quite different than in the previous. Thus, the previous cycle can't by itself predict the next one. There are naturally many factors involving change: technological development, changes in culture and values, economic and market development, political decisions, etc. They all shape our world and, increasingly, our environment.

Thus, each cycle is at once very much the same as and also quite different than the previous cycle. This model has repeated itself since the dawn of the industrial society some 200 years ago and repeats, as mentioned, in 40- to 60-year wave-like cycles. We are moving from one wave to another as we speak, and are currently headed into a new era: the sixth wave.

At the beginning of this new cycle, the old form remains, but the content is different. The primary engine for the fifth wave was digitalization, but something even more powerful is propelling the sixth wave. The purpose of this book is to describe the factors that contribute to the sixth wave, which will extend to the middle of this century. I will elaborate my theoretical framework in Chapter 3.

I analyze future world developments from many different aspects, such as what is happening geopolitically, where our economies are heading, what the state of our environment is going to be, how learning will be renewed, what kind of cultural forces are shaping our society and how human consciousness and the human mind develop in response to changes in society. Development is defined more and more often by technological leaps, which give wings to the human aspiration for a good life. The negative effects of new technology, however, are becoming more apparent: for example, automation and robots are taking over job functions at an increasing speed and there are concerns that iPads in kindergartens may inhibit children from developing through play.

I also present methods and foundations for futures studies. These help the reader grasp how we can — even with imperfect tools at our disposal — manage the future. It is through the use of these various sources of information that we can anticipate the factors that define the direction of our future.

We *futurists* — persons who study the future in order to help people anticipate coming changes — speak of knowledge about the future as a *visionary knowledge*. This is knowledge that combines our information about the past and present with our understanding of the nature of societal, economic and technological development. The product is a vision of the future society with all its complexity.

Even though I've worked in futures studies for a few decades, I don't claim to know the future. No one knows what it will be like. I can, however, give reasoned views on what the future could look like. No one can do more than that.

The name of the book is *The Patterns of the Future*, because **I want to send the reader's thoughts into the future**. Many futures researchers are mostly interested in technology. This book, however, is more focused on societal development. I've tried to explain my views simply but not by oversimplifying. We can't do much about the complexity of the world: My wish is to simply help the reader better understand it. If I succeed in doing that, then the mission of the book has been fulfilled.

So that the reader can understand the nature of futures studies, I will next shed some light on it. Contemplate for a moment the following description of futures studies:

> Futures studies can be mainly characterized as essential interdisciplinary cooperation to develop and adapt systematic scientific methods for evaluating future development trends, opportunities and options.
>
> In addition to creating foresight, which is the ideal result of empirical scientific research, futures studies also aims to identify alternative development goals and opportunities. This aim also firmly includes scientific analysis of the value-based goals of alternative action models.
>
> Futures studies not only aims to establish continuous historic development trends but also to analyze discontinuities, new phenomena and new structures that can be expected and their consequences. The underlying assumption is that it is possible to influence future choices by acquiring knowledge of future options.

The above definition is not mine but rather an extract from a report by the central scientific committee of the Finnish Academy that introduced futures studies into the academic scene in Finland in 1979. It is an excellent definition, and I believe it works to this day. Eventually, Finland Futures Research Centre was founded in 1992.

I joined four years later and have worked there ever since (except for a few short intervals).

Thus, futures studies were initiated in Finland, with only a small initial investment. The goals, however, were set high: to create a world-class cluster of academics working in futures studies. Something new was started within the Finnish academic field. It has now grown to an academic institution of more than 50 researchers, which is unique, even in the international context. There are very few academically orientated futures research centers in the world.

The creation and history of the Finland Futures Research Centre has meaning for the theme of this book. Getting started is the founding requirement for creativity and new thinking. Working as a futurist takes curiosity, looking at things with fresh eyes, questioning the old and deciding what to let go of.

The field of futures studies has many similarities with normal scientific activity, as well as a few differentiating characteristics. Although systematic and scientific analysis are common to both, what differentiates futures studies is its fundamentally interdisciplinary nature and its paradoxically unattainable object of research: the future.

The final justification for any scientific activity is to produce meaningful knowledge — in other words, to make reality understandable. Futures studies attempt to make the invisible, i.e., the future, visible.

The manner and methods of refining knowledge change throughout history, although slowly. Machine computing power continues to increase quite tremendously, as does the amount of help machines can offer us. It has been predicted that in a few decades, we will be unable to tell the difference between the thinking and speaking done by humans and by machines. Could this actually happen?

The most important resource, after all, is still the human, with his and her feelings, intentions and will. Can human behavior be predicted — and how? This was the dream of cybernetics as early as the 1970s; will this become possible in the future world, where machine intelligence increases along with computing power? The computing ability of the human brain is still one million times faster than that of a computer, but the situation could and likely will change in just a few decades. What happens when computers are actually more intelligent than the human brain?

We could say that the most challenging task and the overarching mission of futures studies is to understand change. How does something that has been impossible for 20 years suddenly become possible? How was it that so few could predict the collapse of the Soviet Union, the fall of the Berlin Wall and now the recent global financial crisis? *Why are we so poor at predicting change?*

This is, in fact, the basic premise of this book: how to understand, predict and anticipate change. This is the reason why futures studies, as a scientific approach and a source of knowledge, must be interdisciplinary in nature. In futures studies, information is sought from whichever scientific field is relevant to the current research topic. In other words, if we are studying the future of bicycling, we must understand technological advancement and, in this case, materials technology. But we must also understand the development of our ways of living (sociology), human geography (urbanization), development of businesses that exist in or around our physical environment (business economics) and so forth.

In addition, futures studies has to consider global trends. It has to understand how major trends influence local conditions. The recycling economy, or intelligent collection and reuse of materials, is a growing global trend. The European Union has made circular economy one of its key policy goals. Some countries, like Italy, have banned the use of plastic bags. And how to take that plastic out of oceans, where it is now the most common material? What's the point of shipping blocs of granite from Finland to China, to be shaped there into a refined form and then shipped back to Finland?

Another task of futures studies is to openly reflect upon our values. Is nuclear energy ethically acceptable and something upon which we ought to build our future? Futurists cannot hide under a cloak of neutrality but rather must recognize that all decisions involve the consideration of values. This also means that futures studies is participative and community oriented.

Futures studies is also fundamentally open to evaluating the philosophical basis of science. In other words, we must ask what our perception of reality is based on. *Fallibism*, an important aspect of standard scientific discipline — introduced by Karl Popper, a classic scientific historian — contends that scientific knowledge must always be adjustable in light of new observations. There is no reason to construct mausoleums for science.

We could thus argue that futures studies is focused on understanding dynamism and rapid changes in a world that is becoming ever more complex. In order to develop this understanding, we require methods that are on the one hand flexible enough and on the other hand sensitive enough. The history of research methods in futures studies — for example, scenario and Delphi methods — has its roots in the Cold War era, when the worst-case scenario could have seen complete nuclear destruction within a day's time.

We have been close to this scenario a few times. The true story goes that during the Cuban missile crisis, a Russian nuclear submarine crew member refused to obey an order to launch a nuclear missile and thus aborted the start of a disastrous nuclear war. In the language of futures studies, that moment of truth for that marine was a bifurcation point: a point where two globally very different trajectories for the future were possible. In fact, these Cold War conditions triggered the idea to develop the scenario method to understand the multiplicative effects of a possible nuclear war.

As will become evident later in this book, we also need long time periods and modeling in order to understand the overarching development cycles, i.e., the rhythmic character of the world, if you will. This has been a recent focus of mine. Life and reality on this planet — and, I gather, even throughout the rest of the universe — are rhythmic. It is this rhythm we must strive to understand. That is how the future is made palpable.

In conclusion, seeking to understand the future requires a rather large measure of utopist thinking, power of imagination and courage to disagree. This is what science fiction and fantasy literature traditionally offer up. It's enthralling to think that the future is even more wondrous than what we could have imagined, especially when we stretch our outlook a bit further. More than likely, 30 years ago nobody could have imagined the world we live in today.

Ilkka Tuomi, a very accomplished futurist, has provided an interesting description of the various methods of foresight based on his long experience at the Finnish company Nokia.[7] While working there in the 1990s, he realized that nobody could quite tell what was going to happen next in mobile phone development. The Nokia folks were taken by surprise each time, even though they themselves were part of creating that future. Tuomi calls this surprise an *ontological expansion*.

In plain language, this means that one can't deduce the future from the past. Additionally, what engineers design does not dictate the future application of that particular technology. For example, the first version of the internet, ARPANET, was built for communication between machines, not people. The technology behind text messaging was originally developed purely for receiving voice messages. Our views of the future will always neglect certain factors that nevertheless will play a crucial role in affecting the sequence of events and in creating for each technology its historically bound application.

Tuomi divides foresight into three ways of understanding the future. First is *probabilistic* foresight, which is based on probability and which is practically the sole method used in economics. This method represents the conceptualization of the future as a continuum of the past and is based on Newtonian physics; the accuracy of this type of foresight can be analyzed post-fact. In scientific language, probabilistic foresight is defined by epistemic, or informational, interest: We want to know as accurately as possible what the future will bring. It is founded on expectations, which in turn are based on historical facts.

The other approach is *possibilistic*. Practically speaking, this method involves thinking in scenarios: what kinds of different futures we can envision and what possible paths into the future we can imagine? For example, at the present time several alternative scenarios for the United Kingdom of 2030, after Brexit, can be constructed. We can imagine the present situation continuing where the United Kingdom drifts further away from Europe. But we can also imagine another referendum for a return to the European Union launched by the next government of the United Kingdom.

So we are speaking of possible worlds that aren't subject to probability analysis. The idea is to create a story or a narrative that helps us imagine all possible future scenarios. In futures studies, three to four alternative scenarios are often constructed in order to explore the various dynamics of the future. We don't get fixated on one particular scenario, and our approach is culture-based: We try to regard the future as a result of a host of choices that we make, either consciously or unconsciously.

If the first approach finds inspiration from Newtonian mechanics and the second from art and cultural research, the third is founded on living systems, or organisms. This can be called *constructivist* foresight. In this approach, the future isn't some distant land on the horizon but rather something that is constructed day by day. In other words, the future is formed and created. This is a prerequisite for a future that actually becomes what we have envisioned. This, however, requires tremendous number of trials and quick learning.

Living organisms, unlike human beings, have no long-term goals but rather an ability to adapt to whatever environment in which they find themselves. This kind of action can't be reduced to mathematical algorithms, nor does Turing's machine — the precursor to the digital computer — succeed in such a task. Thus, we're back to the concept of ontological expansion. It means that we prepare for a future that is different from what we had expected. Let's put this in practical terms: for a business, for instance, it means deep collaboration with clients and aiming to provide them with what they desire. In other words, a service business does not assume to know what that is; rather, they discover that together with the client. There is more on this topic in Chapter 7, where I discuss methods along these constructive lines at a company called Reaktor.

Even if at one given moment we can't imagine all the factors that will influence the future, we can nevertheless *create* the future. Many of the various technologies that came into use worldwide and which helped bring about the digital revolution, such as the personal computer, laser printing and the ethernet were created at the Xerox research center in Menlo Park, California. That kind of dissemination could hardly have been imagined by any of the engineers working at the research center.

All of this is as humbling as it gets, but it also illustrates how exciting it is to look into the future. "You reap what you sow" may be true, but how that happens is another matter altogether.

References

1. Lazonick, William. 2014. *Profits Without Prosperity.* Harward Business Review. Accessed September 23, 2016. https://hbr.org/2014/09/profits-without-prosperity.
2. Jacobs, Michael & Mazzucato, Mariana. 2016. Rethinking capitalism: An introduction. In: Jacobs, Michael & Mazzucato, Mariana (Eds.). *Rethinking Capitalism. Economics and Policy for Sustainable and Inclusive Growth.* Wiley Blackwell.
3. Mazzucato, Mariana. 2016. *The Entrepreneurial State.* London: Anthem Press.
4. Mazzucato, Mariana. 2016. Innovation, the state and patient capital. In: Jacobs, Michael & Mazzucato, Mariana (Eds.). *Rethinking Capitalism. Economics and Policy for Sustainable and Inclusive Growth.* Wiley Blackwell.
5. Perez, Carlota. 2016. Capitalism, technology and green global age: The role of history in helping to shape the future. In: Jacobs, Michael & Mazzucato, Mariana (Eds.). *Rethinking Capitalism. Economics and Policy for Sustainable and Inclusive Growth.* Wiley Blackwell.
6. Maxton, Graeme & Randers, Jørgen. 2016. *Reinventing Prosperity. Managing Economic Growth to Reduce Unemployment, Inequality and Climate Change.* Greystone Books.
7. Tuomi, Ilkka. 2012. Foresight in an unpredictable world. *Technology Analysis & Strategic Management*, 24(8), 735–751.

Chapter 1

WHAT IS REALLY GOING ON?

One most wonders about the future during uncertain times: the times when the global economy is hit by a recession; when people get laid off and fired from their jobs; when economists spread gloom and give their analyses with very serious faces; when newspaper headlines are all negative; when people don't buy homes and when they curb their spending. There is less concern about the future when global matters seem to roll along on their own accord and there seems to be certainty that there *is* a future.

It is precisely during the bad times that one should be thinking about the future. This is because thinking about the future can lead to useful analysis about *what* can be changed and *how* one can change it. Looking into the future can mean reanalyzing or evaluating options. Being stuck in the past seems to be a particular problem facing humankind. Reality is a combination of the past and the future that has been condensed into the present. Reality is not contiguous and simplistic but rather requires various perspectives in order for its nuances and shades to be illuminated.

The desire to see into the future is part of human nature, and for as long as civilized cultures have existed, there have been visions of what's to come. Plato's state was perhaps the first idealized vision of a future society. That tells us how far back in history humankind began looking into the future. The Greek philosophers essentially created the spiritual roots for Western science and thinking.

At the end of the day, we are faced with the fact that we don't know anything about the future. It's a secret world. But could we predict the future when we identify the factors that affect it? Possibly.

It's a fallacy to think that one can predict the future with exactness, as chance plays an important role in all events. Quantum physics tells us that particles can simultaneously appear as waves and as separate particles, which tells us that there are also no scientific grounds to believe in a distinctly defined future.

The history of humankind shows us that amidst steady development, abrupt changes suddenly disrupt society and everyday life. How predictable are such changes? For example, who could foresee how much mobile technology was to change daily life? It's now hard to even imagine a world without mobile phones, although it's hardly been 20 years since they first appeared in our lives.

Humans are characterized by the skill to easily adapt to new situations. Evolution has probably strengthened this characteristic and has in part ensured the success of the human race. We currently need this ability more than ever.

The relationship between humans and the future has remained largely unchanged for many millennia. In other words, we've remained unchanged since the origins of advanced civilization in Mesopotamia. The development of cultures requires a dialogue between human beings, and nature: we have molded the environment in countless ways by sowing the land, using forests for timber and by fishing the oceans. Every action shapes the future in some way, but some actions have a more significant impact than others.

The breadth of our effect on our own environment is new. In early history, human action had at most a local effect, with hardly any global impact, but all that has now changed. Paleontologist Tim Flannery describes this change by calling man *the disrupter*, who through technology has accelerated natural selection by an order of magnitude of 10.[1] This has created a whole new direction for cultural evolution.

Thus far, planet Earth's major milestones have been asteroid crashes, sudden climate change and the resultant mass extinctions. Such disruptions have been numerous throughout history, but for the first time the disruption is being caused by a conscious or even self-conscious being: humankind.

Humankind has domesticated planet Earth and enslaved most of its resources in order to satisfy our needs, which, also for the first time, will have global consequences. From the perspective of cultural evolution, this is a completely new situation.

The late futurist Pentti Malaska, spoke of the need for global record keeping.[2] The Thirty Years' War in the 17th century initiated the keeping of statistics. It was then that the first nation-states started to develop and which, for instance, created the need for population censuses. The same principles that have guided the analysis of national resources should encompass the entire planet. These would allow a clear understanding of the actual impact humankind has on its environment. These kinds of statistics, however, are in their infancy.

Naturally, we do know some things already. For example, we know that humans already use about half of the entire amount of energy consumed by nature, which is mostly consumed in photosynthesis. However, the amount of energy produced by humans is only about 0.000001% of the amount of renewable energy produced by the sun.[3] So everything is relative. Compared to the sun, humankind is a minor factor.

Because the scale is changing from local to global, our perspective also has to change. Growth is still largely measured against goals: how much more economic growth or exports we require, for example. At the same time, we must find new ways to understand the global nature of progress, which is best done by developing analytical tools.

One could argue that it's easy to predict the future based on current knowledge: i.e., the prognosis is bad. Global climate change seems to be unstoppable, and the future is about to become unmanageable due to an increasing scarcity of resources and an explosive increase in pollution. This is what the situation looks like from a long-term global perspective.

On the other hand, we've never had as many means to change the direction of our societies — not just technological but also political and cultural means. It's thus useful to reexamine events from 100 years ago: What did the world look like then?

There were at most 50 nation-states 100 years ago. Among them were few — mostly European — giants, some of which could even be called *imperiums.* The relative "backwardness" of China, India and Turkey at that time emphasized the ruling position of Europe. Everything seemed possible during the *Belle Époque.* That is, until from small tinder a vast war broke out, lasting almost 30 years. Even though Europeans did their best to destroy each other in two world wars, the development in the region dominated global progress, including that of the United States. This can be attributed just as much to the weakness of the rest of the world as to the excellence of Europe.

That world seems quite distant now. Back then nation-state thinking was at its strongest, and use of military force was quick-triggered. Nation-states are now waning, although their power has not completely vanished. Use of military power is constantly decreasing and other forms of power, especially economic, are gaining importance. In the world of 100 years ago, borders and time were important. Many boundaries have now disappeared: In Europe, many of the national currencies have been replaced by a supranational currency, and both goods and people cross borders much more easily. Things at a distance affect those nearby. Planet Earth has become flat in a sense that we can easily reach almost anyone by digital means of communication, irrespective of their whereabouts. There are currently 4.6 billion mobile phone users and the number is growing rapidly.[4] Nations, organizations and citizens have become more intimately networked. The virtual world has quickly become almost as vast and complex as the real world. The financial economy continues to grow much faster than the real economy.

These new networks are most often not tightly managed. What do Brazil, Russia, India, China, and South Africa (BRICS) countries have in common? Not much, except for being in a different stage of development than other Western nations. "BRICS" as a term was coined by the banking institution Goldman Sachs, and its use has spread globally, even though we're not dealing with a constellation of countries that would have rather uniform structures, goals and values (such as the Nordic countries, for instance). However, what is important to understand about the BRICS nations, is that all of them — with the exception of the latecomer South Africa — have global ambitions. This common denominator has given them reason to become political allies and thus become more than a simple term to define a market.[5]

It's clear that the era of Western dominance is more or less over. The world is becoming increasingly multipolar. Geopolitically, the next era will differ radically from the past era of Western dominance. However, the United States, no more than Europe, will not disappear from the world map as a result. The result will be something quite different. A lot depends on the preservation of Western unity and mutual trust. How much will Europe and the United States stick together — or will one or both form key alliances elsewhere in the world? Europe has gained a lot from its connection to the United States; history teaches us that much. Fatal consequences followed the one time that Europe forgot that connection, and one only has to consider what happened to Europe after World War I to understand how vital cooperation really is. During World War II, the United States came to the rescue at the last possible moment, when Germany had all but claimed victory over Great Britain. Even if the real reason for United States to enter the war was the attack of Japan on Pearl Harbor, its support helped Europe out of the impasse it had driven itself into.

Nowadays, it may be fashionable to think that the United States is on a major downward slide and that there's no point in focusing on its direction. Asia is growing fast; everything new and interesting starts there. This thinking bears to be criticized for several reasons.

First, even though the United States is no longer "young" and Europe no longer dictates the global pace, they comprise a pair that shares many values and practices. *Second*, neither has a more credible or reliable partner elsewhere. Europe can't become allied with Russia any more than with China. This of course also applies to the United States. At the end of the day, Europe and the United States only have each other. *Third*, there are signs that the strongest growth period in the BRICS countries is about to end: their performance in the last decade was much stronger than what it is so far in the current decade.[6] The gross domestic product (GDP) of Russia has dropped massively in the last years: The year 2015 brought them back to 2007, while it was almost double only two years earlier, in 2013.[7] At the same time, voices calling for a stronger democracy and more attention to escalating environmental problems, including risks related to the use of nuclear power, are becoming more pronounced. Simultaneously, pressure for democracy in China is ever increasing. The leaders of this country must face the fact that their newly rich middle class — not to mention the elite — may not tolerate pseudodemocracy in the future the same way they still do today.[8] India, on the other hand, is plagued by a lack of efficiency created by a period of strong socialism. Its institutions are archaic and can no longer meet the demand for flexibility required by the networked world of today. Brazil is struggling to pay for the welfare state it created in the last decade. Despite its advancements, South Africa has regressed since its success in the post-apartheid years.

Even though China has become another superpower, its GDP per capita trails far behind that of Albania and is not even a fifth of that of Finland. China has a long road ahead, and it doesn't possess even a theoretical chance to reach the Western standard of living with its present consumption model (see Chapter 4). Not to mention the fact that already by now, due to massive economic growth, China's environmental problems have mounted to an intolerable level: the air pollution in Beijing, for instance, has given it the nickname "airpocalypse". Groundwater supplies in most of the cities are classified as "bad or very bad". More than a fourth of the rivers are categorized as "unfit for human touch". China has become the world's largest emitter of greenhouse gases.[9] The economic growth China has experienced already bears a massive price tag.

On the other hand, it's difficult to find the kind of leadership the world yearns for, especially among Western leaders. After a strong start, President Barack Obama's impact on world politics has proven disappointing. Europe has shriveled in its own economic hardship and even its strongest representatives — Germany being the case in point — provide solutions that are not visionary but rather practical. The "golden years" of the last decade (2003–2007) of strong economic growth have become a mere memory as Europe strives to get back on its feet after a carefree accumulation of debt. At the same time, the United States is recovering from the financial condition it was left in by a Republican administration and ultra-liberalist chairman of the Federal Reserve Alan Greenspan. And now Americans have elected a new President, Donald Trump, who will add tremendously to the uncertainty of the world.

Everything is ready for a new era.

But the new era can't begin before enough of the old has been cleared away. This is especially true of the economy. The economy has become a modern Minotaur, holding the world in a state of terror and causing the suffering and death of numerous victims. Exploitation of natural resources has created enormous amounts of pollution and endangered the world's ecosystems. The endless goals and skills of greedy bankers to create huge fortunes have poisoned the general atmosphere.[10]

One must also remember that, more than ever, economic initiatives and new enterprises are needed, particularly in old Europe. They create the well-being necessary for people to self-actualize. Without industriousness and entrepreneurship operating at a much more vigorous level than before, it is simply not possible to support the present state of the welfare society.

A new kind of business thinking is gaining ground that highlights corporate responsibility and sustainability. The pioneer of this thinking, Yvon Chouinard — founder of outdoor clothing maker Patagonia — has said:

> Our planet is warming up because of our own actions. Despite all the knowledge about it, we refuse to take the necessary steps in order to solve the problem. At Patagonia we've started to get prepared for a more local economy. A global economy based on cheap transportation is not sustainable. We must stop using non-renewable energy sources and start to manufacture recyclable clothing. We are taking these steps at Patagonia so that we don't follow the path of the American auto industry and become victims of nonchalance, greed and laziness.[11]

There are other corporate leaders who seem to support this kind of ethos. In January 2016 at World Economic Forum, some key food conglomerates — like Nestlé, Tesco, and Unilever — agreed to start serious efforts to halve global food waste. At present, the level of waste is intolerably high at one third of total production — a major leap in sustainability would result if the waste could be significantly reduced.[12] For companies like Nestlé, that has a very dubious track record in terms of negligence regarding human rights and environmental hazards, these types of initiatives may show a way towards more civilized and ethically tenable business practices.[13] Finnish CEO Mika Anttonen has remolded the gasoline retailer ST1 into a company engaged in developing alternatives to fossil fuel by offering ethanol at his gas stations. This ethanol is made out of organic waste and lends itself well to Northern climates.[14] I believe this type of movement is barely in its infancy and ready to boom in the coming sixth wave. But this does not happen easily: ultimately it depends on how capitalist economic and business practices start changing, as Naomi Klein has recently rightly pointed out.[15]

In this book, I look at one economic–societal era changing into another. I base my study on the theory of long cycles — in other words, the concept that ever since the industrial revolution, the modern world economy has developed in 40–60 year cycles. During each cycle new technologies, practices, professions and ways of life surface. The fifth wave, now ending, has ridden on the tremendous growth of information and communications technology. The sixth wave will bring along technologies that will enable more efficient use of all resources — materials, energy, money, and human power. Digital technology will still have a huge significance in this new era, because it enables the practices that reduce the consumption of materials and energy.

The theory of the long cycles, I believe, gives a more solid foundation for anticipating the future (see Chapter 3). The evolution of humans, organizations and nations is similar to evolution in nature, where one can also see cycles such as that of the seasons. Thus, we can compare the development of railroads to the development of the virtual world. In every historical era, the content changes but not the form.

The reason we are now in the beginning of a new era is to a large extent connected to the development of markets and economic principles. Asia in general and China in particular have contributed tremendously to the reshaping of global markets. This in turn made — in the first decade of this century — raw materials and commodities more expensive than at the end of the previous century. In recent years, we have seen falling prices of commodities and oil due to the global economic downturn, China's excessive production of some key commodities and Saudi Arabia's serious interest in shaking up the oil market. In the long run, however, scarcity and price necessitate the minimization of these factors in production and, hence, in consumption.

On the other hand, the results of pollution and of the exploitation of natural resources are becoming more and more visible. The regularity of the monsoon rains in Asia is a thing of the past, the ice cap on the North Pole is dramatically reduced each summer and fish harvests everywhere are diminishing. Humankind has tampered with the biosphere's thermostat, and median temperatures are rising in various parts of the globe. Scientific knowledge about this is more and more solid.

Humankind is claimed to be a rational being. If this is true, awareness of the breadth of our environmental problems will embolden the growing uprising of the populace. Societal structures offer us two options by which to exert influence: voting and consuming. Nowadays every political party has an environmental agenda. Consumption of ethical goods will increase, despite the additional effort and cost that such products require.

While I sketch out a new era in this book, I also try to explain some of how futures research is conducted. The last 30 years have brought about massive changes: In 1985, the Soviet Union still existed and the Cold War prevailed. There was no email, and in the airport lounges and waiting areas, people were reading books and not flicking through their mobile phones, iPads or laptops.

In the future, the behavior of people in the lounges will change again, but exactly how, it is hard to say. To accurately predict the future is impossible. Even if we could accurately predict future technologies, we couldn't accurately predict how they will be used. We do know that technology will be increasingly integrated into our daily lives, and that in the future we'll have lots of it, not just on our skin but also under it. The gauging of our health is developing with ever-increasing sophistication of equipment that measures our physical condition. With leaps in the development of diagnostics, treatment of diseases also improves. Wind, solar, and wave technologies will become routine means of energy production, and buildings will start to produce their own energy.

The habits and values of people will also change. Respect for nature will increase, and people will want to experience an authentic and direct connection to their environment. In the future, spiritual matters and experiences will perhaps no longer be regarded as weird but understood by everyone and considered to be a natural part of our world. Most likely old social structures and classes derived from previous centuries will disappear as new ones will rise. New political parties will appear on the scene and some old ones will die, together with the baby boomer generation. It will no longer be self-evident for a young adult in the West to get a driver's license.

In 40 years, people will wonder how we could possibly have lived like we do now, just like we now wonder how we could have lived before personal computers and smartphones came along.

It is possible to discuss and foresee the future even though we do not know what exactly is going to happen. It is not just a web of random occurrences but is rather a complicated puzzle that one can perceive when one can see enough pieces of it. So it is my intention to offer my readers a tool or, in today's terms, a user interface with which to orient towards the future.

References

1. Flannery, Tim. 2010. *Here on Earth: A Twin Biography of the Planet and the Human Race.* London: Penguin Books.

2. Malaska, Pentti. 2010. *Planetary Statistical Service.* Helsinki: Futura.
3. *Ibid.*
4. Statista — The Statistics Portal. 2016. "Number of mobile phone users worldwide from 2013 to 2019." Accessed September 9, 2016. http://www.statista.com/statistics/274774/forecast-of-mobile-phone-users-worldwide/.
5. Stuenkel, Oliver. 2015. *The BRICS and the Future of Global Order.* Lanham: Lexington Books.
6. Euromonitor International. 2013. "The BRICs are More Important than Ever to the Global Economy." Accessed September 9, 2016. http://blog.euromonitor.com/2013/08/the-brics-are-more-important-than-ever-to-the-global-economy.html.
7. The World Bank. 2016. "Russian Federation." Accessed September 9, 2016. http://data.worldbank.org/country/russian-federation.
8. Daniel Bell's interesting insight in: The Atlantic. 2015. "Chinese Democracy Isn't Inevitable." Accessed September 9, 2016. http://www.theatlantic.com/international/archive/2015/05/chinese-democracy-isnt-inevitable/394325/.
9. Council on Foreign Relations. 2016. "China's Environmental Crisis." Accessed September 9, 2016. http://www.cfr.org/china/chinas-environmental-crisis/p12608.
10. Luyendijk, Joris. 2015. *Swimming with Sharks: My Journey into the World of the Bankers.* London: Guardian Faber.
11. Chouinard, Yvon. 2005. *Let My People Go Surfing: The Education of a Reluctant Businessman.* London: Penguin Books.
12. Sustainable Brands. 2016. "Nestlé, Tesco, Unilever CEOs Among 'Champions 12.3,' Determined to Halve Global Food Waste." Accessed September 9, 2016. http://www.sustainablebrands.com/news_and_views/waste_not/sustainable_brands/nestle_tesco_unilever_ceos_among_champions_123_determine.
13. ZME Science. 2015. "Why Nestle is one of the most hated companies in the world." Accessed September 9, 2016. http://www.zmescience.com/science/nestle-company-pollution-children/.
14. Focus on Finland. 2016. "Solutions for a healthier planet — Biofuel boom driven by ambitious tragets." Accessed September 9, 2016. http://focus.finland.fi/biofuel-boom-driven-ambitious-targets/.
15. Klein, Naomi. 2014. *This Changes Everything. Capitalism vs. Climate.* Simon & Schuster.

Chapter 2

THE PAIN AND THE THRILL OF UNCERTAINTY

Uncertainty, risk and chance events are an integral part of the human world. It is highly interesting to consider just how important chance or random phenomena have been at various turning points in history and in the lives of ordinary people. Although the advancement of industrial society has given us greater control over many risks, the growing complexity of societies has also increased the possibility of chance events. This chapter contemplates what is needed in order to achieve successful risk management in the future.

The insurance industry has a simple definition of risk: probability multiplied by economic damage. The greater the potential damage caused by a risk, the smaller the probability of it occurring. Insurance policies became an important tool of risk management in the increasingly complex society of the 20th century. The greater risk to the insurance company, the greater the cost.

However, the cost of the risk can only be assessed if the risk is known. If the risk is not known, conditions turn more perilous. For instance, the links between asbestos and cancer were not understood until the 1970s, when the use of asbestos for building insulation was at its height. In other words, building contractors and insurance companies had no idea of the risk they were dealing with. When the problem was finally recognized and then accepted, insurance companies had to pay for their "ignorance" and fork out huge sums in compensation. They had had no way of calculating the cost of the risk.

It is considered a measure of prudent risk management that more and more future phenomena are assigned a probability greater than zero. This is primarily because the complexity of various systems is almost inevitably set to increase with the development of society.

Does this sound familiar? Many people already find the bureaucracy of the European Union, for instance, unbearable. This brings us to a critical point as far as risk management is concerned: Risks can only be managed when their probability can be assessed. The key question with respect to future risk management is whether it is possible to keep the system simple enough. History tells us that without a conscious and determined effort, this cannot in fact be done.[1]

It is easier to tolerate and understand uncertainty and chaos if one can detect some underlying rhythm to it all. Mathematicians identify two extremes in events: *periodic* events, which recur with striking regularity, like a pendulum in a grandfather clock; and *aperiodic* events, which are unique and random, like a bundle of oil-coated spaghetti on a plate.[2]

Observing life around us, it's not hard to see that pretty much all events fall somewhere between these two extremes of periodic and aperiodic events. This seems to involve some degree of regularity: We get up every morning and in the evening go back to bed again. Our everyday experience tells us that almost everything that was yesterday is also today.

But not everything. Sometimes major surprises arrive all of a sudden and we are perplexed. Who could foresee the fall of Soviet Union, the 9/11 event, the financial crisis, the coming of the internet, Facebook? You can go on with this list *ad infinitum*. The answer is: hardly no one. Similarly, in our personal lives: you may win in a lotto or have a heart attack — both would most likely come as a surprise.

An example of an event at the aperiodic end of the continuum is the 2011 earthquake in Japan, which changed the life of the entire nation. This is an extreme phenomenon that does not fit in with prevailing conceptions of normal events. For this reason, it is extremely difficult, if not impossible, to predict such an event. In other words, it is at once highly unlikely but nonetheless possible. The same goes for the sequence of events following the earthquake. If the Fukushima nuclear plant had been better protected, Japan would have been spared at least one dramatic event — the melting of the plant's fuel rods.

One fundamental question, of course, is whether it is possible to predict extreme phenomena. Nassim Taleb says in his book *The Black Swan* that it is impossible to predict extreme phenomena, even if there may subsequently be several explanations for *why* something happened.[3] However, this in itself is a post-mortem analysis of "impossible" events or an exercise in psychologizing events.

Events always have some context, i.e., some environment in which they happen. Yet, sometimes a random variable enters into every scene, sending an event veering off the normal course of things. The scope of possible events is determined by the ever-changing environment. An extreme phenomenon is one where a random variable from outside the context enters the scene. The random variable does not follow any known structure or pattern and therefore cannot be predicted.

However, this does not mean that all events are equally probable. Events may indeed have different probabilities. While some events are more probable than others, a random variable may appear to mix things up, even if beforehand this may have seemed impossible or at least highly improbable.

Extreme phenomena create a situation where there is no information or no model on which to make forecasts or calculate probabilities. On the other hand, these phenomena lead us into a world where an increasing number of possible phenomena must be assigned a probability, no matter how small.

Chance Events Spew Destruction

Let us examine the earthquake in Japan a little closer and see what sense there is to what was said above.

On March 11, 2011, Japan was struck by a 9.0 magnitude earthquake, which was the most powerful quake ever recorded in the country. No one knew to expect it. Scientists are unable to predict individual earthquakes, and they don't yet know the geological signs of an imminent one.

What they can do is assign some probability to an earthquake in certain regions. According to the United States Geological Survey, there is a 38% probability that in the next 30 years, the southern California area will experience a 7.5-or-higher magnitude earthquake. The probability that this will happen next week is 0.02%. That's the best they can do.[4]

The key here is that despite the scientists' best efforts, there is no model, method or signal for predicting the occurrence of an individual earthquake. They have studied changes in electromagnetic radiation, increases in radon concentrations, foreshocks occurring before the actual seismic event and changes in animal behavior. Although all of these have been detected ahead of some earthquakes, these things may also happen even if there is no earthquake.

In other words, none of these signals can actually *predict* an earthquake. As long as this remains the case, it is impossible to locally predict a specific earthquake event. This is why each and every major quake is a surprise of some order. However, it is quite possible that in the years ahead, scientists will succeed in developing a reliable forecasting method. In the United States, National Aeronautics and Space Administration (NASA) scientists are looking at the occurrence of unusual electromagnetic signals preceding major quakes, the theory being that compressions in rock can lead to the formation of positive electrical charges in the earth. This, it is thought, could form the basis of an early warning system.

In this example, natural events or natural catastrophes are one variable that is hard to control. Another one is the way society reacts to the disaster. Just over one year after Fukushima, the commission appointed by the Japanese Parliament to investigate the accident concluded that it was both a man-made and natural disaster in equal parts.[5]

The reason for this conclusion was, firstly, that even though the earthquake was exceptionally strong and 9.0 magnitude quakes have been measured very rarely, these kinds of giant quakes have already happened on two occasions in this century prior to Fukushima: in Sumatra (2004) and Chile (2010). The earthquake itself was exceptional but not unprecedented. Even before Fukushima, poor preparations and slow rescue efforts following the violent earthquake in Kobe in 1995 had alerted the Japanese to just how ill-prepared they were for an earthquake affecting the city center.

Secondly, the 14-meter-high tsunami generated by the earthquake easily washed over the 5.7-meter seawall at Fukushima. This last line of protection was no match for the violent force of the tsunami.

The problem is that hardly anyone foresaw this kind of accident. When the tsunami came to shore, seawater flooded the plant's backup cooling system and because there was no electricity, the emergency cooling system did not start up. Ultimately, the sequence of events spun out of control both because the owners of the nuclear power plant had not anticipated such a scenario and because the regulatory authorities had not required them to do so.

In hindsight, the Fukushima accident could have been avoided if a few conditions had been met:

(1) If there had been an awareness that an earthquake of this magnitude may happen and simulations of the possible consequences of such an earthquake had been made. However, this possibility was disregarded and therefore no attempt was made to assess the direct and indirect impacts of such a disaster on critical infrastructure such as nuclear power plants.
(2) If there had been tools to predict that the quake would be hitting this specific location. However, no tools were available to predict a local earthquake and it therefore came as a complete surprise.
(3) If there had been a swift and effective rescue operation. Instead, the response came too slowly and important information was held back. Furthermore, power plant employees had received no instructions on how to react in this kind of scenario.

For this reason, the accident eventually reached mammoth proportions.

(4) If there had been an awareness that something like this could happen. The willingness to prepare for surprising and extreme yet wholly possible situations was just not there — and this was the most extreme situation of all. The International Atomic Energy Agency (IAEA) classified the Fukushima disaster at the highest level of nuclear accidents. The human, social and economic effects of the disaster are almost unimaginable.

In a world of uncertainty, the only possible salvation is to prepare for any and all eventualities and to mount an immediate response. This is not what happened in Japan. The experts had some idea of the risks nuclear power plants pose, but ordinary citizens were not even aware of such risks. They were not discussed in public. The slow response in the wake of the accident and the withholding of information worsened the situation considerably.

In this regard, a report commissioned by the Japanese government is scathing in its assessment: "It is absolutely unforgivable that a nuclear accident cannot be managed on grounds that a significant event such as a tsunami exceeds expectations."[6] The report commissioned by the Japanese Parliament, for its part, observed that the accident at the Fukushima nuclear power plant "cannot be regarded as a natural disaster. It was a profoundly manmade disaster — that could and should have been foreseen and prevented." In the end, it was ruled that the cause of the accident was willful negligence: "The government, the regulatory bodies and the operator of the power plant should have recognized their responsibility to protect people's lives and society. They effectively betrayed the nation's right to be safe from nuclear accidents."[7]

The 2011 earthquake in Japan alone would have been a huge shock to the country, but since it turned into a man-made nuclear accident, it serves as a crude awakening to the risks created by technology. Nuclear power is a particularly good example because it is the first widely used technology in the marketplace that involves such severe risks that in Finland, for instance, individual insurance companies or even insurance conglomerates would not be prepared to cover them.

So what role did chance play in all of this? Why did the Fukushima nuclear meltdown happen in March 2011?

Ultimately, it was not really a chance event. To suggest that the accident was simply a chance event would be to attribute the blame to instances (such as "nature") that don't deserve to be blamed. As was pointed out earlier, societies have a tendency to become more and more complex. This increasing complexity should be matched by the development of a corresponding management system. Failure to keep the two aligned is bound to lead to problems in compatibility. One such problem exploded in March 2011 and changed the future course of an entire nation. It is no coincidence that something that has been considered impossible becomes possible: It is simply a case of not being prepared for such an eventuality. The only element of chance involved was perhaps the timing of the accident.

It's also not a matter of chance what people know and don't know. The only possible element of chance is how we *react* to knowing or not knowing. Before the United States invaded Iraq in 2002, Secretary of Defense Donald Rumsfeld was asked at a press conference whether there was any evidence that Saddam Hussein was indeed providing support for al-Qaeda. Rumsfeld had this cryptic answer:

> "There are known knowns. There are things we know we know. We also know there are known unknowns. That is to say, there are some things we do not know. But there are also unknown unknowns — the ones we don't know we don't know."[8]

Rumsfeld's reply offers an interesting insight into the way that people can think about what they know. He is probably trying to convey the veiled message that, at the time, the United States did not really know about Saddam Hussein's links to terrorists. There were people in the United States administration who thought they knew, but they didn't know for sure and couldn't admit this.

For the Japanese authorities, the Fukushima nuclear accident was a case of unknown unknowns. It was not understood that they *should have known* about the possibility of such a disaster. And since they didn't understand it, they invested no effort in trying to plan and decide in advance what should be done in the event of such a disaster. We must remind ourselves that Fukushima occurred less than 20 years after the Kobe earthquake.

Fukushima disregarded contingency theory, which has been developed from systems-thinking in the past few decades. Contingency theory posits that organizations should be as open a system as possible and constantly weighing alternative futures. In the case of Fukushima, the possibility of this kind of risk had been consciously excluded from the range of possible events. A nuclear accident had become an "unknown unknown," even though the risk should clearly have been known. This sowed the seeds of true disaster, with dramatic consequences for the Japanese economy. The Nikkei stock market index, fell sharply immediately after the Fukushima disaster as investors withdrew their funds from the market.

Some surprising chance events may be just a matter of lazy thinking, which at certain times may carry a high price. Let us consider some of the most dramatic turning points in world history, such as the outbreak of the first world war. Is it possible that one reason for the unfolding of events leading up to the war was simply that not enough thought was given to the potential consequences of the actions of individual countries? Could anybody really anticipate what Hitler's rise in Germany would lead to? The letter sent by Mahatma Gandhi to Hitler in the summer of 1939, urging him to consider the costs and consequences of persisting with the war, falls into this same bracket. Hitler, of course, didn't heed that advice, with devastating consequences.

How to Navigate in the Uncertain Future

Apple founder Steve Jobs was legendary in his obstinacy. He often presented his engineers and coders with impossible challenges. If the outcomes weren't up to his rigorous standards, he would let people know in no uncertain terms. Jobs was often known to dismiss his engineers' efforts as rubbish, no matter how much sweat they had poured into the project. He had no hesitation in questioning everything. As his biography testifies, even the people closest to him were amazed at how ill-tempered he could be.[9]

However, under Jobs's relentless direction, the impossible often became possible. The fascination with Apple products persists because Jobs had thought them through like no one else. He knew what he wanted, even though he didn't necessarily know what this required. He did not accept the concept of impossible technical problems. This is why Apple became the world's biggest and most successful — though far from being environmentally or socially progressive — technology company.

In his own way, Jobs thought and acted like a visionary: He had a clear view and a vision of a *desirable future*. The future exists as a hope, or at least some kind of aspiration. As the philosopher Georg Henrik von Wright, once a pupil of Wittgenstein, observed, humans differ from animals in that they have intentions.[10]

The future is not determined by aims and objectives alone, although they do have a prominent role to play. In some very fundamental way, aims and objectives do, however, contribute to removing uncertainty from the world. This is mainly because people begin to interpret the world through their aims. Aims provide perspective on and create order in the world. Psychologists have shown that willpower and one of its key components — self-restraint — are absolutely critical to an individual's career development.[11]

The future can also be considered from the vantage-point of *probability*. The world of probabilities is fraught with danger. Most projections of population growth made by the best experts have failed miserably. The same goes for technology forecasts. In 1943, IBM President Thomas Watson predicted that in the future world, there would be a market for perhaps five computers. Also notable is that in 1976, digital technology pioneer Ken Olson could not understand why anyone would want to have a computer at home.[12]

Probabilities steer our thinking more than anything else. Let's take an example: in the early 2000s, the Finnish forest industry invested about 8.5 billion euros in the paper industry by buying up companies in Europe and the United States. These investments were premised on the idea that the world would likely continue to turn as before: people will continue to use paper and the market will continue to remain strong.

As it turned out, demand for paper collapsed, and digitalization proceeded to rapidly take over. All these investments proved to be immensely costly mistakes. Ultimately, the reason why the industry executives got it all wrong was that they had failed to see that the world was changing. They were trapped in a world of false impressions that were based on past developments. It is this that explains why probabilities are so dangerous: They lead us to forming assessments of the future on the basis of past developments.

On the other hand, we need probabilities, because it is through probabilities that we orient to the future. It's important to know that the sun will rise again tomorrow or that we will be paid our salary on a certain day of the month. Probabilities reduce the scope of chance. All predictions, from next spring's fashion trends to the amount of carbon dioxide in the atmosphere, are based on probability calculations.

The future can also be considered a *potentiality.* The likelihood of the Fukushima disaster occurring was extraordinarily low, but it was nonetheless a possible event. People very rarely prepare for a future that is thought to be unlikely and undesirable to boot. However, it was precisely this kind of thinking that led to the development of the scenario-method during the Cold War.

Probabilities were very much brought to the forefront during the Cold War, which stemmed from an ideological confrontation between the United States and the Soviet Union. During these years, it was considered paramount to prepare for an unlikely and undesirable future scenario: the turning of the Cold War into a very "hot" one or a war of nuclear exchange. This preparation was instrumental in the development of the so-called scenario-method (see Table 1) in the 1950s, the notion of "scenario" having been borrowed from the film industry, where it refers to the manuscript of a film or play.[13] The American physicist Herman Kahn, working as a defense and intelligence officer at the Pentagon, was keen to develop a method that could more systematically describe the alternative outcomes of the Cold War.

Table 1. Scenarios: what they are and what they are not?

Scenarios are not	Scenarios are
Forecasts of the future	Justified stories about the future
Unclear Utopias	Clear and consistent
Illogical descriptions	Internally logical
Variations of the same trend	Different from each other
Focused on irrelevant details	Focused on the essential
Overriding basic strategic questions	Related to strategic basic questions
Mere playing about the future	Challenging and meaningful descriptions of the future

In a world threatened by nuclear annihilation, Kahn's basic principle "think the unthinkable" meant thinking about what would happen if nuclear war broke out. From the 1950s onwards, Kahn forced the political and military leadership in the United States to take a stand on what the world would look like in the aftermath of a nuclear war. At the same time, he was opposed to the then-prevailing New Look doctrine, according to which the United States should aim to launch the first nuclear strike, because the Soviet armed forces were so much stronger.

Kahn thought this was an extremely dangerous strategy. Instead, he wanted the United States to convince the Soviet Union that even if they succeeded in launching the first nuclear strike, the United States would still have the capability to mount a counter-strike and would go on to win any nuclear exchange. The Soviet Union, in order to act rationally, would have to take this into account in planning its own first nuclear strike.

First and foremost, Kahn wanted to force the United States political and military leadership into thinking about what the world would be like after a nuclear exchange. He wanted them to understand just how profoundly the world would change, if there would even still be life on earth. It's necessary to face and embrace even the unpleasant alternatives: If one is reluctant or unable to think about and weigh unpleasant yet possible alternatives, then one is probably ill prepared and therefore unable to react when something unexpected happens.

In the business world, the first person to take an interest in the opportunities presented by this kind of scenario method was Pierre Wack, former director for the Shell Oil Company. By the early 1970s, he was convinced of two phenomena that would have momentous future implications: On one hand, changes in the Arab world were severely eroding the stability of oil-producing countries that had lasted 25 years, and this had been absolutely crucial to establishing the dominance of oil companies and to generating their huge profits. On the other hand, everyone in the oil industry was aware of this, but no one was prepared to actually do anything about it. Although pressures in the Middle East were mounting, everyone thought that with time, as before, tensions would subside and the Western hegemony would continue to reign supreme.

Wack was very knowledgeable of world politics and had a deep understanding of different cultures. He soon realized that the Arabs were looking to change the system and that an energy crisis would be inevitable, which among other things would dramatically affect oil prices. Wack's analysis showed that what initially had been a mere possibility was turning into a probable future world. He knew he would now have to convince his fellow directors at Shell about this possibility and help them prepare for future changes. This, of course, was far from easy, as his colleagues were not in the least interested or prepared to hear a message that would challenge their existing worldview.

However, Wack proceeded to force Shell executives around the world to consider what they would do in a world where the price of crude oil went up from 2 dollars per barrel (159 liters) to what was then a staggering 10 dollars per barrel — the equivalent of current oil prices soaring from 40 dollars to 200 dollars. Wack managed to get these executives to prepare for a scenario such as this by beginning to consider the costs that an oil crisis would entail. Above all, however, he helped them to understand a situation where the future is not an extension of the past. "Forecasts aren't always wrong," he said, "because the world is not constantly changing. It is this that makes forecasts dangerous, because they always fail when they are needed most: to predict major changes in an operating environment that makes prevailing strategies outdated."[14]

As Wack had predicted, the oil crisis started in 1973, and the price of oil rose sharply to 13 dollars per barrel in 1975. Wack also helped Shell to predict the second oil crisis in the late 1970s, which was triggered by the Iranian Revolution of 1979. As a result, Shell started to grow much more rapidly than its competitors.

Even today, Shell is known for its comprehensive and pioneering work on scenarios. The last set of official shell scenarios were published in May 2016.[15] Unfortunately, this has not really translated into their operations: for decades, Shell has escaped from all responsibility in its operations in Nigeria, where oil spills have caused massive destruction in the Niger river delta area.[16] Their arctic operations have been widely criticized which is one of the reasons they decided to drop their arctic drilling efforts in 2015.[17] Even if in one of their most recent scenario, called "Building a pathway for net-zero emission future" — shows their radical thinking, it has yet to turn into action.

Risk Management and Long Waves of Societies

Leaps in development during the industrial era can be analyzed from the vantage point of so-called long cycles of 40–60 years. As with the steamer, the railway, the motor car and electrification in earlier decades, so too did the first oil crisis in the 1970s usher in a new era that saw the development of a completely new technological structure in the world (see more on this topic in Chapter 3). It, too, completely changed the lives of people, companies and nations. Computers, mobile phones and the internet created the foundation for new business success stories and changed people's behavior. But the upheavals also laid the foundation for the next crisis.

The roots of the financial crisis that started in autumn 2008 can be traced back to developments in earlier decades. The American economist Nouriel Roubini understood this better than anyone else.[18] Based on his studies of late-1990s economic crises in developing countries — Thailand, Indonesia, Korea, Brazil, Russia, and

Argentina — he found that they all shared one basic element in common: a growing current account deficit. In other words, these countries were spending more than they were earning and then borrowing money from outside sources to keep their economies afloat. Furthermore, they had inadequate mechanisms of banking regulation, thus allowing the banks to get away with irresponsible practices. Old boy networks were going strong.

Roubini turned his focus to countries where he saw similar patterns. By 2004, he realized that the United States economy also fitted this description. The United States was obviously not a developing economy, but in this case it did not ruin the analogy. His key finding was that the United States National Debt was heading toward staggering levels. And his projections were right: In 2008 it stood at 5 trillion dollars (by January 2017 it had reached nearly 20 trillion dollars).[19] At the same time, the Federal Reserve lowered the interest rate to close to zero, and the housing market revealed the true scale of the debt burden.

Roubini — who soon earned the nickname Doctor Doom — insisted that it was imperative that we understand the signs that a crisis was imminent and to take the potential consequences seriously. He expressed his views to the world's leading economists at an International Monetary Fund (IMF) conference in September 2006. Roubini maintained that the United States was headed for an unprecedented housing bubble, oil shock, collapse in consumer confidence and profound economic recession. The events would unfold as follows: As a result of the securitization of housing loans, billions of dollars would end up circulating on the world financial markets at the same time that the economy would move to the edge of the fiscal cliff. This would drive hedge funds, investment banks, mortgage lenders and many other creditors into crisis.[20]

In hindsight, Roubini's forecast is an amazingly accurate description of what happened in the years following the IMF conference. However, his expert audience was skeptical or even dismissive of his ideas. These people might well have arrived at the exact same analysis as Roubini did, but he was not believed, because the world in those days looked different: there was little unemployment, inflation was low and the economy was growing. Roubini did not let his thinking be bound by the prevailing truths of economics. Based on his own experience and expertise, he put together the pieces of the puzzle and offered a more in-depth analysis of the potential consequences than anyone else. Two years after his speech, his vision of the future had materialized in a way that shook the world to its core.

Chance and the Future

A conclusion we can draw from this is that humans, nature and society are shaped and guided by a host of factors, some of which can be clearly understood and observed. These include the long cycles of the economy, natural selection and factors of attraction in relationships. However, there still remain a large number of factors that are either completely random or that exceed our understanding.

The ultimate justification of scientific activity rests in the refinement of knowledge — in making reality intelligible. As we move towards greater intelligibility, chance and curious events slowly but surely disappear from our world. Just as the great explorers in their day discovered new continents, so the explorers of our day are slowly beginning to unravel the mysteries about the birth and evolution of the universe.

However, every answer we find leads to a dozen new questions. In the end, therefore, we're always left with uncertainty. In this world of uncertainty, we have to create the future ourselves — a future where we leave as little to chance as possible.

References

1. Tainter, Joseph. 1988. *The Collapse of Complex Societies.* New York: Cambridge University Press.
2. Casti, John & Wilenius, Markku. 2015. Seizing the X-events: the sixth K-wave and the shocks that may upend it. *Technological Forecasting and Social Change*, 94, 335–349.
3. Taleb, Nassim Nicolas. 2007. *Black Swan. The Impact of the Highly Improbable.* New York, US: Random House.

4. United States Geological Survey (USGS). 2016. “Bay Area Earthquake Probabilities.” Accessed March 8, 2016. http://earthquake.usgs.gov/regional/nca/wg02/results.php.
5. *CNN.* 2012. “Japanese parliament report: Fukushima nuclear crisis was ‘man-made.”’ Accessed March 8, 2016. http://edition.cnn.com/2012/07/05/world/asia/japan-fukushima-report/.
6. Prime Minister of Japan and his Cabinet. 2016. “Report of Japanese Government to the IAEA Ministerial Conference on Nuclear Safety” at TEPCO’s Fukushima Nuclear Power Stations. Accessed September 13, 2016. http://japan.kantei.go.jp/kan/topics/201106/iaea_houkokusho_e.html.
7. The National Diet of Japan. 2012. “The Official report of the Fukushima Nuclear Accident Independent Investigation Commission.” Accessed September 13, 2016. https://www.nirs.org/fukushima/naiic_report.pdf.
8. U.S. Department of Defence. 2012. “DoD News Briefing — Secretary Rumsfeld and Gen. Myers.” Accessed September 13, 2016. http://archive.defense.gov/Transcripts/Transcript.aspx?TranscriptID=2636.
9. Isaacson, Walter. 2011. *Steve Jobs.* New York: Simon & Schuster.
10. Von Wright, Georg H. 1971. *Explanation and Understanding.* Ithaca: Cornell University Press.
11. Baumeister, Roy & Tierney, John. 2011. *Willpower: Rediscovering the Greatest Human Strength.* London: Penguin Books.
12. PC World from IG. “The 7 Worst Tech Predictions of All Time.” Accessed September 13, 2016. http://www.pcworld.com/article/155984/worst_tech_predictions.html.
13. Screenplayology. 2016. “History of Scripting and the Screenplay.” Accessed March 8, 2016. http://www.screenplayology.com/content-sections/screenplay-style-use/1-1/.
14. Wack, Pierre. 1985. “Scenarios: Uncharted Waters Ahead.” *Harvard Business Review*, Sept–Oct 1985, p. 1.
15. Shell Global. 2016. “Shell scenarios.” Accessed September 13, 2016. http://www.shell.com/energy-and-innovation/the-energy-future/scenarios.html.
16. *The Guardian.* 2014. “Shell and Nigeria have failed on oil pollution clean-up, Amnesty says.” Accessed September 13, 2016. https://www.theguardian.com/environment/2014/aug/04/shell-nigeria-oil-pollution-clean-up-amnesty.
17. *The Huffington Post.* 2015. “Shell Comes Up Empty: A Moment of Clarity.” Accessed September 13, 2016. http://www.huffingtonpost.com/susan-murray/shell-comes-up-empty-a-moment-of-clarity_b_8259454.html.

18. *The Guardian.* 2009. "He told us so." Accessed September 13, 2016. https://www.theguardian.com/business/2009/jan/24/nouriel-roubini-credit-crunch.
19. National Debt Clocks. 2016. "National Debt of United States." Accessed March 8, 2016. http://www.nationaldebtclocks.org/debtclock/unitedstates.
20. Mihm, Stephen. 2008. "Dr. Doom." Accessed March 8, 2016. http://www.nytimes.com/2008/08/17/magazine/17pessimist-t.html.

Chapter 3

WAVE OF ADVANCEMENT

The future exists in the conclusions made about it and in the plans made for it. At the moment there is great disagreement about the direction the future is taking. There are researchers who think the future is defined by scarcity.[1] There are others who think we're headed towards a world of abundance, that we are in fact at the threshold of a new era and the most magnificent period within the evolution of humankind.[2] Yet others believe that our rapidly growing structures are so fragile that civilization could collapse at any moment.[3]

Whatever the interpretation about the present situation and the future, very few would deny that humanity has never been confronted with problems of such magnitude and severity. Climate change, soil impoverishment, scarcity of water and energy, waste problems, diminishing fish stocks, disappearance of rain forests and biodiversity are some of the most serious environmental concerns. At the same time, it is likely that the gap between natural resources and their use will widen. Even though population growth has slowed, according to United Nations, the global population is expected to reach 9.7 billion in the year 2050.[4] The Organisation for Economic Cooperation and Development (OECD) estimates that the middle class will grow from 2 billion to 5 billion by the year 2030.[5] This creates tremendous pressure on natural resources due to their increasingly accelerated use. These factors together seem to lead to the inevitable conclusion that the growth of the human race and the limited resources of planet Earth are on a collision course. Too many facts confirm that humankind has already consumed too much of the planet's limited resources in order to meet the needs of the growing population.[6] For instance, Global Footprint Network has calculated that in 2016, August 8 marked the day when humanity had used the amount of natural resources available on a sustainable basis for the year. After that date, the local resource stocks had been drawn down and too much carbon dioxide had accumulated in the atmosphere amplifying global warming.[7] The evolution that has brought humanity unprecedented wealth during the last two centuries is now threatening to destroy the human race.

The problem is mainly ethical in nature: People have carelessly exploited natural resources. It is now time for a change of course. About 10 years ago, a United Nations research project on the status of ecosystems — Millennium Ecosystem Assessment estimated that most of the world's ecosystems have already suffered greatly from human action.[8] According to the World Wildlife Foundation (WWF) Living Planet Index, the number of mammals, fish, birds, reptiles, and frogs has diminished by half since 1970.[9]

Global Footprint Network calculates, we would need one and a half Earths to satisfy the needs of the global population without consuming the reserves of future generations.[10,11] The World Bank reports that around 86% of the global population lives in areas where the environment and natural resources are continuously being depleted. These are but some of the indicators to show that the biosphere is about to reach a pivotal point, due to our excessive use of resources. Once we reach that point, there is no recourse, especially as it concerns climate change.[12]

In the light of this information, a change in thinking is obviously warranted. The creative forces of the world should be directed towards solving the large problems of humankind. For that we need not just new technological solutions but also more intelligent methods of measurement — for analyzing the progress and advancement of welfare more than, for example, gross domestic product (GDP) growth. We must also ask whether the economy has taken too large a role in a society where economic language seems to infuse all interactions. Must everything be evaluated in economic terms? What would actually be the best way to evaluate welfare progress?

This change in thinking may sound like an idealistic and utopist solution. Considering the time we have, it might also be too slow of an advancement strategy. It's difficult to change the behavior of even one person, even when the positive consequences would be obvious. Long overdue international resolution on climate change — even considering the relatively good results of Paris climate conference in 2015 — exemplify how much more difficult it is to effect changes that rely on cooperation among nations. Even so, sometimes things do improve: the action against the depletion of the ozone layer has shrunk the hole in it to the point where it is now expected to be completely recovered by 2050.[13]

Having spent a long time striving to understand societal change, I have concluded that one must approach societal progress and change with a framework that recognizes what is unchangeable and what historically must change. I've found that certain forms and rhythms always repeat throughout history. The content created in each era is new. It's particularly important to understand the dynamics of societal change — its rapid and forceful turns. This would also allow for longer-range predictability.

This thinking has been aided by the so-called Kondratiev wave theory as illustrated in the principle of the long wave.[14] Long waves are a basic concept of futures research. I became more deeply interested in them while working at the largest private insurance company in the world, Allianz. It was the year 2008, and the world economy was headed towards a head-on collision. When the crash truly happened in the fall of that year, I began to wonder how one could fully understand such wild economic dynamics. Kondratiev wave theory from almost 100 years ago came to my aid. The essence of it is that the economy — indeed the whole of society — works in cycles, waves and patterns. Let us explore a little further what this means.

Kondratiev Wave Theory

The Kondratiev wave or cycle, named after Nikolai Kondratiev, the most thorough of the early long wave scholars, is a 40–60-year fluctuation in the economy. What Kondratiev did in his research was to subject the hypothesis of the long waves of economic activity to rigorous and systematic examination. As noted earlier, the main difference between Kondratiev's work and those who had been examining long waves before him was that Kondratiev took advantage of the latest and most sophisticated methods of statistical analysis available at the time. In his empirical analysis, Kondratiev used several key indicators[15] of economic activity, such as commodity prices, work wages, foreign trade turnovers, raw material production and consumption rates and private bank savings.[16]

Kondratiev argued that modern economies fluctuate in cycles of 40–60 years (known as Kondratiev waves or K-waves), always starting with technological innovations that penetrate economic and social systems, thereby effecting a prolonged economic upturn and a steady increase in productivity. This development is then coupled with new value systems, social practices and organizational cultures. At a certain point, however, the new technology networks begin to offer diminishing returns on investment. This results in stagnation of credit demand, with the real interest rate dropping to zero before the cycle begins again. This pattern has been demonstrated by every major economic crisis in the past 200 years, the last financial crisis included. There is, therefore, an observable, structural and temporal pattern that defines our economies (see Figure 1).

There is no consensus about the timing of the waves: different authors rely on slightly different chronologies. Likewise, the key drivers vary somewhat as well, particularly when it comes to identifying the drivers for the sixth wave.

One of the most popular explanations for the existence of the K-waves has come from the examination of the clusters of technological innovation. This causal hypothesis originally comes from Joseph Schumpeter, whose main inquiry regarded how innovation and technology influence economic growth. In his early work, Schumpeter

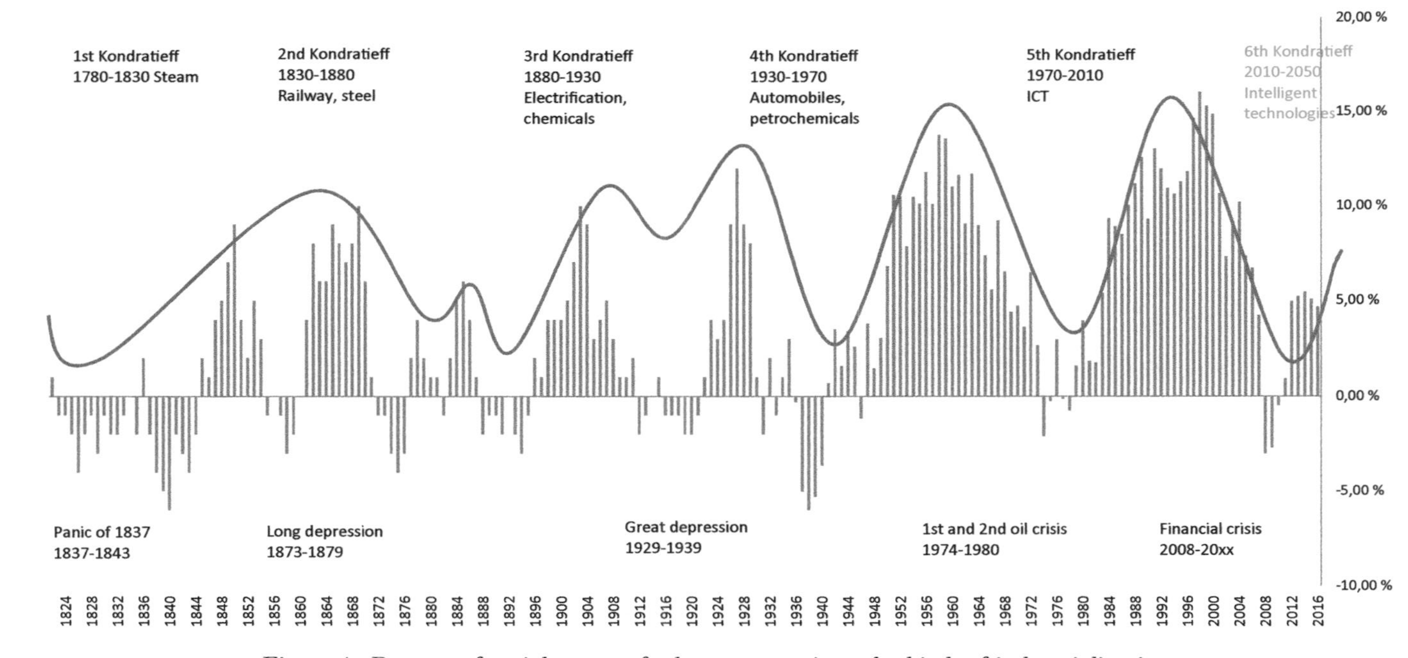

Figure 1. Pattern of social waves of advancement since the birth of industrialization.

Note: Rolling 10-year return on the S&P 500 since 1814 till January 2016 (in %, p.a.).

Datasource: Datastream, Bloomberg, Allianz SE.

Illustration: Helsinki Capital Partners.

approached this by investigating the long-term economic growth patterns and their relationship to innovation. The Schumpeterian framework thus became based on the idea that temporal clusters of major innovations create new opportunities, which in turn accelerate economic growth.[17] Many of the interesting K-wave theories later built upon this by trying to explain historical growth patterns through changes in key areas, such as communications, energy, production or transport technologies.

To complement Schumpeter's original theory, Gerhard Mensch has added the idea that major innovations occur during recessions because of investment behavior. He argues that during prosperity, investors tend to invest in less-risky ventures and that in stagnation or recession, fewer low-risk investment opportunities are available.[18] Together, the Schumpeter–Mensch theory — that technological innovation serves as the key driver to the waves — has inspired the main body of literature related to K-waves.

It is quite remarkable that in a recent compilation of work by Kondratiev experts,[19] none of the authors (and all of the most-esteemed Kondratiev experts were represented) even hinted at the possibility of a crash similar to that of the Great Depression, which at that point was only a couple of years downstream. On the contrary, renowned futurist Harold Linstone expected the upswing phase of the fifth K-wave to last until 2024 — driven by nano- and biotechnology — at which time he expected a change in the curve to the downswing phase of the sixth wave.[20] As we can now clearly observe, the shift to the next wave has already begun, having started with the turmoil of the financial crisis of 2008.

Similarly, Jim Dator, one of the most well-respected futurists ever, did not assume the then current wave would necessarily crash some years later. However, in his article, he pointed out the long trend of increasing consumer spending, which was sparked by the introduction of credit cards to the masses, and thought that this development should have already caused the existing wave to crash. But his real point was that K-waves might be altogether a thing of the past and that we should actually look for alternatives to guide us on our trembling road towards a hazy future.[21] In similar fashion, futurist Jordi Serra expressed doubt as to whether the K-wave theory is too rigid and deterministically loaded to fit into the world of increasing risks and thus growing instabilities.[22] Now, with the obvious benefit of hindsight, we are able to state that it was indeed the mounting risks that eventually materialized as the financial crisis of 2007–2008. In Serra's otherwise reflective article, there was no clear predictive statement about a lurking financial meltdown.

To be sure, from the standard economists, the idea of recurring cycles have been long contested. The key problem they find, is the lack of empirical evidence. Perhaps the best known critic is Angus Maddison who expressed his perspective on the long-cycle theory in the following way:

> My basic conclusion is that the existence of regular long-term rhythmic movements in economic activity is not proven, although many fascinating hypotheses have been developed in looking for them. Nevertheless, it is clear that major changes in growth momentum have occurred since 1820, and some explanation is needed. In my view it can be sought not in systematic long waves, but in specific disturbances of an ad hoc character. Major system shocks change the momentum of capitalist development at certain points.[23]

However, in the field of economic theory, long-term cycles and fluctuations belong to the field of evolutionary economics. When we move more towards understanding innovation, trends, change or generally long-term development — the interest of Schumpeter in particular — we come closer to using Kondratiev waves as tools for understanding the patterns of change rather than proving empirically that history repeats itself in a rigid form. Kondratiev as well as Schumpeter worked within a framework of long-run equilibrium, meant to describe the actual economic growth path.

Maddison agrees with Kondratiev in that systemic shocks are always events that intervene with the economy's expansion. But for him, these shocks are purely random, whereas here the argument is that shocks are of endogenic nature, produced by the system itself.

Table 1 presents a definable pattern of economic performance over 200 years of history in industrial societies. While it cannot claim to be a highly accurate description of our economic history, it sure helps us to understand how modern society develops and gives us an interesting perspective towards the future. German economist Leo Nefiodow has done a great job in bringing together the empirical evidence for long-term cycles.[24] Regarding his analysis of the past waves, I very much agree with his arguments.

As the future is the main topic of this book, it is my intention to provide a picture of the future, which is not completely randomly emerging but rather a consequence of traceable patterns of past, highly dynamic developments, in which different factors from the fields of economy, society, politics and culture are inputs. This approach does not neglect surprises, discontinuities or other dramatic changes. It only says: we should make use of the patterns in understanding the future because that is an indispensable way to have any anticipatory power in our views towards the future.

In what follows, I present my view of K-waves and adopt a rough chronology, in which each wave is defined by a key technology or a socio-technical "revolution." The chronology adopted here is clearly different from what the above-mentioned writers have assumed. But it is my firm belief that my interpretation has the benefit of incorporating the recent financial crisis as a clear demarcation line, indicating a shift from the fifth to sixth cycle.[25]

The first Kondratiev wave (approximately 1780–1830) was dominated by the invention of the steam engine, which signaled a dramatic increase in productivity in the early days of industrialization. The second cycle (1830–1880) was dominated by the proliferation of railways and steel, both of which were crucial to the growth of industrial production. The third wave (1880–1930) saw the electrification of the world and the spread of chemicals in agriculture, which also sped up the pace of innovation in medicine. This wave came to an end with the Great Depression of the 1920s and 1930s.

The fourth Kondratiev cycle (1930–1970) saw the advent of the Ford Model-T — and the entire auto industry, which had been

Table 1. The succession of development waves in industrial societies.

K-waves	First wave	Second wave	Third wave	Fourth wave	Fifth wave	Sixth wave
Period	1780–1830	1830–1880	1880–1930	1930–1970	1970–2010	2010–2050
Drivers	Steam machine	Railroad steel	Electricity chemicals	Automobiles, petrochemicals	Digital communication technologies	Intelligent, resource efficient technologies
Prime field of application	Clothing industry and energy	Transport infrastructure and cities	Utilities and mass-production	Personal mobility and freight transport	Personal computers and mobile phones	Materials and energy production and distribution
Human interest	New means for decent life	Reaching out and upwards	Building maintenance	Allowing for freedom	Creating new space	Integrating human, nature and technology

strengthened by the growth of the petrochemical industry. Most of the increase in productivity in this period derived from that development. The long period of cheap oil and stable economies collapsed with the oil crisis of the early 1970s. At the same time, however, certain key innovations saw daylight, such as the microprocessor, which ushered in the fifth wave (1970–2010). The first microcomputer was built in a garage in California, and a little later the first-generation telecommunications wireless Nordic Mobile Telephone network (the predecessor of the Global Systems for Mobile Communications standard) was set up in the Finnish archipelago. In the years that followed, these basic innovations were developed, refined and distributed around the globe, creating entirely new industrial sectors.

The transformation of Finnish industrial company Nokia into a telecommunications giant was emblematic of the age of information and communication technology (ICT). But we must understand that it was a child of its age. Nokia went surfing on the fifth Kondratiev wave and demonstrated its power. The wave increased the productivity of the economic and social system. Once again, we see how a specific innovation solved certain key problems related to the development of the previous waves while simultaneously creating challenges for future waves. While the fourth wave produced a tremendous expansion for Western economies with massive industrial and economic growth (particularly after World War II), the fifth wave focused on creating a new virtual infrastructure for managing this level of activity. The global redistribution of production capacity and excess supply are among the factors inherited from the fifth Kondratiev wave. When responding to the consequences of the preceding waves — the massive distribution of cars, oil, technology and services — the actors of the sixth wave need to provide solutions for the challenges of the previous phase while also raising economic productivity to an even higher level.

In the previous wave, the excessive use of energy and materials, coupled with insufficient technology, launched a development that was unable to prevent petrochemical pollution. This alone defined an agenda for the sixth Kondratiev wave, which will set the tone for global development over the next 40–60 years. The search for better resource productivity will steer both businesses and societies, thus defining new products and services.

Information and communications technology was pivotal in the fifth wave. It increased productivity, just as the other new technologies in the previous waves did. Simultaneously, we witnessed the rise of investors with available capital who were looking for profitable new investment targets (see Figure 2). The capital ended up flooding the housing market in the United States and elsewhere. The subsequent overheating of the economy resulted in a gigantic banking crisis, or the so-called "financial crisis," with its deepest moments in 2009. The effects of it are still strongly felt, particularly in Europe.

Kondratiev's waves can be understood as the internal dynamics between economics and society: waves that repeat with a certain regularity. Because modern societies are comprised of complex interactions between politics, technology and economics, a post-recession economic boom does not automatically follow. There are prolonged periods of economical stagnation to be found throughout history. There are arguments in the literature about Kondratiev waves proclaiming the mechanism producing the long economic waves has

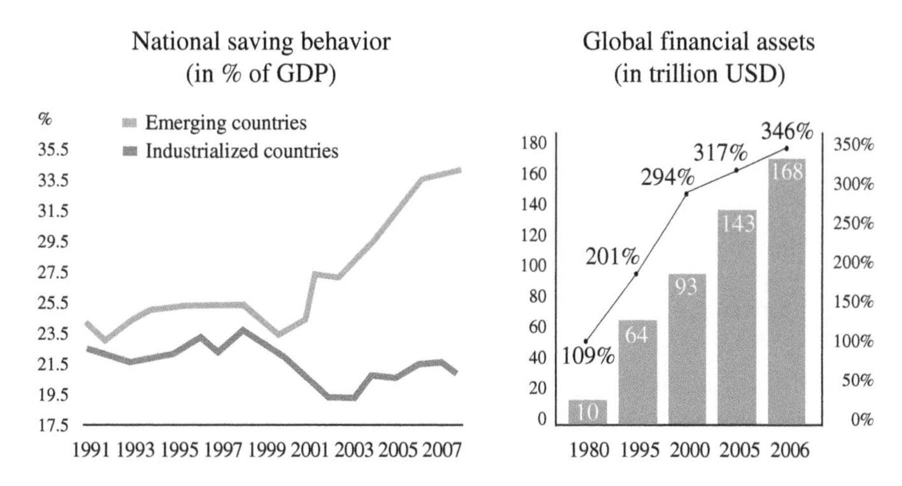

Figure 2. These trends showed the way to the crisis.
Source: Mckinsey Global Institute Global Financial Stock Database.

already changed significantly, because the cycles in technological advancement have become more and more frequent.

It is tempting to think that we've transitioned from long and slow economic cycles to some kind of constant upheaval. I tend to think, however, that the real full-fledged technology revolutions don't come about any faster than before. The generation gap is still about 25 years. As a matter of fact, it can be even argued that there are less disruptive innovations now than there were in the 19th century, when a tremendous number of technical innovations surfaced for the benefit of humankind, starting with steam engine, electricity and the telephone.

Technological advancement opens up new horizons for all-encompassing societal breakthroughs. Those have been envisioned, for example, by Peter Diamandis and Steven Kotler in their book *Abundance*. In the book, they construct a future scenario that far overshadows any current vision of well-being.[26] In this scenario, current technological advancement climaxes in a world of abundance enabled by an unprecedented global nerve system: the Internet of Things (IoT), in which every consumer product and device has its own IP-address. In the future envisioned by Diamandis and Kotler, everything, no matter where it is located in the world, will be part of the web and thus reachable and more efficient to use. In their thinking, the solution to large global problems lies in the resources of information technology and the technological advancements that follow. The technological advancements make it possible to find solutions for climate change and for solving the scarcity of raw materials and energy. According to them, new technologies for creating sustainable development are already here but only just sprouting.

Major technological advances often go hand-in-hand with societal changes. The changes in scientific models and theories alter also the spiritual superstructures of society: the structures and values that the system is built upon. One can presume that the current societal problems and the solutions that are being sought for them will make up a new foundation for the functioning of society. The old divisions and separation of industrial branches no longer apply, because various kinds of industries merge with each other and also with everyday life and leisure in new ways. This is part of an overarching change in societal power dynamics: Power is increasingly becoming decentralized.

The change is possible because humans are capable of innovation — in other words, humans can shape the future. We need a new wave of innovation that brings both technological and political solutions for ending the exploitation of resources. These innovations can represent a completely new kind of thinking, be it based on new inventions or combinations of new and old, such as industrial ecology, green nanotechnology or new energy technologies. In addition to meeting the basic needs of people here on Earth, humankind is looking for intelligent solutions to the problems that we have inherited from our past development.

The sixth wave that is about to take form is truly global in nature. At its formation, competition for the next determining factors of technological advancement, social unity and cultural activity will intensify. Both individual and collective awareness of the limits of our planet will increase. The new innovations of the sixth wave will radically increase the efficiency of the use of natural resources. The impacts of the innovations will be magnified through their firm link with the digital world of the previous wave.

The intelligent solutions of the sixth wave combine physical products, digital communication and human capital. Let's next take a look at the nature of technology.

The Relationship between Technology and Humanity

The relationship between humankind and technology has changed dramatically in the last few decades. It has become more intense and more intimate. In the 1980s, there was still very little personal technology in homes. As I glance around my own living room now, I notice several gadgets that have become common in the last few decades. They belong to me or other members of my family. Some other devices that have been on the market longer appear simple now. Technology has become more multi-dimensional and more intimate.

The nature of technology is such that it lives and evolves with humans. Most often, new inventions are loathed and their impact gets played down. This was the case, for example, with the telephone, the radio, the bicycle and the television. The bicycle was regarded an extremely dangerous vehicle of transportation: Its manual encouraged slow riding. The telephone, invented by Alexander Graham Bell, was not a sensation: It was regarded as some peculiar scientific toy, for which one could not really imagine a use. In the 1990s, when Nokia CEO, Jorma Ollila described a future in which everyone would carry a mobile phone, it sounded to most people like a fantasy from an executive with no base in reality.

In this context, the story of Apple and its co-founder Steve Jobs is particularly interesting.[27] The interaction between humans and machine — the actual touch and feel of the machine — was an obsession for Steve Jobs ever since the beginning. When Jobs and co-founder Steve Wozniak were developing their machines in the garage of Jobs's father, Jobs understood how important it was to fully recognize what a simple, user-friendly interface really meant. Each of the Apple success stories, from the Mac computers to the iPad, is a triumph of humans' relationship with machines. Apple has grown into one of the largest company in the world precisely because Apple understood better than any other company how valuable a good user experience is. Soon after iPhones were introduced to the market, I remember seeing people petting the machines as they would pet a loved one.

This, if anything, proves how design combines technology and liberal arts, which was the very union Jobs sought. Jobs was passionate about shaping technology so that it would follow function as closely as possible and also correspond to human esthetic values. The round corners of Apple computers and the twirling dial of the iPod represent this very idea.

We could pretend that technology can easily be tamed to meet human needs as much as possible. However, in real life, this is hard to achieve. The majority of technology is still so complicated and inflexible that its function is really only illuminated to the engineers that designed it (if even to them). Here we return to the most important foundation, which became an obsession for Jobs: Consumer technology products have to appear in a friendly and simple fashion and they have to be good-looking. In other words, he demanded that human qualities be instilled in technology. That separated him from his contemporaries in a groundbreaking way. Even the insides of the machines, only accessible to the repair techs, had to look beautiful. Even the Apple factory machinery had to look gorgeous!

Ever since our ancestors started to use tools 2 million years ago, the task of technology has been to make life on Earth easier. The entire history of modern civilization is one of facilitation: steam power, railroads, electrification, fossil fuels, cars, and digital technology. All of these technologies, and countless others, have enabled an easier life.

But to some extent, the opposite has also happened: The technological complexity of the environment has grown to such proportions that it causes most people's hair to turn gray. Complexity kills in the end. It kills enthusiasm and vitality and has driven entire civilizations to destruction. Every society that becomes too complex and thus hard to manage has been ruined before too long.[28]

Steve Jobs' main idea in the 2000s, about the interaction between technology and human beings, was that the personal computer was to become a "digital hub" of all the technologies that serve people's needs. Even though Apple's vision changed by the end of the decade (because the hub moved into "the cloud"), the whole idea was still revolutionary and made the company the most valuable technology company of all time.

The last time Steve Jobs introduced latest products in June 2011, he stated with irony that "synchronizing all your devices drives you crazy"[29] but that Apple had found a solution: moving everything (email, contacts, calendar, books, and music, etc.) into the "cloud." In the cloud, one's data and files would be instantly synchronized with any device that was connected to the internet.[30] Simplicity meant seamlessness, ease and speed.

Complexity can be tolerated if there is some order. One could even go so far as to say that some degree of complexity belongs in today's life. People want it: The phone has to work as a phone but also as a text messenger, a music player, a camera, etc. Life requires complexity in order to be rich. The question is: Is the complexity manageable? If it is unmanageable, then the complex reality renders life complicated, chaotic and unpleasant.

Don Norman, an expert in cognitive science who has worked at Apple and Hewlett Packard, has pointed out that the actual goal is to tame the complexity that life predicates.[31] Many wish for the richness of experiences and circumstances that technology can produce. Problems arise because human action is typically different from that of a machine — and that fact is often not recognized in the design and function of the device or machine. Bad design simply destroys the user experience.

The problem doesn't necessarily lie in the complexity, *per se*. But if there is no order to the complexity, then confusion and obscurity will follow. If the desk is cluttered, but you know the location of papers and items on it, then the chaos isn't necessarily bothersome (except perhaps esthetically). It's essential not to feel helpless and powerless when faced with complexity.

In a world that is becoming more and more technological, it is the precise management of complexity that essentially separates the good solutions from the bad. New technologies appear constantly, and the fountain of needs seems inexhaustible. Everyone wants to enjoy a rich life, and that unavoidably brings along complexity. Simplicity, clarity and harmony promote the feeling of manageability in technology, just as in life in general.

In the case of Apple, we should point out that simplicity in the sixth wave will also mean that any device should be easily repaired and reused along the idea of circular economy. As this was not Jobs's aspiration, Apple has performed really poorly in this regard. Let's hope simplicity in the future comprises ease of repair and reuse.

What ultimately matters is whether interaction with technology produces such intelligence and understanding that people thrive on. If one comprehends technology in a way that allows one to manage it, and it functions reliably, there is no issue. On the contrary, it's actually quite pleasurable. But if one doesn't understand how to make the machine work as desired, that creates anger, anxiety, and depression.

The sixth wave focuses on key technologies and innovations for improving the efficiency in utilizing resources.[32] The fifth wave was a giant race towards more flexible technologies and lower expenses. Now the race is towards materially less-intensive products and processes and a more intelligent use of natural resources. Smarter technologies and products based on natural fiber are replacing the current resource-intensive and non-recyclable solutions.

Let's look at Finland in the context of opportunities within the bioindustry. Two of the then largest forestry companies in the world were Finnish: UPM and Stora Enso. A third, Metsä Group, was also among these largest forestry companies. From the environmental perspective, however, Finland is one of the world's most resource-intensive countries, due to the important role of the forest industry in our economy.[a] In the past, the forest industry not only consumed a lot of energy but was also a polluter. This has shifted markedly in the past few decades and will continue to change. For example, from the 1990s to 2012, pulp mill emissions diminished to a fraction of what they used to be; relative to the production of pulp and paper mills, sulfur emissions have declined by 85% and phosphorus emissions into water systems by 70%.[33] Pulp mills produce more energy than they consume and already account for the majority of the renewable energy produced in Finland.

The forest has long been a source of inspiration and income for Finns. Tar has been exported since the 16th century, and in the 17th century Finland was the major producer of tar in all of Europe. Timber, pulp, paper and numerous wood products later became the backbone of the forest industry. However, many key performance indicators of the forest industry have declined by

[a]Resource intensity means the amount of services or products produced per resource (e.g., water, energy, material). It measures efficiency in the use of resources. However, one has to bear in mind the starting point. For example, Finland has an industrial economy based largely on natural resources as a consequence of their abundance.

one-third since the start of this millennium. Exports of paper, saw goods and veneer have fallen, while employment has declined at the same rate. Paper production is especially expected to fall even further in the coming decade.[34] There is tremendous pressure in this industry to renew its product portfolio and find new innovations. Packaging and building industries need more solutions based on wood fiber that are strong, light, durable and wholly recyclable. All in all, the demand for ecologically designed fiber-based products and solutions are increasing, and Finland should be a natural source for these kind of services. For instance, in the future, wood structures will be utilized in buildings much more than now. This evolution stems from the esthetic, economic, and ecological value of wood.

There is now a window of opportunity for the forest industry: Wood products, new biomaterials, forestry services and energy have interesting growth expectations. Finland will live from the forest in the future, as long as we can harness the new opportunities.

Another example is the global Ecotourism industry. In the last 20 years it has grown annually by 20–35%.[35] The reason for this growth is that sun and sand is not enough for an increasing number of people who appreciate experiencing nature in deeper ways. In the context of sixth wave, this is exactly what will move people from being plain consumers to more active prosumers. Properly organized, this type of tourism does not harm nature but connects people more intimately with the wonders of our natural environment. At the end of the day, the ethos of the sixth wave — after all the exploitation of nature we have committed — will be about rehabilitating our relationship with nature.

Why the Sixth Wave?

Why would one study the next decades with the help of Kondratiev's wave theory? Because when one recognizes the wider framework of the forces of societal change, it is easier to accept destruction of the old and birth of the new. We are not just talking about technology but also the dynamics between new organizational structures, values

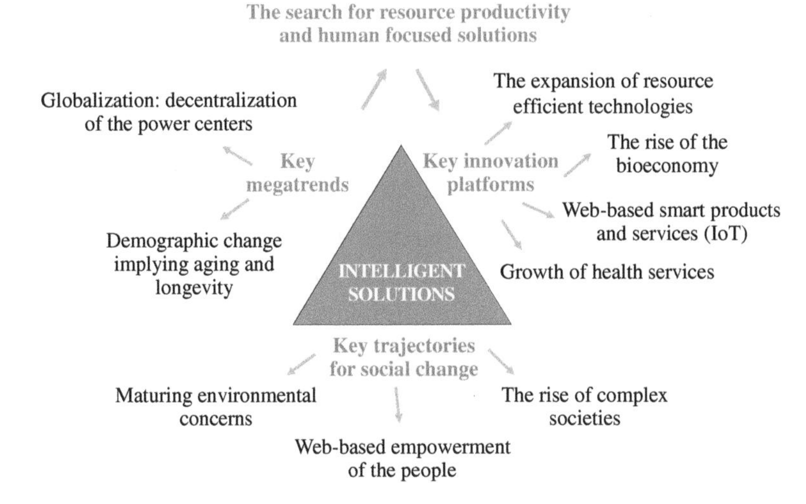

Figure 3. The drivers behind sixth wave (2010–2050).

and cultures. It's a matter of how successfully we avoid the same patterns and create success through new opportunities. It's not enough to build more intelligent products; we must also build more intelligent systems (see Figure 3).

Even though the sixth wave will produce systemic changes, the details of which are impossible to predict, it is possible to pinpoint a few fundamental factors of the change.

Virtual experiences are a given in the everyday life in the future. We will see new business models that dramatically increase the flow of communications between different branches and put in motion the creation of new kinds of partnerships, businesses and concepts. Ever-increasing computing efficiency enables interaction between machines: IoT will have a major impact on people's lives and on economic rejuvenation. How will companies participate in this future advancement? For instance, the way we buy airline tickets and use mobile technology to make the journey smooth in airports have completely changed in the last 10 years. Behind this change is the fact that there is much more machine-to-machine talk than there used to be, enabling us to receive and to provide the information needed.

In order to engage this capital of know-how, we need marketing capability, in addition to investors, business angels and other financiers to bring forth more sixth wave innovations. It is especially crucial to fund the early stages of innovation. In Silicon Valley, I've observed a particularly efficient model for this: Success is built by combining ideas and know-how in tight cooperation by entrepreneurs, risk investors and other key parties. It's a matter of combined skills and a well-functioning platform for innovation. It requires deep sharing of information, understanding the interests of the stakeholders and tight partnerships.

But above all, the ideas must be connected with overall development trends. For example, health care and society in general must prepare for the coming shift in our population's age structure. Japan was the first country to experience rapidly aging population. From 2030 on, others will follow, first in Europe, then Russia, China, United States and eventually the rest of Asia will see 30% of the population to be 60 years or older. Demographic research shows that by mid-century, the probability of reaching the age of 60 is 98% in Japan/Oceania, 82% in Western Europe and even 69% in China. There is going to be continuous aging of the world's population throughout the century.[36]

More often elderly people will want to continue working past the retirement age. This requires new kinds of flexible health care and pension structures that can adapt to individual needs. The public sector, especially health care, needs comprehensive reforms that take advantage of digital technology. Digitalization is an answer to many problems, but only if it meets the evolving human needs and if societies also advance accordingly. Intelligent digital systems are of no use if social and cultural structures don't evolve.

The Culture of the Sixth Wave

Our research shows that regarding cultural values people increasingly appreciate what has to do with openness, transparency, and agility.[37] We consider this as being a sign of culture that will grow stronger in the sixth wave. The new culture also includes constant testing and trials, openness, learning something new and accepting failure. Things are sometimes done in a different order than is customary. Intuition and fast action play a large role in development, since it's not always most efficient to spend time analyzing and planning; one must instead take the direction that *feels* right and then proceed to testing. Quick prototypes result in more innovation than by securing the viability of the idea with time-wasting analyses. Feedback and development are faster. More intelligent and better-functioning solutions can be achieved through the eagerness to experiment.

At the end of the day, the sixth wave is a race against a time bomb. The resource and production structure of the global economy is about to blow up. The bomb is fueled by both an economy that carelessly exploits both material and spiritual resources and by our way of life that supports the exploitation. We are beginning to see the consequences more and more clearly, such as in the pollution of our environment and in unsustainable greenhouse gases, but also in economic indebtedness. In order to find solutions, we must create ecologically sustainable technologies, manufacturing processes and ways of living. Inequality is inevitably growing in many societies.[38] This problem is political in its origin and can be corrected to some extent through societal regulatory mechanisms: taxation and legislation. We must also create a more intelligent model for a welfare society that adapts to the aging population. This requires a reform of the pension system and the dismantling of boundaries between working life and pension systems.

Regarding these time bombs, there are three important questions to take into account when creating the future: How can solving societal and environmental problems be made into corporate goals? How can human needs become corporate goals? And how can the finiteness of global resources become a motivator for technological advancement? If these questions were to be taken seriously, that would mean charting a new direction. We should dismantle obsolete structures that no longer serve our goals. We return to these questions in the subsequent chapters of the book.

References

1. Bardi, Ugo. 2014. *Extracted: How the Quest for Mineral Wealth is Plundering the Planet: A Report to the Club of Rome.* Vermont: Chelsea Green Publishing; Randers, Jørgen. 2012. *2052: Global Forecast for the Next 40 Years.* White River Junction: Chelsea Green Publishing; Sverdrup, Harald & Ragnarsdottir, Vala. 2014. Natural resources in a Planetary Perspective. *Geochemical perspectives,* **3** (2).
2. Diamandis, Peter & Kotler, Steven. 2012. *Abundance: The Future Is Better Than You Think.* New York: Free Press.
3. Casti, John. 2010. *Mood Matters: From Rising Skirt Lengths to the Collapse of World Powers.* New York: Harper Collins.
   Costa, Rebecca. 2010. *The Watchman's Rattle: A Radical New Theory of Collapse.* Philadelphia: Vanguard Press.
4. UN. 2015. "World population prospects." Accessed September 13, 2016. https://esa.un.org/unpd/wpp/publications/files/key_findings_wpp_2015.pdf.
5. OECD Observer. 2015. "An emerging middle class." Accessed September 13, 2016. http://www.oecdobserver.org/news/fullstory.php/aid/3681/An_emerging_middle_class.html.
6. Global Footprint Network, 2015. "Earth Overshoot Day 2015." Last accessed March 8, 2016. http://www.overshootday.org/.
7. *Ibid.*
8. Millennium Ecosystem Assessement. 2016. "Guide to the Millennium assesement reports." Accessed September 13, 2016. http://www.millenniumassessment.org/en/index.html.
9. World Wildlife Fund (WWF). 2014. "Living Planet Report 2014." Accessed March 8, 2016. http://wwf.fi/mediabank/6426.pdf.
10. Global Footprint Network, 2015. "Earth Overshoot Day 2015." Last accessed March 8, 2016. http://www.overshootday.org/.
11. *Ibid.*
12. The World Bank. 2012. "Climate Change Report Warns of Dramatically Warmer World This Century." Accessed March 8, 2016. http:// www.worldbank.org/en/news/feature/2012/11/18/Climate-change-report-warns-dramatically-warmer-world-this-century.
13. *The Guardian.* 2016. "Ozone layer hole appears to be healing, scientists say." https://www.theguardian.com/environment/2016/jun/30/ozone-layer-hole-appears-to-be-healing-scientists-say.
14. Longwave Group. 2016. "The Longwave Principle." Accessed March 8, 2016. http://www.longwavegroup.com/principle.php.

15. Kondratiev, Nikolai. 1984. *The Long Wave Cycle.* Guy Daniels, trans. New York: Richardson & Snyder.
Louçã, Francisco & Reijnders, Jan (Eds.) 1999. *The Foundations of Long Wave Theory. Volume I: Models and Methodology.* Cheltenham, UK: Edward Elgar.
16. Kondratiev's article "The Long Wave Cycle" mentions the following data sets: consumption rates indices of commodity prices in England, France and the United States 1780–1920; quotations of the French rente 1820–1920; quotations of English consols 1815–1920; annual wages of agricultural workers in England 1789–1896; weekly wages of workers in English cotton industry 1806–1906; foreign trade turnover of France 1830–1920; foreign trade turnover of England 1800–1925; coal production in England 1855–1912; consumption of mineral fuel in France 1830–1910; production of lead in England 1857–1918; production of pig iron in England 1845–1925; private savings banks in France (liabilities towards depositors in millions of francs) 1838–1910. Kondratiev believed the phenomenon of the long waves to be inherently tied to the rise of industrial capitalism, and for this reason he recorded data starting only after the industrial revolution. After him, other authors have claimed to identify the same pattern from much earlier times.
17. Schumpeter, Joseph. 1939. *Time Series and Their Normal in Business Cycles: A Theoretical, Historical and Statistical Analysis of the Capitalist Process.* Volume I. Chapter V. New York: McGraw-Hill Book Company.
18. Mensch, Gerhard, Coutinho, Charles and Kaasch, Klaus. 1981. Changing capital values and the propensity to innovate. *Futures,* **13**(4), 276–292.
19. Devezas, Tessaleno. 2006. *Kondratieff Waves, Warfare and World Security.* Amsterdam: IOS Press.
20. *Ibid.*
21. *Ibid.*
22. *Ibid.*
23. Maddison, Angus. 1991. "Business cycles, long waves and phases of capitalist development" Accessed September 15, 2016. http://www.eco.rug.nl/GGDC/maddison/ARTICLES/Business_Cycles.pdf, p. 83.
24. Kondratieff.net. 2016. "The sixth Kondratieff — The new long wave in the global economy." Accessed September 13, 2016. http://www.kondratieff.net/
25. Here it might be noted that I started to develop this theory between 2007 and 2009 while working at Allianz, the world's largest private

insurance company, as Senior Vice President responsible for strategic research.

26. Diamandis, Peter & Kotler, Steven. 2012. *Abundance: The Future Is Better Than You Think.* New York: Free Press.
27. Isaacson, Walter. 2011. *Steve Jobs.* New York: Simon & Schuster.
28. Tainter, Joseph. 1988. *The Collapse of Complex Societies.* New York: Cambridge University Press.
29. Cloud computing. "Quotes from Apple CEO Steve Jobs on iCloud and device synchronization at 2011 WWDC." Accessed September 13, 2016. https://cloud-computing-today.com/2011/06/15/apple-ceo-steve-jobs-quotes-on-icloud-at-wwdc/.
30. Isaacson, Walter. 2011. *Steve Jobs.* New York: Simon & Schuster.
31. Norman, Donald. 2010. *Managing the Complexity.* Cambridge, MA: MIT Press.
32. Moody, James Bradfield & Novgrady, Bianca. 2010. *The Sixth Wave.* North Sydney: Random House Australia.
33. Environmental Statistics for Forest Economy 2012. Accessed September 25, 2016.https://www.metsateollisuus.fi/mediabank/606.pdf.
34. What Science Can Tell Us. 2014. *Future of the European Forest-Based Sector: Structural Changes Towards Bioeconomy.* Oulu: European Forest Institute. Accessed March 8, 2016. http://www.efi.int/files/attachments/publications/efi_wsctu_6_2014.pdf.
35. Ecowanderlust. 2015. "The Growth of the Global Ecotourism Industry". Accessed September 13, 2016. http://ecowanderlust.com/ecotourism-2/growth-global-ecotourism-industry/1487.
36. Lutz, Wolfgang, Sanderson, Warren, and Scherbov, Sergei. 2008. The coming acceleration of global population ageing *Nature,* **451**, 716–719.
37. Kurki, Sofi, Pura, Minna, and Wilenius, Markku. 2016. *Re-acting the Future. New Ways to Work: The Case of Reaktor.* Finland Futures Research Centre, FFRC eBook 4/2016; Kurki, Sofi & Wilenius, Markku. 2015. Ethics in the sixth wave: How new ethical companies will transform our economies in the coming decades. *Futures,* **71**, 146–158; Wilenius, Markku. 2014. Leadership in the sixth wave. Excursions into the new paradigm of the Kondratieff cycle 2010–2050. *European Journal of Futures Research,* **2** (36).
38. Stiglitz, Joseph E. 2016. Inequality and economic growth. In: Jacobs, Michael & Mazzucato, Mariana (Eds.). *Rethinking Capitalism. Economics and Policy for Sustainable and Inclusive Growth.* Chichester, West Sussex, UK: Wiley Blackwell.

Chapter 4

THE PULSE OF PLANET EARTH

The Californian Charles David Keeling, a young and curious researcher, was the first notable climatologist to focus on measuring atmospheric quantities of what is now called greenhouse gas. In the 1950s, he began to construct precision instruments for measuring the amount of carbon dioxide in the atmosphere. Nobody had managed that prior to him. In 1956 he built a small observatory on top of Mauna Loa in Hawaii. Based on his results, he came to understand one of the most essential characteristics of the rhythms of the planet: breathing. The amount of carbon dioxide increases during the day and decreases during the night due to the breathing of plants.[1]

He then discovered seasonal variations in breathing; the sensors detected the highest carbon dioxide levels in May and the lowest in October. After years of analysis, something even more interesting started to become clear: The amount of carbon dioxide in the atmosphere is slowly but steadily increasing overall. Later he started to investigate the reason for the increase in carbon dioxide and found it to be the use of fossil fuels. The so-called "Keeling Curve" was established, which showed that the carbon dioxide count in the atmosphere has increased from 314 parts per million in 1956 (when the measuring began), to 403 parts per million by the mid-August of 2016.[2] Although parts per million sounds small, it signifies a dramatic increase that, more than anything else, speaks of the human impact on the biosphere that sustains our planet.

Geologist James Lawrence Powell published a study in 2014 about climate-change-related articles in scientific publications. He went through almost 10,000 studies and found only one that denied the existence of climate change caused by human activity. This evidence seems to prove that there is little doubt within the scientific community of the existence of climate change.[3]

Powell's study was published immediately prior to the fifth report by the Intergovernmental Panel on Climate Change (IPCC). The conclusions of the report are gloomy: more extreme weather events and droughts that will especially plague farmers are expected. In order to avoid a temperature rise of more than two degrees, we should leave two-thirds of the remaining fossil fuel unused. According to the climate researchers, a temperature rise of more than two degrees is extremely dangerous, because it would result in significant and unprecedented variations in climate conditions.

A four-degree rise, which we'll reach by the end of the century, would be catastrophic to the current "business-as-usual" scenario: Life in the tropics would become extremely difficult, and most of the polar ice caps would melt, resulting in the rising of sea levels by several meters.[4] There would be fewer clouds in the sky due to the warming, which might sound like a good thing, but in reality that means that less heat would bounce off the clouds and radiate back towards the upper atmospheres and into space. This would intensify the heating of Earth's surface. Already at present, a full 75% of daily heat maximums can be attributed to climate change caused by human activity.[5] There is more and more evidence of existing sea-level rise.[6]

Unfortunately, political decision-making is advancing at a snail's pace, even though there is tremendous proof of the harmful consequences of climate change. The last United Nations COP 21 climate change conference in Paris in December 2015 was a modest success story: An agreement was reached to stop global warming before it exceeds the 2° Celsius line, with aspirations to limit emissions to 1.5° Celsius (compared to pre-industrial levels). I say "modest," because in the agreement no real measures as to how to cap emissions on that level were presented. What is particularly painful is the fact that the current annual rate of deforestation is over 50,000 square miles, which primarily takes place in tropical regions. On the positive side, forested areas are increasing in size in Europe and Asia — especially in the latter, due to the planting of forests in China.

Since I began my work on the Finnish program for studies on atmospheric changes in 1992, I've followed the discussion closely. Twists and turns have occurred in both climate change research and political negotiations, but less has been achieved than what was expected in the 1990s. The political progress has stagnated largely due to filibustering by the United States and China, whose combined emissions amount to over 40% of global emissions.

The complicated process of climate change may be affected by factors not yet well understood. A cooling of the climate for other reasons is, in theory, also possible, as happened during the so-called Little Ice Age (from about 1450–1850, when the major European rivers froze over).[7]

The climate system is a complex whole. Based on past observations, a connection between temperature and solar spots can be assumed: the fewer spots, the cooler the climate. However, the correlation is not very straightforward and climate scientists hold that the effect is rather regional than global.[8] Even if the climate were to suddenly start to cool, we wouldn't regret investing in renewable energy technologies and moving away from fossil fuels. Developing new technologies means investments, new jobs, new manufacturing and new opportunities. Being stuck in the old solutions from past industrial eras will become expensive in the long run.

In addition to information and technology, we should also consider our hearts and minds. What does a person experience when seeing birds trying to clean their feathers of oil from a spill? In seeking harmony with nature, we must fight cynicism.

Charles David Keeling was said to have been shocked when he found out how man has disturbed the delicate balance of Earth's breathing. He noticed how Earth breathes according to a certain annual rhythm: the largest concentration of carbon dioxide occurs in the winter in the northern hemisphere before pollination intensifies in the spring. The North dominates the global rhythm, because most of the Earth's land surface area and green cover is there. Keeling also noticed that Earth's breathing becomes deeper little by little as the amount of carbon dioxide increases.[9]

Because the phenomenon is global, its solution has to be as well. This is why we all need to consider the price tag of our current way of extracting wealth from nature.[10] If for nothing else, then at least because the advancement of climate change also destroys the conditions required for agriculture. This is especially true in countries situated on the lower latitudes where most of Earth's population is found.

Water: The Elixir of Life

Humans are mostly made out of water. Water is also the most important condition for life. The significance of water is easily forgotten in the Nordics, because it is practically limitless there. In contrast, when I travelled some parts of Australia, I was reminded of the scarcity of water.

In many parts of the world, things are not so great: Children in Zambia are suffering this very moment due to a lack of clean water, and climate change makes this problem even more severe. The monsoons around the Indian peninsula have started to become less regular and more unpredictable.[11] Climatologists argue there are more changes underway: If temperatures rise the predicted four degrees, torrential rains will become more frequent as storms travel through the warm atmosphere. On the other hand, dry areas will become even drier. It is common knowledge that rainfall has diminished in the tropics and subtropics since the 1970s. The Mediterranean region, the Northeastern United States, Australia and many other areas around the world have turned radically more dry since 1970s and this trend is about to continue.[12]

There are many facets to consider: The oceans have become man's dumping grounds. There are 46,000 pieces of plastic garbage per square kilometer of ocean.[13] After air, water is the most important resource. There should be zero tolerance for wasteful use of water and plastic. We don't need bottled water in Finland. Lake Aral in central Asia was the world's fourth-largest lake only a few decades ago — until it shrank to a tenth of its original size. This is due to agriculture in surrounding countries exploiting the two rivers that feed it, the Amurdarjan and the Syrdarjan. Wheat and cotton farming in nearby countries Turkmenistan, Kazakhstan, Uzbekistan, and Kyrgyzstan have had a disastrous effect on the ecosystem in the entire area. For example, 70% of Turkmenistan has turned into a desert within the last few decades.[14]

How is this kind of destruction of the environment even possible? How do we let an enormous area fall into such a state? The reason, as usual, is shortsighted seeking of economic gain. The countries surrounding Lake Aral are completely dependent on agriculture and oil. Even though the population is educated, inefficiency is sprawling: nowhere in the world is the added value from the use of fresh water as insignificant. In other words, water is being wasted in an incredibly careless way.

A human drinks about two liters of water each day but indirectly consumes 1,500–4,500 liters through the production of their food. Agriculture accounts for two thirds of global water usage but in certain rapidly growing countries like China, India, Pakistan, and Bangladesh, that share is 85–95% of the total water consumption.[15] Simultaneously, some 900 million people lack access to safe water and up to 90% of the wastewater flows untreated into densely populated coastal zones.[16]

Water is also a very politically charged issue. Around 40% of the global population lives along rivers that bisect various countries. Competition for fresh water is intensifying around the globe. Many international conflicts are caused by water; successful water politics bring about peace and stability.

There are many prior examples. The Palestinian/Israeli dispute is but one. An important source of the Syrian conflict is also water.[17] Tensions between ethnic groups in Syria started to escalate after a prolonged drought as farmers rushed to urban centers to escape extreme conditions.

Then, instead of addressing the problem, the ruling Alawite minority, led by President Assad, exacerbated it by protecting their own access to water. These injustices fed the discontent that contributed to the popular uprising, which has now escalated into a full-blown war. The price for poor policies under extreme conditions can be equally extreme.

In fact, most of the major conflicts on Earth are about access to natural resources, the most precious and scarce of them being water. Even though we seldom acknowledge this now, we can count on this being even more true in the future. For instance, the core of the tension between China and India lies in scarcity of natural resources. The transboundary river Brahmaputra is a large river utilized by both countries.[18] However, because of the old territorial and contradictory claims, the countries have not managed to agree how to manage the precious water. In the long run, this lack of institutional management of the precious common resource will result in independent, large-scale utilization projects by China, India and Bangladesh with their own separate interests, without any joint consultation process. The countries have, however, continued negotiations, because they recognize the potential devastation that could result. The negotiations have thus far been unfruitful.

In Europe, there is also a lack of proper water resource management. Right2water has been the first ever successful citizen initiative in Europe.[19] Almost two million citizen signatures were collected by the end of 2014 in support of legislation in the European Commission (EC) for fresh water as a citizen right. Yet, after a lot of promise from the EC, nothing much has been made to secure this basic human right as a public service.

Even though there are some one billion people on Earth who lack secure access to fresh water, there are some positive developments to be observed. Even some former villains are starting to understand the severity of the problem. Nestlé's CEO Peter Brabeck-Letmathe has committed himself and his company to find a solution to water scarcity on our planet.[20] The annual Water Leaders Summit, an exclusive high-level gathering of global water industry leaders, government regulators and policy think-tanks, offers a forum for discussing solutions to pressing water issues.[21]

Climate change seems to have a significant impact on the sufficiency of fresh water on the planet. Global warming itself has an effect on the global hydrological cycle. Rising temperatures lengthen the growing season, which increases evaporation. On an average, precipitation is increasing in the lower atmosphere, but it is distributed very unevenly. Extreme weather events are predicted to become significantly more frequent.[22]

The presumed rising of sea levels is one of the consequences of global warming. By the end of the century, the Gulf of Finland is predicted to have risen by as much as 90 centimeters at its worst (but more likely one-third of that). A larger and more practical problem is the difficulty posed to building activity caused by short-term fluctuations in the sea level. The highest ocean floods have easily been 2 meters.[23]

The most significant global problem, however, is the increase of aridity throughout the world. It seems that the Mediterranean region, the Midwest of the United States, Australia, eastern Brazil, South Africa, and northern India are particularly vulnerable.[24] According to projections by IPCC, significantly more people are going to suffer from chronic scarcity of fresh water in the future. By 2050 it entails the overwhelming majority of the global population.[25]

Because agriculture uses the majority of our water resources, we should look at agricultural solutions for producing food without overusing them. We could start with meat production, which has doubled in 50 years. Producing meat proteins uses up significantly more resources than producing plant proteins. To produce one kilo of meat, 7–10 kilos of feed is required.[26] This supply chain is one of the key reasons for the drastic disappearance of 750,000 square kilometers of the Amazon rainforest — three times the size of United Kingdom — since 1978: Land must be cleared to produce soy, which is mainly used to feed beef cattle.[27]

The other problem is the cost of food, which has risen with the use of fossil fuels. In prosperous countries, where stores are brimming with food, it may be hard to understand the situation in poorer countries, where food is getting more expensive, making access to it even more difficult. The Agriculture and Food Organization of the United Nations (FAO) estimates that by 2050 the global demand for food, feed and fiber will grow by 70%.[28] In addition, there are growing pressures to use agricultural products for biofuels. Also, according to some recent studies, one of the effects of climate change is that the yield of crops will diminish in the future.[29] Thus, as global population is predicted to grow to 9.7 billion by the middle of the century, we have the ingredients for a crisis in our hands. Farmland has also been directed to other use, such as production of biofuel. It's clear that the crisis will strike worse in the countries that don't have the means or will to fight the degeneration. One of the world's most respected asset managers, Jeremy Grantham from GMO, has estimated that a global food crisis is at hand before the end of this decade.[30] Grantham has the reputation of having foreseen all major financial crises in the last decades: the Japanese crash, the dotcom bubble and the global financial crisis.

Summarizing what has been stated above, the increasing consumption of meat is unsustainable in the long run. Meat consumption is, however, constantly increasing and is projected to continue doing so by FAO.[31] Purely from the perspective of resource efficiency, the consumption of plant-based foods requires much less of the life-sustaining global resources, of which water and forests are most important. All living organisms require the former, and in the case of the latter it's a question of the health of the ecosystems. Deforestation destroys Earth's lungs.

Reforestation would significantly advance many environmental goals: carbon capture, precipitation, etc. This is especially true if, at the same time, the complexity of forests is considered. In this regard, there is an important initiative underway: In a project founded in 1971 in the Las Gaviotas area of eastern Columbia, over 30 square miles of new rainforest has been established in the middle of the savannah. Technologies better suited for developing nations have been created there, as well as a social structure established to guarantee work and sustenance for all inhabitants.

I have had the opportunity to visit Las Gaviotas, a unique initiative in sustainability. The society has, for example, been able to "create" water by establishing a microclimate through forestation. A region that was previously completely arid now has stable water resources.[32]

This project opens up interesting opportunities: if the forestation of deserts could happen with the help of methods created in Las Gaviotas, the capture of "excess" carbon dioxide could be significantly increased.

Climate Change and the Future of Planet Earth

Turn Down the Heat: Why a 4°C Warmer World Must be Avoided, a landmark report commissioned by the World Bank, was published in November 2012. The report was written by the leading global climate change research center in Germany, the Potsdam Institute for Climate Impact Research. Its message was desperate: If we continue to allow emissions levels to proceed along the current path towards increasing global warming, it will have a dramatic effect on our societies.[33]

The report depicted a detailed scenario of a world four degrees warmer than present — in other words, the world that awaits us if emissions aren't reduced. That would mean floods, droughts, deforestation, poverty and diseases. Most of the major coastal cities would be faced with dire issues due to rising sea levels. The conditions in this kind of a world would be so difficult and challenging that it would be hard to imagine anyone thriving there. Developing countries will especially suffer.

For these reasons, a process of change must be initiated. The sixth wave, which will last until the middle of the century, will be the absolute last possible moment to do something about it. A lot of evidence suggests that change needs to start within the next 10 years, before it is too late to stop a harmful sequence of events. The common way to address the escalation of the harmful events beyond control is to talk about "tipping points".[34] All available means must be used in order to reduce greenhouse gases.

Our challenge with climate change is how to alter our way of living so that the following generations will not have to suffer unreasonably from the indifference of previous generations. If we continue like we have, such suffering will be wholly inevitable. We are not just talking about climate change but also the future of the entire global system. The United Nations Millennium report from 2005 analyzed the status of Earth's ecosystems and found that most of the world's important ones have already been significantly damaged.[35]

One of the most interesting gambits in the discussion about sustainability is, Jørgen Randers' work *2052* (2012). Randers was one of the authors of the legendary report *Limits to Growth*, published in 1972. Randers was in the group at the Massachusetts Institute of Technology (MIT) that received the commission from the Club of Rome. Forty years later, Randers' compilation highlights two problems: shortsightedness and lack of global management. If we weren't so shortsighted, we could immediately tackle the largest problems. Unfortunately, a lack of strategic grip leads to partial optimization and misguided use of resources. This has become all too clear in United Nations-led climate change policies: Countries are still mostly only interested in their own priorities, and that is why no real change in aggregate emission levels have been detected up until now.

Another large issue is the lack of global management. Our international structures are surprisingly unevolved for solving global problems. It appears that we may need some new global superstructure — more efficient than the current United Nations — with enough authority to create rules for the sustainable use of natural resources.

The third challenge is the massive subsidies for fossil fuels that are responsible for so much pollution. The industrialized nations subsidize energy production in developing nations in many ways. According to the British Overseas Development Institute, 70% of the subsidies given to the 12 largest producers of emissions in developing nations go to fossil fuel projects. They estimate that the 11 wealthiest nations subsidized energy production by as much as 74 billion dollars.

Russia, the United States, Australia, Germany and Great Britain deal out the most subsidies.[36]

The co-existence of human beings and nature on our planet is a fascinating story about the journey of one species. The development of modern civilizations is founded, after all, on harnessing Earth's mineral resources. These resources have been pivotal in all technological advancement: Copper, iron, zinc and many other minerals have made possible the technology that civilizations have been based on.[37] On the other hand, there are some distinctive features for falling civilizations and empires, as carefully argued by geographer Jared Diamond.[38] According to Diamond, there are a number of reasons that might be behind the collapse. First of all, it is about failing to anticipate the problem, secondly about perceiving it once it has emerged, thirdly about failing to organize efforts to solve it and fourthly failing to be successful in solving the problem. Thus, there are many ways not to live up with the challenge. The issues of global warming and plundering of Earth's resources are really calling for successful solutions.

At the current pace of consumption, some raw materials that are currently valuable to various industries will run out within a few decades.[39] Many key minerals are found in only a few locations on Earth. The rare earth metals needed, for instance, for the manufacturing of mobile phones are almost exclusively found in China and a few African countries. Industries that use minerals can currently only recycle less than half of the raw materials, when it ideally should be close to 100%.

The inevitable long-term increase in fossil energy prices, coupled with decreasing prices of renewable sources, means that the industries using metals have to struggle with diminishing returns. Thus, the big question facing the industries based on fossil fuel is: How do we change the structure of industrial production and the use of energy so that dependency on fossil fuel is decisively diminished?

There is no other solution but to take better advantage of solar energy, either directly or indirectly. The time of cheap fossil fuel and minerals is simply over. The future of no nation can be founded on industries that are energy and mineral intensive.

In spite of the need for less resource intensity, nations are now competing to claim the untapped resources of the Arctic environment above the 66th latitude which is thawing due to global warming. The polar ice cap is melting significantly faster than previously predicted. The Arctic region will be completely without summertime ice cover by 2050 but potentially as soon as 2020.[40] The melting has sad consequences: First, certain animals, especially polar bears, will suffer. Second, the lack of ice cap will open up opportunities to tap the Arctic's natural resources, which cannot be done without harm to the ecosystem in the region. Third, researchers predict that the number of storms will increase due to the melting.

The Arctic continental shelves constitute some of the world's largest remaining prospective areas of oil and gas.[41] This is the reason for the tremendous interest in the Arctic. The raw materials, too, could be dug up from the ground. In the scenario of a four-degree warming, the conditions there would change drastically.

The Arctic Council, which is the governing body of countries around arctic region, underscores sustainability in its Arctic region strategy,[42] but is simultaneously permitting and supporting tapping of the Arctic's fossil resources. The possible consequences of oil spills in these distant and vast ocean regions carry much more risk than those inherent to pumping oil from the desert. Although Shell decided to step down from their ambitious arctic drilling plans,[43] there might be others who look for new opportunities in this respect. It would be much safer to consider other types of commercial activities, such as eco-tourism.[44]

The survival of Earth depends on the inviolability of fossil reserves in the Arctic region. In order to stay within the goal of a two-degree warming, the Arctic fossil resources should be left alone. This is the crux of the matter: Scientists have calculated that we can only use up to 565 gigatons of the remaining 2,795 gigatons of carbon dioxide if we hope to have any chance to thrive on Earth in the future.[45] This means, as Naomi Klein has so well described in her *Capitalism vs. Climate*, that we have to do something about human greediness exemplified by oil companies looking relentlessly for new sources for oil.[46]

Tapping the Earth's Resources

A "sustainability deficit," the size of planet Earth has been born not just through environmentally careless production and consumption but also through the appearance of Asia and especially China at the front row of the global economy. Never before have we faced a global shortage of the majority of our resources — not just one or two raw materials, as in previous times. The single most significant reason for this has been the phenomenal growth of China since the beginning of the 1990s and the ensuing increase in demand for raw materials.

At the same time, China has made unprecedented capital investments in infrastructure and real estate in particular. Only at the end of 2014 had this boom started to show signs of a slow-down. And even though oil prices have been in a steep decline since late 2014, we can probably expect the price of raw materials to continue to climb in the long-term.

Our societies have excavated minerals since the earliest days of civilization.[47] Industrialization caused the use of raw materials to increase exponentially, but up until now their prices and supply have remained sustainable, thanks to technological advancement, increased productivity and discovery of new natural resources. We're now surprised to find that many of the raw materials we use are becoming extremely scarce, which of course usually means that their prices will increase.

Mineral resources and biological reserves are our key resources. In the last 10 years, thanks to the steep increase in consumption of raw materials, the question has arisen as to whether there will be a sufficient amount of either. Of equal and growing concern is what will happen to the economy when we're really faced with shortages of important raw materials. Thus far, those who have shared this worry are few. Even so, there is still very little conversation about this topic, because it's hard for people to grasp these kinds of long-term changes.

The finite nature of planet Earth and its resources seems to be easily forgotten. The report by the Club of Rome, *Limits to Growth,* tried to open people's eyes as far back as the 1970s in regards to the finiteness of natural resources.[48] It was the first serious attempt to model the global production and consumption streams according to how sustainable our activity on the planet is. Tapping of natural resources, pollution and population growth were central variables. A research group from MIT did the actual study, and its findings painted the picture of total derailment of society by the end of this century due to overuse of natural resources. Later updates of the report and work by Jørgen Randers have confirmed the original report's basic findings.[49]

Even though those early findings clearly displayed the existence of the critical trends in terms of planetary survival, there was an effort to silence the distress call.[50] Conservative circles throughout society thought the Club of Rome report dangerous and threatening to their business.[51] The findings predicted what is now uncontestable: Wasting natural resources and pollution will lead to stagnation of economic growth. The phenomena listed in the report were expected to occur in the first decades of this century and population decrease in the latter half of the century.

After a heated discussion and a propaganda war, the report was not talked about, its results were dismissed or the results were claimed to be something the report didn't present. For instance, many critics took scenarios built by research group as predictions, which they were not. In fact, the original 1972 report presented 12 scenarios that were built, using system dynamics theory and computer model called World3. These scenarios played out different patterns from 1900 to 2100.

The key message back in 1972 was that we are now able to simulate the future of Earth — for the first time in human history — and it does not look very promising. The decades advanced and a few updates were made along the way. Now we can conclude that the basic scenario outlined in the report was disconcertingly accurate. Global economic problems are accumulating, economic

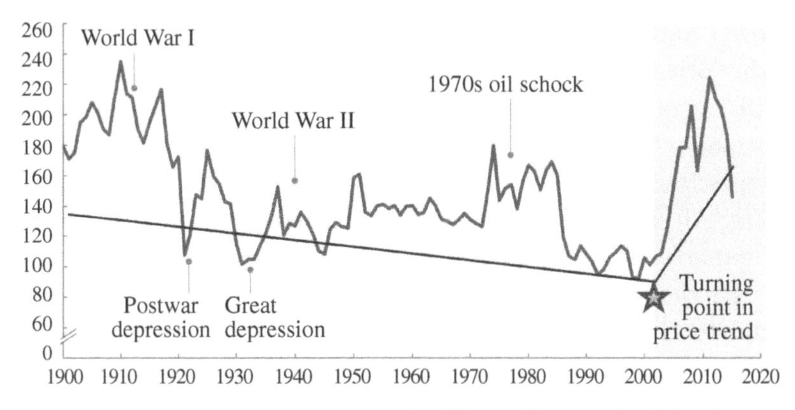

Figure 1. Resource prices have increased significantly since the turn of the century.

Source: Grilli and Yang; Pfaffenzeller; World Bank; International Monetary Fund; Organisation for Economic Cooperation and Development statistics; Food and Agriculture Organization of the United Nations; UN Comtrade; Mckinsey Global Institute analysis.

growth is stumbling in advanced societies and a dearth of resources and increased pollution has started to shrivel economies.

The mineral resources and agricultural products that have kept society and industry going thanks to relative cheapness and accessibility are now becoming scarcer and more expensive.[52] Figure 1 depicts the dramatic increase in commodity prices at the beginning of the 21st century, tamed partly by the prolonged recession in the aftermath of the financial crisis.

This pattern of commodity price increases in the global markets is one of the best indicators of where the global economy is headed in the next decades. Thus, the increasing prices will force a search for alternative products.

History shows us that increasing prices of raw materials can produce considerable changes. The birth of the modern forest industry is a case in point: Up until the middle of the 19th century, cotton rags served as the raw material for paper. As education levels improved and the printing of newspapers and books increased, so did the price of rags, because it was limited in supply. By the mid-19th century, there were certain forward-looking entrepreneurs and engineers in northern Europe who started to look for alternatives to rags as raw material. That material turned out to be the northern conifers. After arduous experimentation and a pursuit of knowledge from experts in the factories of Germany, England and Sweden, new technologies were implemented. This connected countries like Finland to the global economy and created the foundation for the country to grow into an industrial society.

A change in direction has always been necessary whenever a new factor emerges that has an influence on current trends. It's also common to strongly fight the change. So in this day, we continue to live as if information and threats don't exist. However, we know that allowing the current direction to continue means that in 2050, three times as much of our natural resources will be consumed in comparison to today.[53] We already have plenty of evidence that this won't be an option, especially considering the insufficiency of raw materials. The production of uranium, as an example, exceeded its peak in the 2010s, which means that there is no rational basis to think nuclear power would be an answer to our energy challenges.[54]

As a matter of fact, the growth pattern is already changing: The trends in the use of raw materials and in economic growth are starting to become disconnected, as Figure 2 shows.

Gross domestic product (GDP) growth and the use of raw materials started to become disconnected in the 1970s. This chart shows us that the economy is slowly but surely becoming less material dependent. Even though the use of natural resources per production unit is diminishing, relatively speaking, the absolute increase in consumption eats up that gain. The background for this is the phenomenal growth in excavation and production of minerals in the last century. The use of building materials increased 34-fold, excavation of ores and minerals 27-fold and the use of fossil fuel 12-fold.[55] During the same period, prices of raw materials decreased by almost one-third.

If we look at the material intensity of the world economy, a major shift has taken place since the turn of millennium. That is

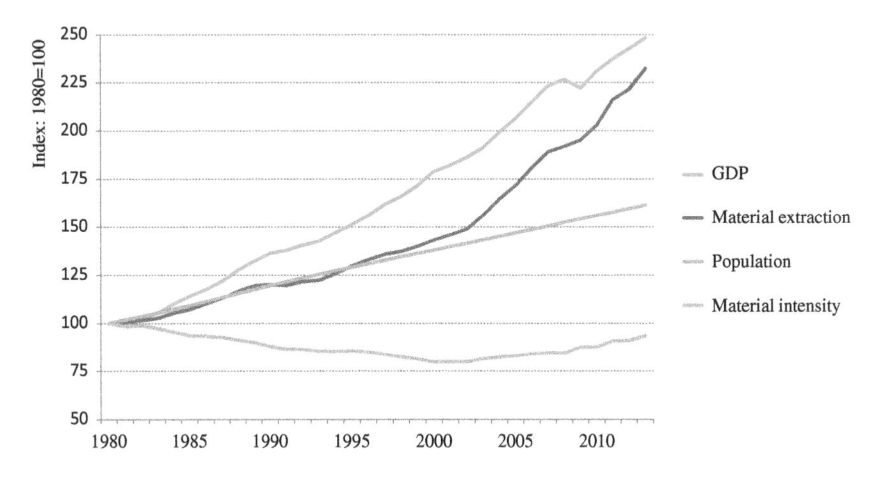

Figure 2. Key long-term resource indicators.
Source: Wu (2016).[59]

when production started to shift increasingly from material-efficient countries to countries that have low material efficiency. As companies from Japan, South-Korea, and India have been eager to relocate their production to China, India, and Southeast Asia, the overall result has been the decline in material efficiency. Counter-intuitively, at present, the global economy needs more material per unit of GDP than it did at the turn of millennium.[56]

Mineral resources have not been distributed evenly. In 2012, 95% of earth metals sold came from China,[57] 60% of the iron ore in the world came from Australia, Brazil, and China, while 83% of the world's exploitable phosphate rock came from Morocco, China and South Africa.[58] Phosphorus is a typical example of a raw material that is becoming increasingly scarce, thus creating ample opportunities for new innovations to take over the marketplace.

All of the above information makes it easier to understand that in the sixth wave, which is now beginning, we are without any doubt going to be faced with both the scarcity of resources and pollution due to the wasteful use of minerals. The most significant innovations of the next few decades will be those that raise resource efficiency one way or the other as new materials are developed. Material consumption must become five times as efficient, or, conversely, consumption

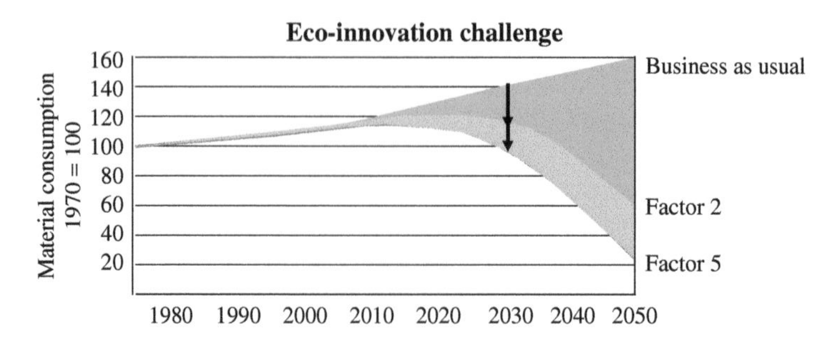

Figure 3. The eco-innovation challenge and material consumption.
Source: O'Brien, M. & Miedzinski, M. 2011. Closing the Eco-Innovation Gap. Eco-Innovation Observatory, Annual Report.

must decrease by 80%. This is a tough goal in economies that are geared towards growth, but humanity has no other alternative.

Figure 3 shows that the curve of material consumption should begin to decline within the current decade if we wish to preserve our environment and safeguard for the next generations the same opportunities that we've enjoyed.

The message is clear: In the strategic development of our societies, all attention should be focused on fundamentally increasing resource efficiency on all fronts in an effort to move away from fossil fuels and to prepare for climate change. This requires a global effort, our next topic.

References

1. Find the the story of Charles Keeling in: Weiner, Jonathan. 1991. *The Next Hundred Years*. London: Bantam Books.
2. Climate Central. 2016. "400,000 Years of Carbon Dioxide." Accessed August 10, 2016. http://www.climatecentral.org/gallery/graphics/400000-years-of-carbon-dioxide.
3. DESMOG. 2014. "Why Climate Deniers Have No Scientific Credibility: Only 1 of 9,136 Recent Peer-Reviewed Authors Rejects Global Warming." Accessed September 13, 2016. http://www.desmogblog.com/2014/01/08/why-climate-deniers-have-no-scientific-credibility-only-1-9136-study-authors-rejects-global-warming.

4. *The Guardian.* 2014. "Planet likely to warm by 4C by 2100, scientists warn." Accessed September 9, 2016. 2016https://www.theguardian.com/environment/2013/dec/31/planet-will-warm-4c-2100-climate.
5. *Bloomberg.* 2015. "75% of heat waves are attributable to climate change". Accessed August 10, 2016. http://www. bloomberg.com/news/articles/2015-04-27/like-that-heat-wave-75-of-them-attributable-to-climate-change.
6. *The New York Times.* 2016. "Flooding of Coast, Caused by Global Warming, Has Already Begun." Accessed September 13, 2016. http://www.nytimes.com/2016/09/04/science/flooding-of-coast-caused-by-global-warming-has-already-begun.html.
7. Read more about the interaction of humans and nature in: Flannery, Tim. 2010. *Here on Earth: A Twin Biography of the Planet and the Human Race.* London: Penguin Books.
8. NASA Science. 2013. "Solar Variability and Terrestrial Climate." Accessed September 13, 2016. http://science.nasa.gov/science-news/science-at-nasa/2013/08jan_sunclimate/.
9. Keeling, Charles. 1998. Rewards and penalties of monitoring the earth. *Annual Review Energy Environment*, **23**, 25–82.
10. Bardi, Ugo. 2014. *Extracted: How the Quest for Mineral Wealth is Plundering the Planet: A Report to the Club of Rome.* Vermont: Chelsea Green Publishing.
11. Yi, Lo, Lawal, Billab and Ajit, Singha. 2004. Effect of climate change on seasonal monsoon in Asia and its impact on the variability of monsoon rainfall in Southeast Asia. *Geoscience Frontiers*, **6**(6), 817–823.
12. Dai, Aiguo. 2011. Drought under global warming. A Review. *WIREs Climate Change*, **2**, 45–65.
13. United Nations Environment Programme. 2011. Plastic Debris in the Ocean. In *UNEP Year Book 2011*, 20–33. Accessed January 23, 2017. http://www.unep.org/yearbook/2011/pdfs/plastic_debris_in_the_ocean.pdf.
14. Varis, Olli. 2014. "Resources: curb vast water use in Central Asia." Published in Nature. 1 October 2014. Accessed August 10, 2016. http://www.nature.com/news/resources-curb-vast-water-use-in-central-asia-1.16017.
15. Global Agriculture. "Agriculture at a crossroads" Accessed September 13, 2016. http://www.globalagriculture.org/report-topics/water.html.
16. United Nations Environment Programme & United Nations Settlement Programme. 2010. "Sick Water. The Central Role of Wastewater Management in Sustainable Development." Accessed August 10, 2016. http://www.unep.org/pdf/SickWater_screen.pdf

17. Smithsonian.com. 2016. "Is a Lack of Water to Blame for the Conflict in Syria?" Accessed August 10, 2016. http://www.smithsonianmag.com/innovation/is-a-lack-of-water-to-blame-for-the-conflict-in-syria-72513729/.
18. The National Interest. 2016. "Water War: This River Could Sink China-India Relations." Accessed September 13, 2016. http://nationalinterest.org/feature/water-war-river-could-sink-china-india-relations-15829.
19. Wasser ist ein Menschenrecht. 2016. "Right2Water campaign lives on: EPSU call on Commission to act now on ECI Right2Water in Brussels action, World Water Day 2016." Accessed September 13, 2016. http://www.right2water.eu/de/news/right2water-campaign-lives-epsu-call-commission-act-now-eci-right2water-brussels-action-world.
20. Nestlé. 2016. "Water Challenge blog." Accessed September 13, 2016. https://www.water-challenge.com/.
21. Singapore international water week. 2016. "Water leader's summit." Accessed September 13, 2016. http://www.siww.com.sg/water-leaders-summit.
22. Fisher, E. M. and Knutti, R. 2015. Anthropogenic contribution to global occurrence of heavy-precipitation and high-temperature extremes. *Nature Climate Change*, **5**, 560–564.
23. Finnish Meteorological Institute. 2013. "Climate change will raise sea level in the Gulf of Finland." Accessed September 13, 2016. http://ilmatieteenlaitos.fi/tiedote/650329.
24. Geophysical Fluid Dynamics Laboratory (GFDL). 2016. Accessed March 8, 2016. http://www.gfdl.noaa.gov/about.
25. See IPCC latest (2015) report on freshwater resources: http://www.ipcc.ch/pdf/assessment-report/ar5/wg2/WGIIAR5-Chap3_FINAL.pdf. Accessed September 25, 2016.
26. UNCCD — United Nations Convention to Combat Desertification. 2016. "Worsening factors." Accessed September 13, 2016. http://www.unccd.int/en/programmes/Thematic-Priorities/Food-Sec/Pages/Wors-Fact.aspx.
27. Mongabay.com. 2016. "Amazon Destruction" Accessed September 13, 2016. http://rainforests.mongabay.com/amazon/amazon_destruction.html.
28. FAO. 2009. "How to feed the world in 2050?" Accessed September 13, 2016. http://www.fao.org/fileadmin/templates/wsfs/docs/expert_paper/How_to_Feed_the_World_in_2050.pdf
29. EurekAlert! 2016. "Crop breeding is not keeping pace with climate change." Accessed September 13, 2016. http://www.eurekalert.org/pub_releases/2016-06/uol-cbi061716.php.

30. Think Progress. 2012. "Jeremy Grantham on 'Welcome to Dystopia': We Are 'Entering A Long-Term And Politically Dangerous Food Crisis." Accessed March 8, 2016. http://thinkprogress.org/climate/2012/08/16/681571/jeremy-grantham-on-welcome-to-dystopia-we-are-entering-a-long-term-and-politically-dangerous-food-crisis/.
31. FAO Corporate Document Repository. 2015. "Livestock commodities" Accessed September 13, 2016. http://www.fao.org/docrep/005/y4252e/y4252e05b.htm.
32. Friends of Gaviotas. 2016. Accessed September 13, 2016. http://www.friendsofgaviotas.org. A video can be seen at: https://youtube.com/watch?v=xogJew_nlko.
33. The World Bank. 2012. "Climate Change Report Warns of Dramatically Warmer World This Century." Accessed March 8, 2016. http://www.worldbank.org/en/news/feature/2012/11/18/Climate-change-report-warns-dramatically-warmer-world-this-century.
34. By tipping point we refer to the term used for describing the point at which world climate crosses a certain threshold, triggered by some factor of change. See *Scientific American*. 2012. "Is Earth Nearing an Environmental 'Tipping Point'"? http://www.scientificamerican.com/article/is-earth-nearing-environmental-tipping-point/.
35. Millennium Assessment. 2005. "Guide to Millennium Assessment Reports." Accessed March 8, 2016. http://www.millenniumassessment.org/en/index.html.
36. Overseas Development Institute. 2015. Empty Promises. G20 Subsidies to Oil, Gas and Coal Production. Accessed September 25, 2016. https://www.odi.org/sites/odi.org.uk/files/odi-assets/publications-opinion-files/9957.pdf.
37. Bardi, Ugo. 2014. *Extracted: How the Quest for Mineral Wealth is Plundering the Planet: A Report to the Club of Rome.* Vermont: Chelsea Green Publishing.
38. Diamond, Jared. 2005. *Collapse: How Societies Choose to Fail or Succeed.* New York: Penguin Books.
39. Sverdrup, Harald & Ragnarsdottir, Vala. 2014. Natural resources in a planetary perspective. *Geochemical Perspectives*, **3**(2).
40. The Verge. 2015. "Arctic will be basically ice-free by summer 2050, NOAA study says" http://www.theverge.com/2013/4/12/4217786/arctic-ice-free-summer-2050-noaa-study.
41. IAEA. 2013. "Resources to reserves." Accessed September 13, 2016. https://www.iea.org/publications/freepublications/publication/Resources2013.pdf, pp. 135–155.
42. Arctic Council. 2015. "Environment and Climate." Accessed September 13, 2016. http://www.arctic-council.org/index.php/en/our-work/environment-and-climate.

43. *Bloomberg.* 2015. "Why Shell Quit Drilling in the Arctic." Accessed September 13, 2016. http://www.bloomberg.com/news/articles/2015-09-28/why-shell-quit-drilling-in-the-arctic.
44. GRID-Arendal. 2014. "Tourism in the Polar Regions." Accessed September 13, 2016. http://www.grida.no/publications/tourism-polar/page/1421.aspx.
45. McKibben, Bill. 2012. "Global Warming's Terrifying New Math." *Rolling Stone* magazine. Accessed March 8, 2016. http://www.rollingstone.com/politics/news/global-warmings-terrifying-new-math-20120719?page=2.
46. Klein, Naomi. 2014. *This Changes Everything. Capitalism vs Climate.* New York: Simon & Schuster.
47. Bardi, Ugo. 2014. *Extracted: How the Quest for Mineral Wealth is Plundering the Planet: A Report to the Club of Rome.* Vermont: Chelsea Green Publishing.
48. Meadows, Donella H., Meadows, Dennis L., Randers, Jørgen, and Behrens III, William W. 1972. *The Limits to Growth: A Report of the Club of Rome's Project on the Predicament of Mankind.* New York: Universe Books.
49. Meadows, Donella H., Meadows, Dennis L., and Randers, Jørgen. 2004. *Limits to Growth: The 30-year update.* White River Junction, Vermont: Chelsea Green Publishing.
    Randers, Jørgen. 2012. *2052: Global Forecast for the Next 40 Years.* White River Junction, Vermont: Chelsea Green Publishing.
50. Solutions. 2010. "The History of The Limits to Growth." Accessed September 13, 2016. https://www.thesolutionsjournal.com/article/the-history-of-the-limits-to-growth/.
51. Bardi. Ugo 2008. "Cassandra's Curse: How The Limits to Growth Was Demonized." Accessed March 8, 2016. http://www.theoildrum.com/node/3551.
52. Resource Revolution. 2013. *Tracking Global Commodity Markets.* McKinsey Global Institute.
    Bardi, Ugo. 2014. *Extracted: How the Quest for Mineral Wealth is Plundering the Planet: A Report to the Club of Rome.* Vermont: Chelsea Green Publishing.
53. OECD. 2016. "Measuring Material Growth and Resource Productivity." Accessed March 8, 2016. http://www.oecd.org/environment/indicators-modelling-outlooks/MFA-Guide.pdf.
54. Bardi, Ugo. 2014. *Extracted: How the Quest for Mineral Wealth is Plundering the Planet: A Report to the Club of Rome.* Vermont: Chelsea Green Publishing.

55. Krausmann Fridolin, Gingrich, Simone, Eisenmenger, Nina, Erb, Karl-Heinz, Haberl, Helmut, and Fischer-Kowalski, Marina. 2009. Growth in global materials use, GDP and population during the 20th century. *Ecological Economics*, **68**(10), 2696–2705.
56. UNEP. 2016. "Global Material Flows and Resource Productivity. Assessment Report for the UNEP International Resource Panel." Accessed August 23, 2016. http://unep.org/documents/irp/16-00169_LW_GlobalMaterialFlowsUNEReport_FINAL_160701.pdf.
57. Progressive Economy. 2013. "China's share of rare-earth production: 97% in 2010, 85% in 2012." Accessed September 13, 2016. http://www.progressive-economy-org/trade_facts/chinas-share-of-rare-earth-production-97-in-2010-85-in-2012/.
58. Vaccari, David. 2009. "Phosphorus: A Looming Crisis." Scientific American. June 2009. Accessed September 15, 2016. http://www.nature.com/scientificamerican/journal/v300/n6/full/scientificamerican0609-54.html, pp. 54–59.
59. Global materials flows database. Available at http://www.materialflows.net. Vienna University of Economics and Business. Vienna

Chapter 5

THE ROAR OF THE PEOPLE

Since 2010 the world has been shaken by a wave of democratic movements. The Arab world has been in turmoil for a long time, and the wave of protests that began in Western Sahara was simply a superficial indication of a deeper change that is currently sweeping across the world. It affects not only countries whose people are rising up to demand their rights but also all others who either directly or indirectly have given their silent consent to authoritarian regimes.

Let us briefly contemplate what this is all about. The pattern of a revolution is approximately as follows: Initially, societal issues accumulate, which then breed hopelessness and a riot mentality. These all create pressure, to which people react both individually and collectively. Then something comes along that triggers a wave of protest. People are swept along and compelled to take part in the resistance. Before anyone can really understand what is going on, the old system starts to break up and a new one emerges to take its place. This is what took place in Tunisia, where the Arab Spring got its start — and which now has spread all over the region.

The transformation I describe above is similar to the transition from one societal wave to another (see Chapter 3). What is this change all about? Where will this phenomenon lead us? The idea here is to provide a broader context of these recent events as part of an international systemic change and to examine the reasons why popular sovereignty will become the focal issue in the coming decades.

We are talking about democracy, power, freedom of expression and human rights. Dictatorships, along with modern progressive democracies, will be challenged in the coming decades.

What I call "the roar of the people" takes many forms in different contexts. While turmoils in the Middle East and Northern Africa have brought the very idea of democracy into the fore and produced a massive number of refugees, there are other sorts of situations worth our concern. The rise of right wing politics in many parts of Europe is noticeable. For instance, in Germany the Alternative for Germany (AfD) party has proceeded swiftly from its inception in 2003 to now having representatives in European Parliament, support from 12% to 14% of German voters, and greater visibility in the media.

Then there is "the roar of the educated" that started with WikiLeaks operations in 2007. Massive amount of secret information has been released producing a totally new platform for us to know what is happening behind the scenes. In 2013, Edward Snowden, a former employee to National Security Agency (NSA) decided to release via the *Guardian* and the *Washington Post* a huge amount of information describing how national security agents have secretly followed communication of top political leaders in the world. In 2016, a consortium of newspapers reported about the Panama Papers, obtained secret data about shell companies used by wealthy individuals to hide their assets in tax-havens around the world. This leak points to the necessity to build an internationally harmonized tax-system to stand against fraud. According to a survey, a clear majority of multinational companies would even endorse it.[1]

Thus, the emerging sixth wave comes with new standards of transparency made possible by the information technology leaps created in the fifth wave. In the coming years and decades we are going to see a massive amount of disclosures at every level. All of this helps us in the end to build a society built on trust and transparency. As the evolution of human societies is based on ever improving quality and quantity of communication, what we have seen in the last 10 years is but a short chapter in making that possible (see Chapter 14).

The Sixth Wave of Global Politics

As mentioned before, the driver in this cycle will be an improved and more effective use of materials and energy. Economic development will be fundamentally affected by climate change and both the growing scarcity and rising prices of some key raw materials. Improving resource productivity — increasing human capital, raw material and energy usage productivity — will become the key instrument for economic and social development, particularly because globalization is inexorable and increases global trade. This will lead to a scarcity of many key raw materials, with the demand exceeding the supply.

Although there are different ideas concerning the point in time of the global peak in oil demand, the graph in Figure 1 clearly shows that we have come close to the point where supply will begin to tumble. As a result, the price of the raw materials — oil in particular — will inevitably rise. This in turn will put pressure on us to decrease consumption and find alternatives. This might be hard to understand in February 2016 (at the time of this writing), when the price of oil is a record low, but fundamentals point to this direction in the long run.

Scarcity of cheap oil — together with growing environmental concerns — will ultimately be the key factor of the energy revolution in which the world will inevitably shift to the use of renewable energy. Chinese oil imports are predicted to grow from 2.5 million barrels in

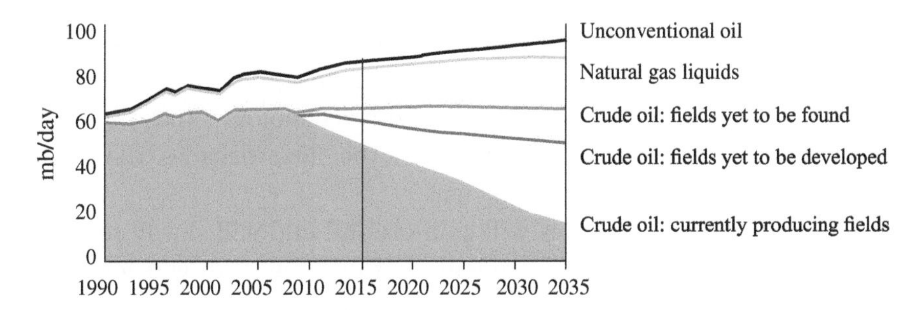

Figure 1. World oil production by type in the new policies scenario.
Source: International Energy Agency (2010).

2005 to 9.2 million barrels in 2020. According to the same estimates, China will surpass the United States as the largest importer of oil within the next few years.[2] China will need to increase its import of oil, while all the world economies will face a situation where demand exceeds supply. The rapid growth of Asia leads to a rapidly growing consumption of raw materials, and there is no end in sight. The growth in China in particular is unprecedented: if its economy continues to grow even at diminishing pace, it will surpass the United States economy somewhere during the next decade.[3]

At the same time, the population in many countries (especially in Europe) is aging, and as the baby boomer generation retires, the dependency ratio will change rapidly. By the year 2030, nearly one-third of the population in some European countries will be over 65 years old, which is radically different than the present situation. This will not only slow down economic growth, it will also lead to a considerable shift in demand for services. In addition to increased pressure on the public sectors that are charged with maintaining basic services (including healthcare), a graying Europe will also lead to the breakdown of the old industrial model. That model clearly defined the length of active working life, and the structure of the welfare state was based on a distinct division between the public and the private sector.

These two megatrends, globalization and demographic change, together create a world in which the key engine of societal advancement is resource productivity. At the same time, technology is advancing in leaps and bounds. The spread of digitalization and the Internet of Things (IoT) bring along intelligent solutions that save resources, such as fuel, as well as money and time. The new combinations of human capital, digital technology and physical products will bring about solutions in the next decades that will make services radically more efficient.

New energy technologies will gain ground and will slowly replace the fuel economy that is dependent on fossil fuel. We will learn to replace organic materials with synthetic ones, thanks to advancements in biotechnology. Nanotechnology already allows us to modify the properties of products so as to make them more durable.

New diagnostic methods are being discovered in healthcare, and we will be better able to predict the occurrence of illnesses and therefore be better able to prevent them. This will allow for more intelligent allocation of healthcare resources. Healthcare and the connected businesses will grow to be the largest field of business in the world.

It would benefit us to take a historical perspective when looking at future changes. During the previous fifth wave (1970–2010, see Chapter 3), which started with the oil crisis in the early 1970s, a power shift occurred. Previously, the United States and the Soviet Union were juxtaposed, and it appeared after the cold war that the United States would dominate alone. However, quite soon after the fall of Berlin Wall, the new situation saw a power balance between the United States, an enlarged European Union and a newly strengthened Asia take form in quick order.

It is interesting that there was a steep rise of democracies between 1970 and 1992. The number of countries with democratic regimes, defined as political participation of citizens, constraints on executive power and guarantees of civil liberties, more than doubled, up to 74. The breakup of the Soviet Union further sped up the movement and by 2005 we had already 89 democratic states.[4] This shift towards democracy will intensify in the sixth wave, in which we will witness the challenging of representational democracy by supporters of direct democracy. Pressure for more transparency and a widening of the base of decision-makers will challenge the existing political systems.

The world has also become increasingly complex, and the fight for political and economic power has continued to escalate. The enormous progress in ICT has in no way canceled out the driving force of the preceding wave (1930–1970) of the petrochemical and automotive industries. The world economy is still dominated by the alliance between oil and money. In fact, the world of oil lends us a useful perspective for understanding the hypocritical Western policies in relation to the Arab countries that are rich in oil.

Up until recent years, countries in which the West has a vested interest — i.e., the oil-producing countries — have been able to exercise their dictatorial regimes freely, without any fear of Western intervention, for as long as they have remained faithful oil suppliers. As late as the spring of 2011, there was hardly any global reaction when Saudi Arabia proclaimed, "The regulations in the kingdom categorically forbid all demonstrations, marches and sit-ins, as they contradict Islamic Sharia law and the values and traditions of Saudi society."[5] The proclamation was followed by a massive mobilization of security forces to enforce the ban. In Yemen, Kuwait, Bahrain, Syria, and many other Arab countries, any unrest was subject to a brutal crackdown.[6]

In January 2011, just before the ruler of Egypt, Hosni Mubarak, was overthrown from his position, United States Vice President at the time, Joe Biden, stated in an interview that he "would not refer to [Mubarak] as a dictator."[7] Even back then it was widely known that Mubarak and Gaddafi had collaborated in the brutal oppression of their own citizens who had dared to demand basic democratic rights. However, it is becoming increasingly clear that the policy of the West — which for more than 30 years has supported the self-proclaimed dictators of the Arab world largely because of the thirst for oil — has to come to an end at some point in time. The growing pressure from citizens will make the coming decades hard for those within democratic regimes who deliberately continue to deal with dictators of any sort. Thus, the Arab countries, whose autocratic leaders have had to face the anger of their citizenry because of perceived injustice and violations against human rights, are not the only countries in crisis. The crisis is a much deeper one and involves the entire international system. This crisis is two-dimensional.

The root of the current crisis in the geopolitical system lies in the lack of a clear global structure of governance. The G20 summits, intended to function as a platform for building a new and better international structure, have become stages for ineffectual, factional bickering. The global pendulum has shifted in a major way as Asian countries have marched to the forefront of development during the last 20 years, while the financial crisis hit the Western world particularly hard. Even so, the United States is trying to do everything in its power to preserve its global economic dominance.

A veritable drama is unfolding as we ask, "How will the new geopolitical landscape evolve in the next few decades?"

The roots of the crisis can be traced back to the excessive exploitation of natural resources and the imbalance between supply and demand of agricultural products. The extraordinary growth of the Asian economies in particular has brought on an entirely new situation in resource utilization. It has resulted in an increasing demand for raw materials, which in turn has amplified the competition for basic resources. For example, the United Nations Food and Agriculture Organization food price index increased over 100% in the first 10 years of this century (although it has decreased somewhat in the past few years).[8] The increase in prices of basic food commodities has an enormous impact, because some 1.5 billion people — or one in five — live on less than 1.25 dollar a day.[9] For them, the food price matter enormously.

The situation is much the same in regard to raw materials. To be sure, there is plenty of oil in the ground, but it is increasingly more expensive to exploit the new finds. Harnessing shale gas and shale oil, especially in the United States, has increased supply since 2008. The price of oil has dropped from 100 dollars per barrel in the summer of 2014 to 46 dollars by the mid of August 2016. This is more than likely a result of Arab oil politics, as they have become dissatisfied with being the designated oil price regulators. In the past, they have decreased production in the face of price drops but not this time. However, oil prices increases are likely in the long run.[10]

As a whole, the oil dependency of the world has entered a new phase. The game is getting tougher, as evidenced by Organization of Petroleum Exporting Countries' (OPEC) actions in the fall of 2014.[11] Decisions by OPEC, initiated largely by Saudi Arabia, brought the price of oil tumbling down. Even if OPEC is no longer acting with common interests in mind but rather is acting solely in the interest of the powerful member nations, we still are sure to see more of the same kind of action. A key aim seems to be disabling United States shale oil production thereby increasing dependency on Arab oil production.

From an environmental perspective, this would seem to be a good development. The United States's production is much more harmful to the environment than the Arabs', due to the technology used to extract the oil from the earth. But there are other things at play in that alternatives to oil and fossil fuel in general are feverishly being sought as both energy sources and as raw material.

A group of researchers has recently calculated that it would be more economical for China to move to an energy system wholly based on renewable sources, such as solar and wind energy. These energy sources will become fully price-competitive within 10 years. In other words, in the near future, Northeastern Asia would be ready for an energy production system that may even end the region's dependency on imported energy. The basis of the calculation is the assumption that each time production is doubled, prices fall by 20%.[12] As for China, a wide country but very centrally led, it would be possible to make fast moves towards an energy system based on renewable sources, once there is a political will for it.

It is therefore a question of geopolitics and natural resources — and their coupling, for these factors together constitute the framework of the next Kondratiev wave. We have learned from the previous serious economic crises between waves that a rebound will take quite some time. It took until 1954 for the world economy to return to levels of 1929, prior to the Wall Street crash. Even though the shock was milder in the early 1970s, the oil crisis, heavy stagflation and other factors contributed to a poor economic performance. Next, I take a closer look at those factors and their connection to global politics.

The Global Political Crisis

Renowned economists Nouriel Roubini and Ian Bremmer have remarked that we live in a so called "G-Zero world," or one in which no individual country or block has either the leverage or the willpower to genuinely pursue an international agenda that sincerely benefits every country. Thus, instead of cooperation we are likely to see more international conflicts, whether in the context of macroeconomic coordination, financial system regulation, trade policy or the most far-reaching of all, climate policy.[13]

This is due to the G20 (a forum for international cooperation that brings together leaders, finance ministers and central bank governors from 20 major economies) having evolved into a group that is pushing its own selfish agenda, rather than the network of nations that it was prior to the worst stages of the financial crisis and which worked to strategically build international cooperation. China and the United States — what could be called the G2 — is also ineffectual, because China has never accepted the responsibility for international politics that has accrued in the wake of its economic success. A cooperation between the United States, Europe, and Japan — or G3 — is quite unlikely due to Japan's recession, earthquake and nuclear disaster (see Chapter 2).

And yet we have nothing better to offer than G20, reborn in 2008 in response to the shared threat of financial crises. In the space of just six months, significant initiatives were brought forth for new regulation of financial institutions. The IMF was awarded a new role and additional funding to support it. When the acute crisis abated, however, the United States administration fell into a virtual coma in terms of international matters, as it dealt almost exclusively with two domestic issues: leading the country out from the recession caused by the crisis and the upsurge of extreme right-wing forces. Meanwhile, the laboriously constructed euro zone has continued its drift from one crisis to the next, owing both to reckless spending by the member states and lack of discipline. Market speculation, which, for example, had an important role in the Greek crisis, has also complicated the situation.

From the 2010s onward, the arena of international politics has become colored by growing discord between the United States and China, due mainly to China's unwillingness to react in any way to the mounting pressure to appreciate its currency, which has been kept artificially low by the Chinese Government. This has caused a rift inside the G20, where even this conflict has been discussed.[14] The actual problem lies in the fundamental shift in the nature of global cooperation. In spite of all disagreements, cooperation in the past 20 years has been based on rising Asian economies: China's and India's means of growth, in particular, are their export channels with the West. At the same time, the developing nations have served as places where production can be shifted, thanks to low labor costs. Correspondingly, China and other Asian countries have gained market size in the West for their exports thus creating stronger dependencies.

This configuration has started to shift, because the structure of Asian economies have evolved to more closely resemble those of the West, thus making them more like competitors than (unequal) partners. This new situation will undoubtedly continue and even deepen over the coming decades. It is clearly visible already in, say, international climate negotiations, where over the years the competitive situation has brought the negotiations to a deadlock. WTO negotiations have also almost come to a standstill because of this. Instead, a new deal for transatlantic trade and investment cooperation (TTIP) between the United States and Europe is being negotiated. This would open up both parties' free access to each other's markets.

There are major concerns that the TTIP agreement would eliminate Europe's effort to keep up high standards in environmental regulation. In July 2016, Greenpeace leaked 250 pages negotiation drafts that proved European Union precautionary principle to be threatened by the agreement.[15] The principle dictates that any product's access to the market can be hampered if there is fear that it may cause harm to consumers. United States-grown genetically modified food (GMO) has not been allowed to be sold in European markets for this reason.

Apparently, through TTIP, United States government tries to lift these barriers. And they do have ways to squeeze European governments. For instance, they have threatened to block the easy entry of European car producers to United States markets, if Europe does not give open entry to United States agricultural products.[16] There is a fear that once such permit is given, United States companies could charge European Union for breaking the agreement even if products would not fill European standards.

A new wave of nationalist selfishness has followed the above trends. The key actors in global economy are fighting against each other in order to protect their own industries and jobs. This is happening in a situation where the world needs global cooperation perhaps more than ever before. No one wants the world economy to face another shock like the recent financial crisis. To avoid it, a new regulatory structure is required that will take into account the global nature of financial economy. In fact, the world needs an entirely new kind of superstructure with sufficient power and resources to implement supervision and control.

Opinions about this are deeply divided, however. The developing economies in particular are not interested in binding financial regulations created by the West, which, quite justifiably, the developing economies blame for creating the crisis in the first place. The United States, on the other hand, is reluctant to give up their trump card, the United States dollar, to any other new currency basket. Europe, on its side, faces such serious internal problems that it is quite unable to serve as the engine for the global system.

Is the American Hegemony Over?

Joseph Nye, advisor at the time to President Clinton and a professor at Harvard University, has an interesting view of the future development of international power. He posits that the world will need ever-stronger management of global issues in the future.[17] Ironically, he predicts that the three economies likely to be the strongest in 2050 — the United States, China, and India — will have adopted strong measures to defend their own positions. They can therefore hardly be expected to put forward any significant initiatives for a new international system.

The United States has played a decisive role in international politics since World War II. There have been arguments that American power has been on the decline since the Vietnam War and that trend will continue into the coming decades.[18] Although the return of Asia to the forefront of the world economy (after a break lasting 300 years) is inevitable, it is clear that United

States will continue to have a major global impact in the decades ahead.

The development of the geopolitical system can be considered from three different power perspectives: military, economic, and transnational. From the military power perspective, the United States will retain its position for a long time to come, and no other actor on the world stage is likely to challenge that position in the foreseeable future. In the economic sphere, the world has been multipolar for at least a decade now. The major players have been the United States, Europe, China, and Japan, while the economic powers of many other countries, such as Brazil, have been on the increase. Transnational relationships are increasingly splintered, due to a growing number of actors from the world of business, international aid organizations to international terrorist networks.

It is, however, unlikely that the United States would fall from its leading position in global politics like the British Empire did a century ago, for the simple reason that the situation is different. The power of the United States, unlike the power of the British Empire, has never been based on acquisition of territories but rather on military and economic might, which in turn were significantly supported by the dynamism inherent to the American economy. This gives the United States a much stronger competitive position against the performance of Asian economies, as the economic strength is based on technological supremacy rather than access and ownership to natural resources.[19]

Professor Charles Glaser from Washington University has asked whether the growing influence of China in world affairs will lead to an inevitable conflict between China and the United States.[20] Although this is not likely, peace is far from being guaranteed. For the time being, relatively stable political relations, nuclear weapons and the Pacific Ocean between the countries are helping to maintain the balance. How peacefully will the inevitable growth of China happen? That, in turn, hinges on China's ability to respond to the demands of the country's growing middle class — demands like freedom of speech and a true multi-party political system — and change what is, at its core, a pseudodemocratic political system.

The recently toughened internal measures against its own dissidents suggest that the Chinese Communist Party leadership fears the spread of hitherto sporadic demonstrations. Witness the surge of dissidents placed under house arrest in China soon after the start of unrest in the Arab world. On the other hand, growing access to information, particularly online, is making it increasingly difficult for Chinese political rulers to control popular opinion. Chinese leadership has no alternative in the long term. They must gradually relinquish the country's pseudodemocracy to create a fully democratic system, either peacefully or through conflict.

While the Chinese gross domestic product (GDP) may surpass the United States in the next few decades, its societal structure will continue to be very different. China is still likely to consist of a very large and extremely poor rural population. Despite the size of the Chinese economy rising to equal the level of the United States, the per capita GDP will trail far behind at that point. This could actually be good news for the international system, because whatever we may say about its scruples, the United States remains an open society at its core — a society that supports individual expression of views and is governed democratically.

Could there be a serious crisis between the United States and China in the future? I do not believe in the likelihood of a real conflict, if only due to simple geography: The two countries are separated by the Pacific Ocean, which is conducive to keeping the superpowers each in their own sphere. While China has clearly positioned itself against the United States by keeping its yuan undervalued relative to the dollar, it is still a far cry from an international conflict. That being said, we must recognize that nuclear weaponry and the deterrence afforded by them are part of the Chinese strategy.

We must also question whether the United States is prepared to relinquish at least part of its hegemony to others and especially to China. The United States must learn to make certain concessions, especially as the economic center of gravity is shifting from the West towards the East and South. A broader question regarding the future would be: "Who is building their economy on sand, and who is building theirs with a view of the coming generations?"

The United States economy has been powered by massive borrowing, which has been financed to a large extent by China. Based on huge federal budget deficits, the public sector cannot continue borrowing in such a manner for very long. It would seem to undermine the financial basis of United States military hegemony, thus contributing to the inevitable, gradual abandonment of the country's role as global police. Ever since the United States got involved with allied forces in Libya in 2011, we have seen strong signs of a new United States foreign policy — one that will increasingly be based on coalitions with willing partners, rather than on unilateral measures.

The United States economy may experience another crisis at the end of the 2010s, which will be the result of a constant increase of its public debt; in February 2017, the number stands close to a massive 20 trillion dollars. This will probably give rise to values that support a healthier economy. It is possible that even in the United States, a broader and deeper hand will need to direct politics, taking into account sustainable economic growth, aging of the population and effects on the environment. Borrowing, both private and public, will have to be curbed. Saving and healthy investment strategies will renew their appeal.[21] This will largely depend on how important a change in direction is felt to be necessary by the government.

But besides China, there is a question of the role of other BRICS countries in the sixth wave. What is the type of role Russia, India and South Africa will take in global politics considering that all of them — with the exception of South Africa — have truly global ambitions? What is more, how will those countries that comprises over 40% of global population and occupies quarter of earth's territory be active players in redefining the global agenda? The fact is that, particularly ever since 2009, the cooperation between BRICS countries has widened considerably with regular meetings and some efforts to build a common agenda. By and large, BRICS-formation has been the first real effort to build a political umbrella under South–South relationships.[22]

Russia has seemingly taken a dangerous trajectory. Ever since Putin started to take measures to regain strong influence over some former countries of the Soviet Union in the early part of the 2000s, there has been a growing tension between Russia and Europe/United States. Unfortunately, it seems as if Russia is on track to face really hard times, if not collapse. Its economy is poorly managed, contracting and suffering under European Union sanctions, sending off foreign investors.[23] The definite turn at the beginning of 2000 to dismiss an industrialization strategy and to rely on hydrocarbon exports seemed a good option while fuel prices had swung upward and global demand surged. Russia had also the political motive to make Europe dependent on Russian energy. Today Russia is the main supplier for European Union countries of crude oil and natural gas.[24] For any longer term, the chosen strategy will prove to be rather short-sighted. Russia has not been focusing on alternative energy sources besides hydrocarbons and nuclear power. Relying almost totally on natural resources has left its strategy to resemble that of most developing countries. With the lingering oil prices and increasing international efforts to put a cap on greenhouse gas emissions, we shall probably see Russian efforts to expand their portfolio away from fossil fuels.

Its mission in Ukraine to occupy Crimea and to convert its West-bound politics back to more Russia-favoring politics, is clearly proving to be a rather disastrous affair. From a purely geopolitical perspective it is understandable that Russia is worried about Ukraine's moves towards NATO and Western allies. For Russians, Ukraine and Belarus provide an essential buffer against Western invasion. History proves that what is now deemed possible, will not necessarily be so in 20 years. Having said that, according to the polls, the majority of Ukrainian people want to be more closely connected to West.[25]

As George Friedman has argued, it is more likely that in the 2020's we are going to see a lot of chaos around Russia which will lead to further fragmentation of former Soviet countries.[26] If this happens, it probably means Ukraine will do everything to tie its future to Western allies in the same way Baltic countries have done.

Brazil is the powerhouse of Latin America. In the first decade of 2000 Brazil shone as a bright example of a country that rose from relative poverty among countries of the rich. The Brazilian president, Luiz Inacio da Silva ("Lula") was immensely popular and heavy investment in public services helped him to appear as national champion. Commodity prices were on the rise and Brazil, which leans heavily on exports of commodities was enjoying the upward ride. In the current decade, the Brazilian economical situation has changed considerably. The economy went into a recession in 2014 and 2015 showed almost 4% drop in GDP. Key reasons have been a stagnating Chinese economy — Brazil's principal export partner — and a lousy European economy. The country has greatly suffered from the political crisis that forced president Dilma Rousseff to be suspended from her office as of May 2016. She is accused of spending government money, borrowed from the state bank, without authorization, to a poor farmer's program.[27]

Brazil has been elemental in forming UNASUR, South America equivalent to European Union.[28] It needs to be stated however, that UNASUR is just in the beginning stages of a path potentially leading to an European-like integration. Brazil's role in building the BRICS-coalition has also been very important. A more institutional phase of BRICS collaboration started from the meeting in Brazil at the height of the financial crisis. It turned out that the BRICS countries saw themselves as the ones keeping global economy on track at the time of the crisis.[29] Brazil at that time was still growing fast.

Brazil's true strength is its vast natural resources. It is rich in minerals and it has a lot of human capital, median age being only 30 years. The Amazonian rainforest covers over 5 million square kilometers. However, the annual deforestation rate — although dropping last 10 years — is still a whopping 100,000–150,000 square kilometers. After finding a giant supply of petroleum under the ocean some 100 km east of Rio de Janeiro in 2007, Brazil started to fancy becoming a major producer of oil.[30] President Lula called this finding "a second independence for Brazil".[31] From another perspective, exploiting this finding is another step towards making Brazil more stuck with "dirty commodities" and the country more deeply dependent on using precious natural resources in spite of the menace of global warming. In fact, Brazil's economy and society has suffered immensely from a great drought in 2014–2016. It has created a lot of shortages to electricity production which is 75% based on hydropower. It has been suggested that there is a link between deforestation, drought and climate change.[32]

Since 1960's Brazil is generally known as "a country of the future". The question is when is the right time for Brazil to reclaim its nickname. The country is vast, almost the size of the United States but lacks the infrastructure of a developed country. It has tough geographic conditions that make logistics demanding.[33] However, it has become a major agricultural exporter and it is now investing heavily into renewable energy sources beyond hydropower. Due to a coastline 7,400 kilometers long, Brazil has an immense 143 GW of wind power potential and it has set a goal to produce at least 20 GW wind power by 2020. Brazil is also endowed with plenty of sunshine and its solar energy markets are among the fastest growing in the world. Developing these sectors would help Brazil to get rid of its crippling electricity shortages.[34]

Brazil's true strength may still lie in its vast biological resources. As we move towards the end of this century, we shall find that the world will need ever new ways of understanding how our biological diversity and our understanding of physics and science of nature can bring new kinds of solutions. While the plain truth is that we are in many ways indeed racing for last resources on this earth,[35] we still have a huge amount of capacity totally underused. It is possible to find materials and solutions that do not plunder nature or human collectives. In most cases this means we need to replace non-renewable materials with natural ingredients. Gunter Pauli, the author of *Blue Economy*, has given some extraordinary examples of solutions that use natural materials innovatively. For instance, entrepreneur Lucio Ventania in the north of Brazil has invented 100% bamboo hangers, to replace hangers normally made either with steel wire or plastic requiring lots of chemicals in the process (and creating a terrible waste problem).[36] Bamboo is typically grown on land that was formerly used for sugar cane production. The workforce has been found among those left unemployed as a result of mechanization and automatization of agriculture. Since the market for hangers is about 25 billion dollars annually, we are not talking about a small opportunity here. Since our future is all about this type of innovation, Brazil could be a source for new and more sustainable production based on natural materials.

India is a natural partner for BRICS alliance. As with Brazil, India stands out with a promise of a prosperous future. But as Brazil suffers with its colonial past, so has India its own shortcomings. British rule did not help India as its industry didn't do well under British trade laws and forced Indian manufacturing out of business. The ongoing tension with Pakistan has caused four wars since the independence, and has crippled India. Additionally, the decades with socialism, while it had some noble goals, left India with an overbearing bureaucracy.

However, India may still be a surprise factor of this century. It has world's second largest population and is the seventh largest economy in the world. It has, as does Brazil, vast natural resources and a young population. It has clear global ambitions and with the current energetic prime minister Narenda Modi, India seeks to modernize itself. India has a massive youth population of 800 million (under 35) and is determined to make education available to all its people. In addition, India has an advantage that China has not: it is a democracy and thus the politics, even if in turmoil at times, is based on the idea of an open society.

During last two decades, India has positioned itself as the backoffice of the world. In recent years, however, the growth of the outsourcing business has been somewhat weaker. One of India's key opportunities are in the renewable energy sector with a huge amount of potential. The revolution has not happened as of yet, but a report shows that India could stop using almost all fossil fuels by 2050, with the benefit of creating 2.4 million new jobs already by 2020.[37] Prime minister has acted upon that, aiming at additional 100 GW solar PV and 60 GW wind capacity until 2022.[38]

India's real challenge lies, however, in providing a sustainable livelihood for its vast population. Ashok Khosla, a founder of

Development Alternatives — organization in India, has shown how this could happen: by creating already millions of jobs with his concept of social enterprise. Development Alternative cooperates with various local communities. For instance, it has commissioned a Clean-India project, where the idea is to engage students and young professionals in counteracting environmental degradation.[39] In Delhi, for instance, it aims to increase the green spaces to 20% of the land cover. The whole idea is to partner with colleges, school and NGO's to improve conditions everywhere in India.

India might the next superpower[40] in the world but it has a long way to go. The last couple of years have shown a steady progress. India has taken an active role in BRICS-development and will host BRICS-meetings in various parts of India later in 2016. As with Brazil, its greatest asset, even over massive natural richness, is its youth: 65% of its population, over 800 million people are under 35 years. If India can harness that capacity to build and equitable and sustainable society, nothing can stop it.

South Africa has been a part of BRICS since 2011. South Africa's entry was a success both to its foreign policy as it was for the BRIC-alliance. On some international fronts, such as climate change negotiations, it has already been evident how easily South Africa, Brazil, India, and China are able to find joint standpoints. By including South Africa, BRICS greatly expanded its leverage, becoming a truly global alliance with a stronger capacity to speak for developing countries.[41]

South Africa is another country blessed with an abundance of natural resources, extending from minerals, such as gold and diamonds, to a rich variety of agricultural products. It is by far the most developed country in Africa with well developed telecommunication, finance and transportation industry. It has its troubled history with apartheid but is now set for democratic development. For instance, in October 2015, university students in Johannesburg started to protest in the streets after the government announced 10% increase in university tuition fees. After a heavy wave of protest marches, President Jacob Zuma agreed to withdraw the plans. The voice of the people had been heard.[42]

South Africa may suffer from sluggish economy, high unemployment and poor education system. Still, in many ways, it has a lot of attractions: a reasonably advanced infrastructure, natural charm and a favorable demographic profile. While most assessments regarding the future of South Africa appear rather pessimistic,[43] there seems to be, for instance, a huge potential in moving from carbon-intensive energy production into using renewable technologies, as the country has a surplus of both sun and wind.[44] In the wake of non-OECD countries becoming key players for the future of global economy, South Africa can play a crucial role if it opts to take advantage of future opportunities. The projection of OECD holds that at the end of sixth wave, i.e., around mid-century, the share of non-OECD countries may rise close to 60% of global GDP.[45]

Toward More Responsible and Interactive Politics?

The greatest challenge for nations, which are democratic at least in form, is the capacity of these countries to establish new forms of interaction between citizens and the political system. This is particularly challenging at present, as alarmingly many countries are heading into a downwards spiral of debt — countries like Greece, Italy, Spain, Portugal, and France. It is only when such interaction is in place that a new kind of sustainable economy can be constructed. This model can only be constructed, however, with the active participation of people. And such activity is greatly enhanced with digital technologies, which enable consumers to become more motivated, civilly engaged citizens.[46]

The growing economic inequalities in societies are a global phenomenon exacerbated by reckless economic policies. The bloated financial economy that began in the mid-1980s has created enormous wealth for a small portion of the financial elite. Economic inequality has increased dramatically everywhere in the West. It is estimated that the wealthiest 1% of the global population controlled half of all global assets in 2015.[47]

From a civic society perspective, the recent years have shown that current models for democracy, governance and international agreements are irrevocably outdated. In the last Finnish parliamentary elections, one in every five voted for True Finns, the populist protest party. This, too, is a sign of the times, indicating that politics have drifted far from the world of ordinary people. Since the early 2010s, right-wing parties have been celebrating success throughout Western countries, for instance in Austria, Denmark, Finland, Netherlands, France, and United Kingdom.[48] The UK departure from EU (Brexit) and the election of Donald Trump as US president have further brought populism and conservatism into the center of political activity.

Yet, a new political current is already forming. Non-governmental organisations (NGOs), whether they are promoting ecological concerns or providing international aid and charity, have significantly grown in importance during the last few decades. A famous quote from Kofi Annan declares the "21th century is an era of NGOs."[49] I also strongly believe that these trans- and sub-national networks will be at the center of the next Kondratiev wave cycle. They provide a channel for the often-idealistic energy abandoned by prevailing political institutions. Modern technology, education and increased awareness have strengthened NGOs and are becoming the breeding grounds for global democracy, which is inexorably moving forward.

Global democracy can only develop if the pressure from below grows strong enough. Arab Spring and Occupy Wall Street exemplified the power of autonomous popular movements. It seems, however, that there is little need to worry about this, because in many countries the arrogance of the elite has created such pressure for change that it is inevitable. The toppling of dictators in Egypt and Libya was only a matter of time, although we now know that it wasn't quite enough to bring about a real democracy and lasting peace. Nor does this concern only the Arab countries, China or Russia. There are fine examples even in Europe. For one, a businessman who turned Western democracy and rule of law into a farce ruled Italy for a long time.

Thus, we arrived at the notion of creative destruction, coined by Joseph Schumpeter. The old systems no longer work, a new forward-looking energy and spirit have sprung from them and small corrections and improvements no longer help. When the old elite tries to reform the system through old-school thinking and bolstering of old institutions, the result is disappointing at best.

In the financial sector, companies such as AIG and Lehman Brothers were brought down by their erroneous assumptions about the market, and to a certain degree, by their arrogance. They began devising products whose true impact on national economy, popular welfare and finally their own business was either not understood or was simply ignored. In the United States, Ireland, and Spain, real estate developers and financiers artificially inflated housing prices, taking money from people who did not know what they were getting into and creating the housing bubble.[50]

The basic problem in all this is that "economic-speak" permeates all public discourse. This despite the fact that, ironically, neo-classical economic theory has time and again proven how little it can truly explain the functions of economy and society. In the center of the theory is the notion of a rational consumer, which does not explain human decision-making any better than it does human political choices. Economic-speak simplifies views into numbers and thus effectively squelches any strategic discourse.

The mantra of economic growth is connected with the outdated idea of a free-market economy, where those who can get their product to market with the greatest profit are the ones who most succeed. Although the majority of businesses and even politicians still adhere to this principle, an increasing number of the best companies in the world derive their corporate *raison d'être* from collective, social needs. They have understood that we are moving at an increasing pace towards an economic order where the value of businesses is determined by their social utility and degree of genuine concern for the needs of consumers.[51]

Operative Principles of the Sixth Wave

The sixth Kondratiev wave will also recreate organizational operating principles. This involves a new way of operating in a world that is radically different from the one based on the industrial model. Businesses, authorities, researchers, and NGOs alike will eventually embrace this new philosophy, because success in the future will increasingly depend on it. The basic principles of such a social order are the same that underlie the world's most popular encyclopedia, Wikipedia. We could actually talk about a kind of "wikinomia" based on a collaborative philosophy and extensive use of virtual communication technology.[52]

We are, in other words, witnessing a shift into a new and richly networked social operating model and thereby into a wholly new era that might be called "the age of intelligence." This new era is dominated by five key principles.

(1) *Collaboration*

This refers to the integration of consumers into product development, examples of which include Google and its customers; the collaboration between NGOs, authorities and businesses to build better care for the elderly; or enhanced cooperation between environmental organizations and international negotiators in climate policy. I predict an increase of unlikely coalitions: An energy giant might join forces with a civic organization opposing logging, or a tobacco manufacturer could mend their ways and enter into collaboration with a county hospital. Organizations of all kinds will see that collaboration yields more and better results than going it alone. Collaboration means that organizations will become increasingly self-governing, without the rigidity of hierarchies and command structures, and will operate on a basis of trust. Responsibility and power can infuse the organization.

(2) *Openness*

As do businesses establish systems of open innovation to acquire external ideas in order to help innovation, so do popular movements demand transparency of the political system. Authoritarian leaders are doomed in this new era, because it's no longer possible to keep citizens in "information darkness" and thus subjected to ruthless power politics. The change may be fast and savage, but there are precedents: Franco's dictatorship in Spain only ended a few decades ago, but for the average person in Madrid, that world already seems quite a distant place. Once we have entered open society, the authoritarian regimes begin to look ancient. With the dramatic change in the level of education and communication systems, the demand for transparency will color all societal activities in the sixth wave.

(3) *Sharing*

In an explosive burst, the internet has created a new culture of sharing in which people who previously only spoke to those close to them are now sharing their views with others across the globe. The rapidly expanding blogosphere, or opinions written on the internet, itself is a prime example of this development. The corporate world, even beyond the digital pioneers, is gradually realizing the benefits of sharing. For instance, the pharmaceutical company Novartis has placed its research material on type 2 diabetes online for others to access and further develop. In the future, it will become increasingly important to share expertise across various divides, be it professional groups or generations. Working over the internet affords great opportunities for this.

(4) *Integrity*

Both financial and political scandals have proliferated in the past few decades. One could say that integrity has not featured high on the list of preferred virtues. However, what was tolerated merely a few decades ago is no longer accepted. According to value barometers, popular trust in politicians, companies and authorities has eroded to a truly low level. Only 30% of the British believe politicians speak the truth, whereas 92% believe their doctors.[53] The financial crisis and other high profile cases of business fraud have shown the extent and scope of greed within the financial and business sectors. In the age of the internet and social media, secrecy and dishonesty are considerably more difficult. Moreover, public tolerance for such behavior is decreasing, while honesty, responsibility, and authenticity are rising in value.

(5) *Interdependency*

It is becoming increasingly clear that artificial boundaries between sectors, countries, and cultures are a thing of the past. Just as greenhouse gas emissions recognize no national boundaries, so the challenges and opportunities of our age cannot remain confined to human-created structures. The financial crisis made it abundantly clear how interdependent national systems really are. Moreover, only a few members of even the most radical NGOs protest against globalization itself but rather against the wrong kind of globalization. Migration is the other aspect of increasing global flows bringing new kind of interdependencies. The global stock of migration grew from 70 million people in 1960 to 243 million in 2015.[54] As Professor Paul Collier from Oxford University has pointed out, the migration from poor countries to rich is bound to increase and there is no reaching an equilibrium in sight: on the contrary, he foresees the beginning of disequilibrium which will be of epic proportions.[55] As with money flows, people flows will mean more interdependencies in the global system.

New Consciousness Arising

I believe that these principles will be at the core of the social and political transformation of the sixth Kondratiev wave in the course of the next 40 years. In light of the points raised above, however, it is also clear that these principles do not yet guide world politics, although a few pioneers are already implementing them. We face a long road before these principles are fully actualized in society. Take, for example, the 2016 report from Freedom House (an organization that assesses the status and progress of democracy throughout the world), which states that the level of global democracy has actually declined 10 years in a row. Freedom House also reports increasing incidents of violations against the freedom of the press.[56]

Meanwhile, the forms of repression are becoming subtler. In China, Russia and Iran — and regrettably in many other countries — top leadership manipulates and controls what is written about them in public media and ruthlessly denies their own citizens access to information. One way of illustrating this is to compare Google search results for "Tiananmen Square" in Finnish and in Chinese: using the Finnish term produces images of the dramatic demonstrations in Tiananmen Square in 1989, whereas the Chinese term yields harmonious pictures of the historical square in Beijing.

However, many countries coping with traditionally authoritarian rulers — Arab countries in particular — share one extremely interesting dimension: young demographics. The fact is, the population age structure in these countries varies greatly from the West. For instance, over 60% of Iranians are under 30 years of age. This represents an enormous resource, but it is also a risk unless a political system is developed in which human rights are valued and there is greater access to education and work.

It has become increasingly clear that violent extremism rises out of the marginalization of young people.[57] The sole sustainable prevention against proliferation of such organizations as Al-Qaeda or ISIS is the construction of political structures that respect democracy and human rights and provide youth with peaceful pathways to a good future.

Collective movements often originate from a shared grievance that needs to be solved. The rise of the Nazis, drawing its power from the "humiliation of Germany" in the preceding decades, mushroomed into a force that started a world war. The questions back then, just as they are today, were: "What circumstances breed such frustration that all sense of proportion becomes blurred? What makes young men and women resort to desperate measures?" A key reason is undoubtedly their perception as to whether their life has any human dignity.

The world knows no limits when an inwardly turned collective consciousness randomly vents its anger outward. There is, however, another possibility: *Collective* consciousness can evolve into a *social* consciousness, which highlights awareness of the surrounding world. There is a new, historically fresh force affecting collective consciousness today: the explosive growth of communication networks. The Arab Spring protests and the preceding ones in Iran were enabled by a dense undergrowth of virtual communication. The communications ecology enabled by the internet and mobile telephony provided pivotal leverage for the revolution as revolutionaries were able to connect, share ideas and plan collective action.

The key social and political force of the sixth Kondratiev wave — upcoming 40–50 years — is this renewed consciousness, which has been made possible by the proliferation of digital technologies as well as with the rise of the education systems worldwide. Combined with the protests arising from the ranks of the young (the key message of which is: "Let us decide what kind of a society we want to build"), it will alter society with increasing speed in the coming decades. This is especially true in countries where authoritarian regimes are maintained via fear and manipulation. The consciousness can also lead to uncontrollable eruption, in which case the collective wrath can target any old-world institution whatsoever.

The Intertwined Fate of Democracy and Natural Resources

In addition to the perceived lack of democracy, another future incitement of collective expression is the dwindling of natural resources, which will be accelerated by population expansion. The growing scarcity and rising prices of water, grain, basic food commodities and fuel will lead to increasing misery around the world in the years and decades ahead. In addition to resource scarcity, climate change will continue its inexorable progress. The extreme weather events resulting from climate change will force people to find new regions in which to settle and earn their living.

The fate of democracy and of natural resources are already quite firmly intertwined, and will only become more so in the future. The less democratic the country, the more unequal the division of resources is likely to be. The equality produced by genuine democracy enables widely spread welfare in a society, even when the country's per capita GDP does not match the levels in the West. This has been demonstrated in countries such as Botswana and Costa Rica.[58] A high standard of living is not only dependent on a certain level of per capita GDP but on structures and practices that genuinely aim to serve the common good.

Scarcity of raw materials and energy will inevitably become an important motivator for social action. Thus, it is increasingly important to realize that economic growth or a certain level of GDP is not the sole means for advancement in society. We must bring productivity gains to the structures that produce societal well-being. Welfare productivity, in other words, measures the effect of investments on sustainable increases in human welfare. For example, what produces more well-being: investing in new hospital equipment or investing in preventative medicine and educating people about healthy lifestyles? Many variants of GDP (such as the United Nations' Human Development Index, which is based on the Human Development Report),[59] while clearly better indicators of the standard of living than traditional GDP, do not sufficiently measure societal progress towards better human well-being. A perfect measurement for this has yet to be developed.

The Era of Responsible Global Politics?

The international superstructures increasingly fail to meet the expectations placed upon them. The regulatory architecture of the financial system distinctly exemplifies the existing discrepancy between the complexity of the controlled system and the actual abilities of the institution built to exercise that control. The globally freewheeling financial capital cannot be controlled through national institutions, as has been done thus far. An entirely new kind of architecture might be needed that would adequately reflect the international nature of the financial system. While European Union has avoided total catastrophes, it is still an open question if its financial system will weather the next years. The institutions of the European Union have concentrated on building yet more institutions and centralizing power instead of genuinely trying to create a common future and to leverage the joint economic and social capital of the member states. Decision on moving out from European Union did not make this challenge easier.

Ultimately, this is about the pains humanity is experiencing as it acclimates itself to responsibility and sustainability. We have inexorably entered an era of interdependency, where selfish interests cannot blindly be pursued. A rude wake-up call awaits those who have not fully pondered the consequences of pursuing selfish, unscrupulous actions at any cost. The financial crisis was a shining example of what happens when you not only mix a cocktail containing greed, arrogance and blind self-reliance, but also when you applaud the mixologists.

In the next four decades, a driving force in the world economy will be the continuous attempt to correct the undesirable outcomes of the industrial era, such as depletion of natural resources and pollution of the air, water and earth. That means a sharp decline in oil and coal consumption. It also means detaching ourselves from nuclear energy, due to its ever-more evident risks and harmful effects. New intelligent energy sources, versatile and recyclable materials and sophisticated digital products and services are going to elevate our economies to new heights and, therefore, intelligence.

The structure of the global economy is more fragile than is often understood. Even though the German economy is strong, it relies on the Asian economies for growth. Growth in Asian economies, for their part, depends on whether the supply of raw materials is enough to remain stable and match demand. But what if there is a change in this equation? What happens to Asian growth if China slows down? It slowed down to 6.9% in 2015 and is expected to continue.[60] This means that Europe will not experience the same level of growth stimulus as before. And what happens when the environmental problems in China's metropolises simply become unbearable — when there is not enough fresh water for everyone and life is made nightmarish because of the horrific quality of the air?

"Each oil dollar is a cursed dollar," said an Iraqi oil businessman to me years ago. I've come to see that there was a definite truth in his words. The Arab uprising showed that the people have grown tired of the dictators who were made fabulously wealthy with the kind assistance of the West. The rage of the people was mostly directed at the inequalities of the actions of the dictators.

The level of inequality varies. Some Arab monarchs, reigning by virtue of inheritance in Jordan and Morocco have in fact attempted to expand the liberties of the people, as shown in Arab democracy index where these two countries lead the comparison.[61] Observing what has happened in Egypt, Tunisia and Syria: a wave of change will rattle all countries that have trampled on basic human rights.

References

1. Taxand. 2013. "Is a 'Harmonised' International Tax System Viable?" Accessed September 13, 2016. http://www.taxand.com/taxands-take/media/harmonised-international-tax-system-viable.
2. *Forbes*. 2013. "Within Four Years, China To Consume More Oil Than U.S." Accessed March 8, 2016. http://www.forbes.com/sites/kenrapoza/2013/08/25/within-four-years-china-to-consume-more-oil-than-u-s/.
3. *The Economist*. 2014. "Catching the Eagle: Chinese and American GDP Forecasts." Accessed March 8, 2016. http://www.economist.com/blogs/graphicdetail/2014/08/chinese-and-american-gdp-forecasts.
4. Rosner, Max. 2016. "Democracy." Published online at OurWorldinData.org. Accessed September 13, 2016. https://ourworldindata.org/democratisation/.
5. *BBC New*. 2011. "Saudi Arabia imposes ban on all protests." Accessed September 13, 2016. http://www.bbc.com/news/world-middle-east-12656744.
6. Chomsky, Noam. 2011. "Libya and the World of Oil." Accessed March 8, 2016. New York Times Syndicate. http://inthesetimes.com/article/7146/libya_and_the_world_of_oil.
7. *The Christian Science Monitor*. 2011. "Joe Biden says Egypt's Mubarak no dictator, he shouldn't step down..." Accessed March 8, 2016. http://www.csmonitor.com/World/Backchannels/2011/0127/Joe-Biden-says-Egypt-s-Mubarak-no-dictator-he-shouldn-t-step-down.
8. FAO. 2016. "World food situation." Accessed September 13, 2016. http://www.fao.org/worldfoodsituation/foodpricesindex/en/.
9. Global research. 2015. "One and a Half Billion People Live on Less Than $1.25 Per Day." Accessed September 13, 2016. http://www.globalresearch.ca/one-and-a-half-billion-people-live-on-less-than-1-25-per-day/5443472.
10. Barron's. 2015. "Jeremy Grantham Divines Oil Industry's Future." Accessed March 8, 2016. http://www.barrons.com/articles/SB513675781168750046937045804437727345313 24.
11. *Oil & Gas Journal*. 2014. Accessed March 8, 2016. "EIA: OPEC's actions bring huge uncertainty on crude oil price forecast." http:/ www.ogj.com/articles/2014/11/eia-opec-s-actions-bring-huge-uncertainty-on-crude-oil-price-forecast.html.

12. Breyer, Christian & Bogdanov, Dmitrii. 2014. "North-East Asian Super Grid: Renewable Energy Mix and Economics." Accessed March 8, 2016. https://www.researchgate.net/publication/268743535_North-East_Asian_Super_Grid_Renewable_Energy_Mix_and_Economics.
13. Bremmer, Ian & Roubini, Nouriel. 2011. "A G-zero world: The new economic club will produce conflict, not cooperation." *Foreign Affairs* March/April 2011.
14. Zero Hedge. 2016. "G-20 Meeting Ends With Rising Discord Between China And US." Accessed September 13, 2016. http://www.zerohedge.com/news/2016-07-24/g-20-meeting-ends-rising-dischord-between-china-and-us.
15. Deutsche Welle. 2016. "Climate concerns around new leaked TTIP document." Accessed September 13, 2016. http://www.dw.com/en/climate-concerns-around-new-leaked-ttip-document/a-19393318.
16. Deutsche Welle. 2016 "Leaked papers allege US pressuring EU over TTIP free trade deal." Accessed September 13, 2016. http://www.dw.com/en/leaked-papers-allege-us-pressuring-eu-over-ttip-free-trade-deal/a-19228527.
17. Nye, Joseph. 2011. *The Future of Power*. New York: Public Affairs.
18. Wallerstein, Immanuel. 2003. *The Decline of American Power*. The New Press; Zakaria, Fareed. 2008. The Future of American Power. How Can America Survive the Rise of the Rest? *Foreign Affairs*, May/June.
19. Sharma, Ruchir. 2013. *Breakout Nations: In Pursuit of the Next Economic Miracles*. New York: W.W. Norton & Co.
20. Glaser, Charles. 2011. Will Chin's Rise Lead to War? *Foreign Affairs*, March/April 2011.
    Glaser Charles. 2010. *Rational Theory of International Politics: The Logic of Competition and Cooperation*. New Jersey: Princeton University Press.
21. Coyle, Diane. 2011. *The Economics of Enough: How to Run the Economy as if the Future Matters*. New Jersey: Princeton University Press.
22. Stuenkel, Oliver. 2015. *The BRICS and the Future of Global Order*. Lanham: Lexington Books.
23. Focus Economics. 2016. "Russia Economic Outlook." Accessed September 13, 2016. http://www.focus-economics.com/countries/russia.
24. Eurostat. 2016. "Energy production and imports." Accessed September 13, 2016. http://ec.europa.eu/eurostat/statistics-explained/index.php/Energy_production_and_imports.
25. Pew Research Centre. 2015. "Ukrainian Public Opinion: Dissatisfied with Current Conditions, Looking for an End to the Crisis."

Accessed September 13, 2016. http://www.pewglobal.org/2015/06/10/3-ukrainian-public-opinion-dissatisfied-with-current-conditions-looking-for-an-end-to-the-crisis/.

26. Friedman, George. 2009. *The Next 100 Years. A Forecast for 21st Century.* London: Allison & Busby.
27. The Conversation. 2016. "What is Brazilian President Dilma Rousseff's real crime?" Accessed September 13, 2016. http://theconversation.com/what-is-brazilian-president-dilma-rousseffs-real-crime-59363.
28. UNASUR. 2016. "UNASUR News." Accessed September 13, 2016. http://www.unasursg.org/en.
29. Stuenkel, Oliver. 2015. *The BRICS and the Future of Global Order.* Lanham: Lexington Books, p. 15.
30. Klare, Michael. 2013. *The Race for What's Left. The Global Scramble for the World's Last Resources.* Picador.
31. Upstream. 2009. "Tupi oil is 'second independence for Brazil". Accessed September 13, 2016. http://www.upstreamonline.com/live/article1173884.ece.
32. *The New York Times.* 2015. Accessed September 13, 2016. http://www.nytimes.com/2015/10/11/opinion/sunday/deforestation-and-drought.html?_r=0; Laurance, William & Williamson, Bruce. 2001. Positive feedbacks among forest fragmentation, drought, and climate change in the amazon. *Conservation Biology*, **15**(6), 1529–1535.
33. Marshall, Tim. 2015. *Prisoners of Geography. Ten Maps that Tell you Everything You Need to Know about Global Politics.* London: Elliot & Thompson, pp. 212–217.
34. Renewable Energy World. 2016. "New Developments in Brazil's Solar Power Sector." Accessed September 13, 2016. http://www.renewableenergyworld.com/articles/2016/02/new-developments-in-brazil-s-solar-power-sector.html.
35. Klare, Michael. 2013. *The Race for What's Left. The Global Scramble for the World's Last Resources.* New York: Picador.
36. Pauli, Gunter. 2010. *Blue Economy. 10 Years, 100 Innovations, 100 Million Jobs.* Taos, NM: Paradigm Publications. Accessed September 15, 2016. http://www.theblueeconomy.org/uploads/7/1/4/9/71490689/case_86_from_reforestation_to_hangers.pdf.
37. Asia Biomass Energy Co-operation Promotion Office. 2016. "Release of the India Energy Revolution Report." Accessed September 13, 2016. https://www.asiabiomass.jp/english/topics/1302_02.html.
38. *The Huffington Post.* 2015. "The Economics of Renewable Energy: Falling Costs and Rising Employment." Accessed September 13,

2016. http://www.huffingtonpost.com/adnan-z-amin/the-economics-of-renewabl_b_7452996.html.

39. Development Alternatives. 2016. Accessed September 13, 2016. http://www.devalt.org/images/L2_ProjectPdfs/CLEAN-India_Brochure.pdf.
40. *Fortune*. 2015. "India: The next superpower?" Accessed September 13, 2016. http://fortune.com/2015/01/25/india-the-next-superpower/.
41. Stuenkel, Oliver. 2015. *The BRICS and the Future of Global Order*. Lanham: Lexington Books. pp. 40–41.
42. *Boston Review*. 2016. "What Future for South African Democracy?" Accessed September 13, 2016. https://bostonreview.net/world/vito-laterza-ayanda-manqoyi-future-south-african-democracy.
43. The Conversation. 2015. "Why South Africa's economy is likely to grow more slowly than its potential." Accessed September 13, 2016. http://theconversation.com/why-south-africas-economy-is-likely-to-grow-more-slowly-than-its-potential-46158.
44. ASSAF. 2014. "The State of Green Technologies in South Africa." Accessed September 13, 2016. http://www.assaf.co.za/wp-content/uploads/2015/01/8-Jan-2015-WEB-526305-ASSAF-Green-Tech-mail.pdf.
45. OECD. 2016. "Policy challenges for the next 50 years." Accessed September 13, 2016. http://www.oecd.org/eco/outlook/lookingto2060.htm.
46. Gorbis, Marina. 2013. *The Nature of the Future. Dispatches from the Social-Structured World*. New York: Free Press.
47. *BBC News*. 2016. "Oxfam says wealth of richest 1% equal to other 99%" Accessed March 8, 2016. http://www.bbc.com/news/business-35339475.
48. Ackermann, Tjitske, de Lange, Sarah L., and Rooduijn, Matthis (Eds.) 2016. *Radical Right-Win Populist Parties in Europe. Into the Mainstream?*. New York: Routledge.
49. Lang, Sabine. 2013. *NGO's, Civil Society and the Public Space*. Cambridge University Press.
50. Sorkin, Andrew Ross. 2009. *Too Big to Fail. The Inside Story of how Wall Street, and Washington, Fought to Save the Financial System — and themselves*. London: Viking.
51. Porter, Michael & Kramer, Mark. 2011. "Creating Shared Value." *Harvard Business Review*. January–February 2011.
52. Tapscott, Don & Williams, Anothony. 2010. *Macrowikinomics: Rebooting Business and the World*. London: Atlantic Books.
53. Edelman Trust Barometer. 2016. "2016 Edelman Trust Barometer." Accessed March 8, 2016. http://www.edelman.com/insights/intellectual-property/2016-edelman-trust-barometer/.

54. The World Bank. 2012. "International migrant stock, total." Accessed September 13, 2016. http://data.worldbank.org/indicator/SM.POP.TOTL.
55. Collier, Paul. 2013. *Immigration and Multiculturalism in the 21st Century.* Penguin Books, p. 50.
56. Freedom House. 2016. "Freedom in the world 2016." Accessed September 13, 2016. https://freedomhouse.org/report/freedom-world/freedom-world-2016.
57. UNDP. 2015. "Preventing and responding to violent extremism in Africa: A development approach." Accessed September 13, 2016. https://data.unhcr.org/syrianrefugees/download.php?id=10059.
58. *The Economist.* 2007. "The Economist Intelligence Unit's Index of Democracy." Accessed September 13, 2016. http://www.economist.com/media/pdf/DEMOCRACY_INDEX_2007_v3.pdf.
59. United Nationals Development Programme. 2015. "Human Development Reports." Accessed March 8, 2106. http://hdr.undp.org/en.
60. *The Wall Street Journal.* 2015. "China's economic growth in 2015 is slowest in 25 years." Accessed March 8, 2016. http://www.wsj.com/articles/china-economic-growth-slows-to-6-9-on-year-in-2015-1453169398.
61. Arab Reform Initiative. 2014. "Arab Democracy Index IV" Accessed September 13, 2016. http://www.arab-reform.net/en/node/289.

Chapter 6

THE MEANING OF ECONOMY

In a way, the economy is the elephant in the living room: Its role in our society and media has grown disproportionately. Indeed, economic parlance has taken over all arenas; it has become part of the everyday language. We "invest" our time. Caring about environmental matters is referred to as the "recycling economy." Caring for the sick is the "welfare economy." Economic experts are called upon when something significant happens in society; they are the clergy of our time.

The finance sector — banks, insurance companies and other financial institutions — are the circulatory system of the society. Without it the economy simply won't function. For just as blood transports oxygen to the farthest reaches of the body in order to sustain life, the financial sector helps society to advance and create new business. Blood circulation doesn't function properly if too much blood surges into one part of the body or ceases altogether to make it to another part. The financial crisis illustrates the same phenomenon in economy: Initially, there was a flood of money to one part of the economy (the housing market), and in the next phase it was running almost completely dry in many other sectors of the economy. That is when the financial crisis truly hit in September 2008. As a result, the entire circulatory system froze. It hasn't recovered yet, almost 10 years since (see Figure 1).

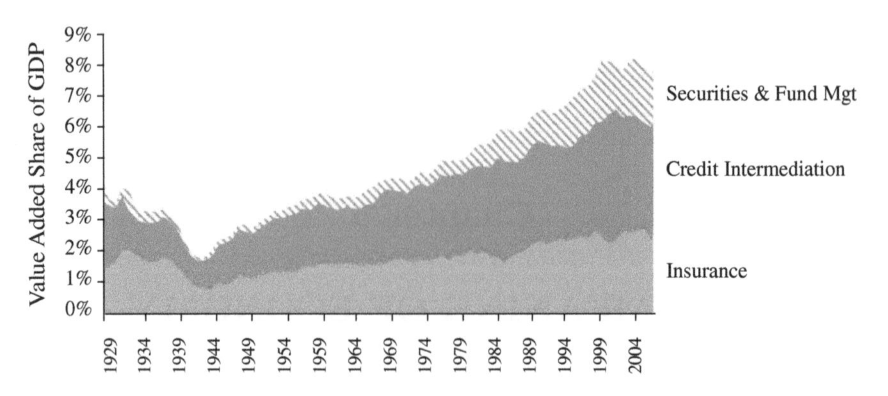

Figure 1. The growth of financial services.

Source: Greenwood & Scharfstein (2012).[1]

The Idea of a Market Economy

When Scottish economist Adam Smith wrote about the wealth of nations at the end of the 18th century, he managed to create a new approach for examining the role and significance of the economy in the society.[2] Up until then, sovereign wealth had been measured by the amount of gold and silver in the nation's coffers. When he observed the advancement of the industrial society in Great Britain and in continental Europe, Smith stated that this was a very antiquated view of wealth. It would be much more intelligent to observe the generation of wealth from the point of view of production and commercial activity. Smith also adopted an idea originally attributed to Plato that posited that the distribution of labor in the society was the driver of advancement.

In the times of Smith, the economy was highly regulated, and there he saw how the regulation was restricting the economy and entrepreneurship. Thus, his view of a free-market economy was far-reaching: Exchange across national and societal boundaries was necessary for economic advancement. The only way to significantly increase economic productivity was to permit free exchange and to allow wealth creation and self-actualization as widely as possible.

For it all to benefit society as a whole, a mechanism Smith called the "invisible hand" was required to ensure fairness and justice in society. Smith's reasoning and strong views reached far beyond the economy. Indeed, he was laying the foundation for a form of societal enlightenment. He foresaw what we can now prove: Societies with small income differences have the fewest conflicts between societal classes. Smith's major concern was liberating trade and expanding the markets in order to increase wealth. He wanted to disassociate economies from the feudal and hierarchical system dating back to the Middle Ages. It was the task of the invisible hand to ensure congruence between private and public interests.

Smith's thoughts about a liberal market economy have surfaced in the last few decades, whereas his views about the positive effect of the invisible hand have gained less attention. The collapse of Wall Street in 2008 led to the decision to impose more detailed regulation of the financial markets. Tight regulation lasted for several decades, until neoliberal politics reared its head at the end of the 1980s, especially in the Anglo-Saxon countries. Liberties in trade and financial markets were added little by little. A key proponent for this thinking was the Chairman of the United States Federal Reserve, Alan Greenspan. He thought bankers so sensible that they wouldn't do anything to cause harm to the system itself. This was an extremely naïve and baffling presumption, considering that it was coming from one of the mightiest economic decision-makers of the time.

In the spring of 2012, Greg Smith, an executive director at Goldman Sachs (one of the most revered banking firms in the world) wrote a column in the New York Times announcing his resignation from the firm whose values had become foreign and distasteful to him.[3] The incident created great commotion in the banking world. According to Smith, the company culture at Goldman Sachs had changed — perhaps quite some time earlier but certainly after the financial crisis — into a culture of vultures. The salesperson's greed came first and the interest of the client last. In his 2012 book *Why I left Goldman Sachs*, Smith encapsulates the rollercoaster ride on the road toward the financial crisis from the viewpoint of a prominent player.

Smith tells us that Goldman Sachs originally became the world's mightiest investment bank precisely because of its corporate culture.

Humility and respecting the clients' interests and needs were always valued above anything else. In other words, the Goldman Sachs of the past valued honesty and openness. That attitude started to change in the 2000s, and it was all but forgotten when the financial crisis erupted and all the firm's employees started to protect their own income by all means possible.

Smith's tale is typical in a recession of the modern economy. The mood of the markets and people is grim. What is more, the future also looks bleak to many. We know that the collective state of mind somehow predicts the future development of the markets.[4]

Smith offers inside information about the mysterious world of investment bankers. I find Smith's conclusion most interesting: There has been no attempt to bring to justice those who caused great losses to ordinary people and to large financial institutions like pension funds. Not one of the key actors was legally charged. The aftermath of the depression of the 1930s was different: The United States Senate organized hearings to determine the causes leading to the crash, and the result of the investigation was that banks were to blame and a new financial system was created.

This time that did not occur, although the total damage was at least as great.

Allianz is the world largest private insurer. When I joined Allianz's strategic unit in December 2007 and was tasked with the responsibility for strategic research and development, there was hardly any talk of major problems looming in the horizon of financial markets, although the first signs were there. Towards the spring of 2008, sheer nervousness could be observed in the markets, and Allianz started to prepare for bad times. Still, afterwards, and in hindsight, one can be astonished how poorly the actual extent of the financial crisis was understood at the time. No one could see the dramatic knockout blow that was going to bring the financial world to its knees. Allianz fared quite well in those storms.

This illustrates the nature of reality. The world consists partly of surprises or events that drastically change our circumstances. In the situation and moment when something happens, we are often helplessly lost, even though we might believe that the situation is under control. This was true also at Allianz, where we were supposed have the sharpest financial wisdom in the world. Even so, the crisis took us by complete surprise.

That surprise moment was partly linked to the kind of unique events that occur in the markets from time-to-time. Let's look at the developments at Lehmann Brothers that lead to bankruptcy in 2008, which in turn triggered the most dramatic phase of the financial crisis.

The value of the company stock had diminished from 76 dollars in November 2007 to 3 dollars in the middle of October 2008, when the company ended up in receivership and the value of its stock was nullified. To those who wanted to see and understand the developments, the situation was clear: Trust in the company was gone, as evidenced by the tumbling stock price. During the morning of the crash, the stock was being bought for mere dimes. It's important to recognize that everyone was having a bad time back then.

When we now look at the events from a bit of a distance, we can clearly see that years earlier low interest rates and the selling of mortgages in secondary markets — pre-packaged in investor-luring products, or the so-called "structured products" — were contributing to an excess of liquid assets in the market. The United States Federal Reserve had started to push money into the markets soon after the terrorist attacks of September 11, 2001 in order to avoid a recession.

Events evolved quickly. Investment bankers were quick to come up with new financial products, one more alluring than the previous and the contents of which even the producers weren't fully aware. Sumptuous returns were, however, promised, and for several years they did produce well. The financial world buckled at its knees in the fall of 2008, and for a while it looked like the entire financial world was going to crumble.[5]

From the economic perspective, the biggest challenge of our time is that the entire Western world, including Japan, has become hugely indebted in recent years and decades. The pace of indebtedness started to increase during the financial crisis, when the income of many nations, including Finland, started to decline. The indebtedness of Greece, Italy, Spain, and Portugal has become massive. Japan is in a worse situation, as its relative debt has grown over 200% relative to its gross domestic product (GDP).[6]

The glorious boom in Japan that started after World War II waned as a result of the financial crisis at the beginning of the 1990s. After that, Japan did not manage to return to the growth path it was on prior to the crisis. Japan wasn't able to modernize its society, the strong currency was slowing down exports and the aging of the population was starting to have an effect. Thus, with the exception of a few rays of light, Japan has been in a recession for almost 25 years. 30 years ago, Finland was called the Japan of Europe, and back then that was a positive characterization.

Japan's debt is comparable to the losses of the United States pension funds in the financial crisis that started in 2008. The increase in the United States debt has also been phenomenal, as it doubled to 14 trillion dollars in 2012; it is now approaching 20 trillion dollars. Counting private debts, total United States indebtedness climbed to 70 trillion dollars. Part of the great national debt's origins lie in the financial crisis, when the United States government massively shored up banks in order to prevent their collapse. The supportive measures were well timed and scaled, as the United States economy is now growing at a pace of 3% and the rate of investment is high.

The larger scope of the problem is that many nations are now over-consuming and will have to curb their consumption by the end of the decade. Banks will have to reduce lending due to their weak position. The baby boomers might have to live on much leaner pensions than anticipated.

The value of European or United States companies is not likely to grow like it did in the previous decade. This is going to be the case with companies producing products that are sensitive to market shifts: housing, boats, cars, etc. In tough times, people primarily spend on basic necessities.

Economic researchers are debating whether the climax of steady growth has been reached. I encountered this topic in 2009. My colleague at the time, Bill Gross, one of the executives at Pimco (an American capital investment firm owned by Allianz) and one of the leading investment experts in the world, introduced the notion of "the new normal." With that he meant that the era of steady growth that preceded the financial crisis is now over.[7] We are drifting into an era of uncertainty.

When considered from the perspective of long waves — the idea of "the new normal" seems quite, well, normal. The old wave is ending and the new one is beginning, and this sets new standards for the next decades. Many factors are going to be different in the beginning of the new wave, such as the aging population. OECD anticipates a sluggish economic growth for developed countries — under 2% average — after 2030 and lasting all the way through the sixth wave, up until 2060.[8] The next decades will be different, due not only to economic changes but also to the increasing scarcity of raw materials, global warming and the crises in welfare nations. The economic rise of China has produced an enormous increase in the demand of natural resources, such as coal, as well as massive environmental problems with global implications. We must change our perception of what is acceptable societal advancement and thus change our standards accordingly.

While some industries are in tremendous difficulty, some others will be winners, even if the economy would recede even further by the end of the decade. The winners are, for example, the kind of technology companies whose products advance the intelligence of their clients' business by increasing the effectiveness of resource use. In Cleantech, the more energy cost savings are sought, the more inverters are sold, for instance. The top education service producers can also expect success.

I see the winners in the coming decades to be the leaders in the following sectors:

(1) Those profiting from *accelerating globalization*: companies selling information-intensive and digital services, including for the Internet of Things; educational organizations that move information regardless of location; companies offering human resource services that allow businesses greater flexibility; various logistics

services that enable smarter production and distribution chains; security professionals who profit from the complexity of global risks; and the gaming industry, which creates new leisure-time options other than TV.

(2) Those profiting from the *changes in population age structure*: health care companies; medical technology; biotechnology solutions such as gene therapy; and financial services linked to pensions and health care.

(3) Those profiting from the *holistic health care services founded on people's interest in their personal well-being:* health products; consulting; wellness training; and organic food.

(4) *Those in the markets of sustainability and recycling economy:* bio materials; renewable energy production and services; refining of natural resources; wood-based construction; consulting in material and energy efficiency; and water purification technology; recycling technology.

(5) *Those focusing The integration of microstructures* into products and services: harnessing nanotechnology in its various forms, such as graphene, which is one-atom-layer thick but up to 300 times stronger than steel.[9]

The economy and technology will become increasingly intertwined in the sixth wave. Technological advancement will intensify: the new information technology, the industrial internet, the Internet of Things (IoT); a new phase of development of the information society; robotics and automation; smart traffic; energy technology; and new materials technology. The new era of intelligent biotechnologies will find forms that are bound to change our world. The technological opportunities for increasing system intelligences are endless. Simply put, the physical, digital and biological drivers of the next decades and their potential to push technologies even further seems almost endless. In terms of technologies, we are approaching what Karl Schwab, the founder of World Economic Forum, calls the fourth industrial revolution.[10]

Let's take the future of traffic as an example. As problems with present traffic are rising to an unacceptable level in many metropolises, a new generation of automobile users is adopting the three zero-principle: zero emissions, zero accidents, and zero ownership.[11]

As we've stated in previous chapters, the use of automobiles really started to grow in the fourth Kondratiev cycle, between 1930 and 1970. It was a period of immense advancement in mobility. Hardly anything else, except perhaps the invention of electricity, has changed people's everyday lives as much as the personal automobile. Even though the car has lost its position as a status symbol in many parts of the developed world, it still remains the centerpiece of the modern way of life for many.

The traditional internal combustion engine has become inexorably outdated. It pollutes (although ever less, due to advances in engine technology), there are insupportably many accidents on the roads, and congestion is ever increasing. Although more roads are being built, it doesn't make much sense for a private person living in an urban environment to own a car. The heap of metal stays unused by most of us, sitting either on the street or in the garage. There are many reasons for a change, as we can see. The premises are increased by the fact that Generation Y (current 14–27 year-olds) is less interested in obtaining a driver's license than previous generations.[12] They are also much more acutely aware of the detrimental effects of car use.

We can predict that a young person born in 2015 will not necessarily procure a driver's license once they become an adult, as has been customary thus far. Young people prefer mass transportation, bikes or to purchase transportation as a service. At a minimum, they will use car sharing: renting a car when needed. This is already a reality today.

In the future, cars will be loaded with more and more intelligence to prevent accidents. Volvo already has a system that algorithmically calculates whether a car is on a collision course with a particular object. If that is the case, the car will make an autonomous emergency braking action. Similarly, the car will sound an alert if the driver is about to change lanes without using the directional signal.

The intelligent transport system will look like this in the future: *First*, cars won't pollute. Electric cars will multiply rapidly once the necessary infrastructure is established. In Finland some are already in place: There is a network of pre-existing outlets in parking areas for cold-weather car warmers which could be repurposed as EV chargers, and there are more and more rapid charging spots at gas stations. The range of today's electric cars is mostly sufficient, because people average about 50 kilometers daily with their personal cars and only some 20 kilometers more with company cars.

Second, increased intelligence in cars means that there will be fewer accidents. Volvo, the pioneer of car safety, has made an "accident-free" car its goal. Google's driver-less intelligent car has driven over 300,000 test miles; the only accident occurred when a human happened to be behind the wheel. Today more than one million people die in car accidents annually — driving is one of the 10 leading global "killers". Human error is the cause in 90% of accidents. There are many good reasons for eliminating the human from behind the wheel. Not just from behind the wheel of cars but also trains, metros, etc. All kinds of cargo handling and transportation will also be automated in the future.

Third, owning a car as a private person will not be common or a smart choice in the future. Most car owners will belong to a car club, much like we belong to a health club or a banking service. This change will naturally happen more quickly in the cities than in rural settings. When cars don't need to be conducted by a human, they can just as well proceed to a destination in the countryside. The new and cheap taxi services like Uber are already using the private car stock more efficiently. These type of new services are creating the new economy of sharing. Provided that their social standards are adequate, they will create much needed new job opportunities.

The future advances in motoring are a terrific example of old industrial sectors becoming services. This will give our economy a new life force while simultaneously destroying the old and useless. The economy in all nations will become more service-driven. Even within manufacturing industries, service will become an ever more important part of the revenue model.[13] For example at Xerox, the service business contributes more than 50% to total revenue. Industry is turning into services.

We'll continue to need industrial production, but in order to earn its existence it will have to have a high production value, and that production has to be efficient. A more important point is that industry will gain more and more attributes typical to service: a close connection to the customer and the option to customize the product to their needs. The future production facility will function much like a café, with a large variety of drinks and delicacies to choose from and a salesperson to help with the transaction. And one can add jam if one wishes.

For industries and their technology development, this new phase of accelerated change is calling for a certain kind of strategic foresight. Moreover, the tone of economy should be much more collaborative. In fact, the real ethos of the economy is not so much of competition but that of solidarity and partnership. It also calls for a new kind of entrepreneurship to which we next turn our attention.

References

1. Greenwood, R. & Scharfstein, D. (2012). The Growth of Modern Finance. Harvard Business School and NBER.
2. Smith, Adam. 1776. *A Wealth of Nations.*
3. *The New York Times.* 2012. "Why I'm leaving Goldman Sachs." Accessed March 8, 2016. http://www.nytimes.com/2012/03/14/opinion/why-i-am-leaving-goldman-sachs.html.
4. Casti, John. 2010. *Mood Matters: From Rising Skirt Lengths to the Collapse of World Powers.* New York: Harper Collins.
5. Lewis, Michael. 2009. *The Big Short: Inside the Doomsday Machine.* New York: W.W. Norton & Company.
6. Trading Economics. 2016. "Japan Government Debt to GDP" Accessed September 13, 2016. http://www.tradingeconomics.com/japan/government-debt-to-gdp.
7. PIMCO. 2016. "On the 'Course' to a New Normal" Accessed March 8, 2006. http://global.pimco.com/EN/Insights/Pages/Gross%20Sept%20On%20the%20Course%20to%20a%20New%20Normal.aspx.
8. OECD. 2014. "Policy challenges for the next 50 years." Accessed March 8, 2016. http://www.oecd.org/economy/lookingto2060.htm.

9. Graphenea. "Graphene - What Is It?" Accessed September 13, 2016. http://www.graphenea.com/pages/graphene.
10. World Economic Forum. 2016. "The Fourth Industrial Revolution, by Klaus Schwab." Accessed March 8, 2016. http://www.weforum.org/pages/the-fourth-industrial-revolution-by-klaus-schwab.
11. Neckermann, Lukas. 2015. *The Mobility Revolution: Zero Emissions, Zero Accidents, Zero Ownership*. London: Matador.
12. Deloitte. 2014. "2014 Gen Y automotive consumer study." Accessed March 8, 2016. http://www2.deloitte.com/us/en/pages/manufacturing/articles/2014-gen-y-automotive-consumer-study.html.
13. Deloitte. 2011. "The Service Revolution in Global Manufacturing Industries." Accessed August 23, 2016. http://www.apec.org.au/docs/2011-11_training/deloitte2006.pdf.

Chapter 7

SINGING THE PRAISES OF ENTREPRENEURSHIP

In Silicon Valley, you always seem to find people who practically do the impossible. Take, for example, a young man by the name of Elon Musk, who had already decided during his college years in the 1990s that he would look for solutions to the great problems facing humankind. He chose three interesting topics: the internet (which was in its infancy at the time), space, and clean energy.

Musk started with the internet. He had been a graduate student at Stanford University for two days in 1995 when he came up with something more interesting to do. He left his studies and founded a company, ZIP2, which developed and marketed online city guides for the newspaper publishing industry. That company was sold for 300 million dollars. He later bought another company, which itself became the first internet payment solution, PayPal (which eBay bought in 2001 for 1.5 billion dollars). Next he focused his attention on the real target of his passion: space. He then founded SpaceX, whose commercial spacecraft was the first to dock on the International Space Station. Musk's goal is to build a vehicle that will allow the populating of Mars and thus take life beyond Earth. According to Musk, the major technical problems are close to being solved. While NASA hopes to have manned missions to mars by 2030, Silicon Valley entrepreneurs may accomplish this monumental goal even sooner.[1]

Musk also founded Tesla Motors, which is developing a new generation of electric automobiles. It created the first electric sports car to exceed 186 miles per hour. The family Model S came to the market after that. In Finland, for instance, it costs about 100,000 euros. The battery is advertised to have capacity for over 300 miles. It resembles a spaceship on the inside. Musk has promised to bring a much better-priced and smaller vehicle to the market called Model 3.

To advance clean energy, Musk founded SolarCity, which designs solar electricity systems. The ingeniousness in the business model of SolarCity is that the homeowner doesn't have to buy the equipment; rather, he or she can rent it. That way the business model serves the interest of both parties. SolarCity is now the leading installer of solar panels in homes. SolarCity also builds charging stations for electric vehicles and offers energy efficiency audits. In the beginning of May 2015, Tesla revealed the Tesla Power Wall concept, which according to the company solves the problem of energy storage.

Musk is very much like Steve Jobs but with better manners. Both have founded companies that have been exceptionally successful somehow or other. They represent the entrepreneurial dream and have what it takes: stubbornness, will and discipline. They are the hero entrepreneurs of our time. As Ashlee Vance puts it in his recent biography, *Elon Musk*, "Musk's ready willingness to tackle impossible things has turned him into a deity in Silicon Valley."[2]

Entrepreneurship is perhaps more broadly about offering people the opportunity for self-actualization. As recently as a few decades ago, entrepreneurs in most part of the Western world were regarded as dubious "businessmen." The current mentality now allows for more acceptance and appreciation of entrepreneurship.

It is clear that old Europe in particular, needs more entrepreneurs in the future. The capability of big industries to employ people will diminish in the coming decades, as has already been happening in the last five decades. Especially in the last two decades, creating new jobs has mostly rested on the shoulders of small and medium-sized businesses.[15]

There are three requirements for starting a new company: a good business idea, performance capability, and financing. The latter is especially an issue for many. If we take the United States as a standard, there should be six times more "angel investors" in Finland, meaning investors who back companies in their startup phase. Norway, for example, has three times as many investors as Finland. Because new jobs are increasingly created in new companies, we need more and more investors who can also support entrepreneurs during their startup phases.

Digital gaming has experienced a significant boom, and thus a large portion of the investments in the digital arena has gone towards the gaming industry. Digital business ideas are growing fast, and there are tremendous growth opportunities in digital technology solutions. The growth opportunities for digital technology are also supported by *Slush,* the largest and most important conference for startups and investors in Europe, organized annually in Finland.

Entrepreneurship is gaining strength everywhere: in Bangladesh, Muhammad Yunus started its Grameen Bank already 1980s. The mission of the bank is to lend small sums to rural people, particularly to women who don't have access to institutional sources of money or they are forced to borrow money with sky-rocketing interest rates. Grameen Bank became rather successful and its model has been used in over 100 other countries.[16]

In Africa, microfinance is developing on three levels of the financial system — micro (financial service providers), meso (support service providers) and macro (policy, regulatory framework, and supervision) and it has gained a solid ground for providing solutions for poor people to earn their living.[3] It seems as if conditions for these types of new models have become more suitable and microfinance has already brought access to financial services to countless people. It may bring new problems as well, such as increasing the debt loads of poor women.[4] However, though it is hard to measure exactly the impact of microfinance schemes, there seems to be a lot of positive action that has concretely helped poor people. In India, for instance, microinsurance is spreading rapidly, helping poor farmers to secure their income in case of harvest loss.[5]

In the next few decades — as the sixth wave of technological advancement takes the world into a new era — new enterprises will be mushrooming in the sectors with the most compelling needs and thus also the largest growth prospects. Options abound in health and wellness businesses, new materials development, new energy production, digital solutions and caring for the elderly. There is clearly a battle for increased enterprise activity and investors in these sectors.

This, however, is a phenomenon much wider than just clean technology. Material and energy efficiency concerns will inevitably lead to new innovations regarding material and service cycles in society. During my visits to Silicon Valley in recent years, I have found many interesting enterprises that have directed their activity towards finding new ways to add intelligence to consumer products.

One of the most interesting Silicon Valley entrepreneurs I met was Neal Gorenflo. He was a successful financier on Wall Street in the beginning of the 2000s. During a business trip to Europe, he suffered a nervous breakdown — in the middle of a parking lot in Brussels. Gorenflo understood then that his life had brought him nothing meaningful. He was fed up with work that was based on greed and selfish solutions. He decided at that moment to change his life.

Gorenflo traded his career on Wall Street for one along his own passions and moved to the town of Mountain View, near Silicon Valley in California. He founded Shareable, a digital platform for public and private development initiatives. Shareable has been successful, and thousands of people have shared their ideas for building a more sustainable and tolerable future. Many of the initiatives are non-profit, and it has contributed to the new culture of "sharing economy."

Sharing economy refers to new, more efficient ways of utilizing resources. At its most basic, it involves renting your car or home to others when you yourself don't need it. In the last few years, an enormous number of organizations and business models based on sharing and joint usage have risen in California. All of the projects that Shareable supports exude the new ethos of entrepreneurship that is founded on the idea that the world can become a better place if we dare to take initiatives.

One of the most interesting enterprises of this new era is Airbnb, a company founded by a couple of students in San Francisco. They came up with the idea while trying to find lodging for a few conference attendees at a time when every single one of the local hotels was fully occupied. The students then accommodated the visitors in their own homes, which brought about the realization that this allowed the visitors the professional experience of attending the conference, but one that was enriched by something completely different than that of a normal hotel stay. A business idea developed: Ordinary people would rent unoccupied rooms and homes. This allowed a chance to avoid "death by hotel," to find reasonably priced accommodation and to get acquainted with locals. The service works well for the owner of the accommodation, as the paperwork, marketing and other practical tasks that the private person does not want to deal with (or perhaps is not even capable of doing) gets handled by the broker. In this model, everybody wins. Airbnb is now the largest hotel chain in the world, functioning in 191 countries by the end of 2016.[6]

What makes Silicon Valley the most dynamic economy in the world and the most dynamic center for new businesses? It looks as if it is the way people share their ideas and collaborate. This is actually the secret of Silicon Valley — not that there are many investors, passionate entrepreneurs and sharp tech gurus. These actors are important, of course, but collaboration is the major differentiating factor in Silicon Valley when compared to other metropolises. It is no wonder that the first business of the sharing economy were founded there. Thus, we can regard Silicon Valley as the melting pot for new technologies and a place where new ideas get wind under their wings, thanks mainly to a culture of sharing.[7]

Advances in digital technology have provided entirely new possibilities for creating services with a more human touch and experience. Data processing allows the opportunity to provide each client with precisely the information he or she needs. I've never been better informed than I was when using Airbnb to book a place to stay. On top of that, I received pertinent and helpful information about the cities I was visiting. When I stayed in a hosted home, I also gained an authentic connection with the local population.

Is Europe ready for the culture of sharing economy? Do our culture, institutions and way of life support the principles of sharing? I would say yes. Crowdfunding, for example, provides opportunities for investing and lending in a way that was accessible to only a very few in the past. In the United States, there are billions of crowdfunding dollars circulating. In some other countries, the growth of crowdfunding has been restricted by laws and regulations. A balance is needed between providing consumer protection and supporting the advance of this innovation funding tool.

As a matter of fact, many of the most successful companies are founded on the idea of sharing. For instance, Google's search service is free, so in principle the company is sharing its resources with the user. Facebook doesn't cost anything to use. The price you do pay is getting exposed to advertising. It's no surprise that these companies also have flourished in Silicon Valley.

The culture of sharing epitomizes the ethos of Silicon Valley: If you share, you will also earn. Even if daily life in Silicon Valley is far removed from the ideals of the hippie culture and Woodstock groove, something permanent from the 1960s remains in the Silicon Valley cultural DNA. I can imagine that many representatives of the coming generation welcome these ideals.

I've also become acquainted with many other socially oriented companies in Silicon Valley, Give Something Back being one example. It's an ordinary company that sells office goods, but it donates the majority of its profits to charity. The funds are channeled to non-profits that do civic work in the customers' neighborhoods. Founder Mike Hanningan says:

> "I'm an incurable world-improver, but somehow I must put bread on the table for my family. So, we decided to combine the two. One evening, I was making pasta with my business partner using tomato sauce made by Paul Newman's company, whose profits go to charity. I said to my partner: 'We don't have Paul Newman's blue eyes, but we know everything about office goods and, on the other hand, we want to improve the world. Let's do both!"'[8]

The company has been successful for 22 years.

The Culture of Silicon Valley

The secret of Silicon Valley is *precisely* its culture: a culture that favors entrepreneurship and co-creation. The roots of this culture were established by a few Silicon Valley pioneers from the 1960s who renounced the hierarchical business model. The culture combines the Western belief in entrepreneurship and the lack of hierarchy of its pioneers with the Eastern, more communal business models — "Each for his own" but "standing shoulder to shoulder."

I noticed at closer examination that the sharing of information was the foundation of all Silicon Valley activity. Creativity flourishes in a culture that combines technological know-how, innovation and new service concepts into a rich stew. The best talents from around the world are attracted to Silicon Valley, adding spice to this richness; for example, one-third of the entrepreneurial population has an Asian background.[9]

In order to understand technology, it is crucial to recognize that technology is more about extending human capacities than about the technology itself. In other words, technology should be regarded as a product of culture. We may hypothesize here that Silicon Valley is the birthplace of the so-called "CARE culture" which encompass the following characteristics:

(1) *Readiness to exchange information and cooperate.* The quality of cooperation is crucial. People in Silicon Valley strongly believe that in giving one's all to cooperation, more is achieved. This is described as the *karmic management*-principle: Joint action — when conditions are right — always pays off, because it is rewarding. This is probably the most crucial element of the cultural structure of Silicon Valley.

(2) *A fresh take on core knowhow.* What each person can do or achieve is not most important; rather, it's what can be achieved together as a team. Technological knowhow is not necessarily most crucial; rather, it's the capability to synthesize, question, observe, network and test.

(3) *Systemic relationship to development.* I took notice of how deeply committed the companies were to continuous innovation. This has allowed investors some extraordinary success: One-third of all investment activity in the United States is directed to Silicon Valley. For example, thanks to the support of investors, cloud technology was being developed long before the opportunity it offered was globally recognized.
(4) *Passion for disruptive innovation.* Many Silicon Valley entrepreneurs are inspired by the thought that global issues could be solved through their work. As mentioned earlier, Elon Musk set out to solve three great challenges for humanity, cleaner technology, reaching other planets, and developing the internet.
(5) *The desire for sustainable solutions instead of short-term gain.* While one should not underestimate the yearning for money, the business in Silicon Valley is focused on sustainable value creation. This could be a departure from common practices elsewhere in many ways. Failure isn't terminal; rather, it is regarded a necessary and instructive experience.
(6) *Willingness to take risks.* In Silicon Valley, there seems to be a high tolerance for risk. This, too, is the product of the culture: Investors are accustomed to taking on high risk and the entrepreneurs themselves are risk-tolerant.
(7) *Focusing on the future.* Past merits are not so important. What matters is the degree of passion for developing your product. In Silicon Valley, feelings matter as much as reason. The most valuable business card for a company is the abundance of energy that springs from confidence in your idea or product.

The emerging sixth wave will bring about more than enough challenges for the creative mind. The post-industrial society stands to be created through application of new business models and new technologies, such as digi-, bio-, nano- and energy technologies. This new society will recycle materials and energy, structures will be examined holistically and the focus will be on increasing business intelligence and efficiency in the use of resources. Taxation should shift from labor to raw materials, as this would ease the transition towards a more entrepreneur-friendly society. Giant technology leaps are needed to make this shift possible. Thus, we will also need technology pioneers in the future — determined entrepreneurs who can create opportunities for a new, more sustainable society, economy and culture.

The biggest problem of society today is, after all, not greedy bankers or even environmental issues but the wasteful use of resources. We need not look too far back in history to see that this has not always been the case. In rural areas, where the majority of the population used to live, it was common to borrow tools. This was sensible, as resources were limited. Many of us may vividly remember how much the previous generations loathed buying something new whenever the old one was still somewhat working. One could prolong the life of a washing machine by months or even years with a rubber band. Now it does seem though, that a certain kind of "culture of repairing things" is making a comeback.

A European consumes 15–20 tons of material annually.[10] That's over 40 kilos per day. A cup of coffee, which contains seven to eight grams of coffee, uses 140 liters of so-called "hidden" water, the amount needed to grow the coffee beans and to produce the final product. In order to reach a sustainable level, we should reduce our consumption to eight tons per year. Now we are headed in the wrong direction: If we continue along the same continuum until the year 2050, our consumption will be three-fold.[11]

The situation must change. We may assume that the new generation of entrepreneurs will create the opportunities to make the shift possible. For the economy, it will imply new products and services, which enable new business models. All the time, more share-economy models are rising all around the world and people are becoming familiar with its basic principles.[12] In both its forms — non-profit and for-profit — sharing economy will certainly be one of the solutions to bring forth a more sustainable economy.[13]

For the new generation, it appears that entrepreneurship is a natural choice. Digital service enterprises have led the way. Many small service businesses with entrepreneurial spirit have sprung up in the last few years, and some of those have gone from tiny to having a staff of hundreds.

Within the deepest core of entrepreneurship is systems thinking. This can sound surprising, so let me explain. An entrepreneur starts a process, does his or her best and waits to see whether the business will succeed or not. Often success lies in being able to sustain all the failures, learn from them and push onwards.

This is an application of systems thinking. Organizations that don't apply systems thinking are unable to import new thinking into the organization, as the pioneer of systems thinking, Russell Ackoff, has stated.[14] In those organizations, errors are punishable and not to be learned from.

An entrepreneur must learn from his or her mistakes — and learn quickly, or the business will fail. However, when an organization grows and becomes stable, innovation is forgotten and errors become something to be feared. This is when leadership is needed. And that is the topic of our next discussion.

References

1. TED. 2013. "Elon Musk: The mind behind Tesla, SpaceX, SolarCity." Accessed March 8, 2016. http://www.ted.com/talks/elon_musk_the_mind_behind_tesla_spacex_solarcity#t-71731.
2. Vance, Ashlee. 2015. *Elon Musk: Tesla, SpaceX, and the Quest for a Fantastic Future.* New York: Ecco Press.
3. Microfinance in Africa. 2013. "United Nations Office of Special Advisor to Africa." Accessed August 23, 2016. http://www.un.org/en/africa/osaa/pdf/pubs/2013microfinanceinafrica.pdf.
4. Africa Renewal. 2011. "Microfinance: What role in Africa's development?" Accessed August 23, 2016. http://www.un.org/africarenewal/magazine/august-2011/microfinance-what-role-africas-development.
5. *The Hindu Business Line.* 2016. "Future Generali eyes 30% growth in rural, micro insurance biz this fiscal." Accessed August 23, 2016. http://www.thehindubusinessline.com/money-and-banking/future-generali-eyes-30-growth-in-rural-micro-insurance-biz-this-fiscal/article 8505158.ece.

6. *Business Insider*. 2013. "Airbnb Is On Track To Be The World's Largest Hotelier." Accessed March 8, 2016. http://www.businessinsider.com/airbnb-largest-hotelier-2013-11?IR=T.
7. Piscione Perry, Deborah. 2013. *Secrets of Silicon Valley: What Everyone Else Can Learn from the Innovation Capital of the World.* New York: Palgrave McMillan.
8. Give Something Back. 2016. "A Kinder Corporation." Accessed March 8, 2016. http://www.givesomethingback.com/CustomLandingPage.aspx?cpi=Founders.
9. Piscione Perry, Deborah. 2013. *Secrets of Silicon Valley: What Everyone Else Can Learn from the Innovation Capital of the World.* New York: Palgrave McMillan.
10. Materialflows.net. 2014. "Material consumption and economic development by content." Accessed August 23, 2016. http://www.materialflows.net/fileadmin/docs/materialflows.net/factsheets/matflow_FS1_update2014_web.pdf.
11. UNEP 2016. "Global Material Flows and Resource Productivity. Assessment Report for the UNEP International Resource Panel." Accessed August 23, 2016. http://unep.org/documents/irp/16-00169_LW_GlobalMaterialFlowsUNEReport_FINAL_160701.pdf.
12. PWC. 2015. "The Sharing Economy." Accessed August 23, 2016. https://www.pwc.com/us/en/technology/publications/assets/pwc-consumer- intelligence-series-the-sharing-economy.pdf.
13. See a great article of sharing economy by Prof. Julia Schor, Accessed August 23, 2016. http://www.greattransition.org/publication/debating-the-sharing-economy.
14. Ackoff, Russel. 2006. "Why Few Organizations Adopt Systems Thinking." Accessed March 8, 2016. http://ackoffcenter.blogs.com/ackoff_center_weblog/2007/03/why_few_organiz.html.
15. Global Entrepreneurship Monitor (GEM). 2016. "Country profile: Finland." Accessed March 8, 2016. http://www.gemconsortium.org/country-profile/61.
16. Yunus, Muhammed. 2011. *Building Social Business. The New Kind of Capitalism that Serves Humanity's Most Pressing Needs.* New York: PublicAffairs.

Chapter 8

THE FREEDOM OF LEADERSHIP

When the Finnish telecom company Nokia was at the height of its glory at the end of the 1990s, a reporter from *Fortune* magazine came to Finland to root out the secret to Nokia's success. At the time, the business world was baffled by the incredible strides Nokia had taken to move to the forefront of the most successful global companies. The reporter started his investigation by interviewing several upper-level managers. The conversations revealed several possible explanations for the success story, and among those mentioned were superior technology, efficient distribution channels and fine-tuned processes. These reasons, however, failed to convince the reporter. He knew there was some other reason behind the success.

In his last day at the Nokia headquarters, the reporter headed to one final interview with the CEO at the time, Jorma Ollila. The discussion was interesting, although it revealed nothing really new that the reporter had not yet come across. At the end of the interview, Ollila asked if the reporter would like to have something to eat. The reporter nodded in agreement and the two headed to the employee cafeteria. When they stopped at the checkout line, the reporter noticed that every employee, no matter their level in the company, had an easy and natural rapport with Ollila.

There he was, the esteemed CEO with his employees, and everyone was greeting him by his first name. It suddenly became clear to the reporter that he had just been witness to Nokia's secret weapon in action. What had emerged as the secret behind Nokia's culture of progress and innovation was its non-hierarchical organizational structure, exemplarily upheld by Ollila at the time.

Unfortunately, the recent history of Nokia proves that what has been created can be destroyed. The shining organizational culture slowly became shadowed by rigidity, poor leadership, bonus structures that treated people unfairly and communication problems. By the beginning of the 2000s, Nokia had grown into a global behemoth with the highest brand value of any non-American company in the world. The flagship of Nokia, mobile phones, was not ultimately destroyed by rising competitors like Apple and Samsung but by its eroding corporate culture. It's not enough to create a wonderful corporate culture: It also has to be maintained.

The example of Nokia shows that the success or failure of an organization depends more on internal rather than on external factors. Everything starts with leadership.

This was also true with the 2015 Volkswagen (VW) test-fraud episode. Although it all started due to an external event when their cars were found to have extraordinarily high emissions by an external research group in the United States, the scandal revealed that the real problem with the company was an over-ambitious CEO, Martin Winterkorn, who abhorred failure and wanted to make VW the world's largest car manufacturer. Within the company, a culture of fear was created that drove into unsustainable decisions. In this case, in order to pass the high United States emission standards, VW created software that hid the results, all in order to get a larger share of United States market. But the real problem was the corporate culture that allows these sort of events to happen.[1]

Moving from Profit Seeking Towards a Humanistic Understanding of Capital

In the corner suites of the global corporations, there is growing awareness that companies are not simply business units whose purpose is to churn out profits for the owners. Even the legendary Jack Welch, former head of General Electric (also known as Neutron Jack), has leaned towards this view. He used to ruthlessly drive for increased shareholder value and profits, without much sympathy for employees or environmental concerns. For example, he fought long and hard for GE to avoid taking responsibility for dumping a massive amount of waste into the Hudson River. He has since then accepted that there is more to business than companies dodging responsibility for the environmental harms they cause.[2]

In the end, business is founded on the organization and its people. A company is not a separate island; rather, it is part of a network that includes society, nature, customers, vendors, employees and of course shareholders.

In business you can be smart as can be and have the best possible product or technology, but if you don't know how to work with all these stakeholders, then sooner or later trouble arrives. Seeking to understand business from a humanistic perspective leads to an entirely different take on the role of human capital in an organization. And human capital longs for intelligent leadership.

What is leadership actually? From the organizational perspective, there are three key factors in any organization that affect the level of employee commitment, as noted by Kenexa Research Institute (now known as IBM Smarter Workforce Institute), a global research organization:

(1) *Company vision and strategic goals.* Certainty about the company's future is in direct correlation with the level of employee commitment. This in turn makes a great deal of difference as to whether company directors are able to start a process whereby the company purpose becomes clear and the employees can connect that with their own goals and future. The importance of a vision is illustrated by the following case: John Mackey founded and heads a chain of grocery stores, Whole Food Markets, which sell mostly organic food. The company has a growth story from the last few decades that is even more impressive than that of Wal-Mart's. According to Mackey, a business must have a higher purpose — that is, something higher than a business-related purpose. This is why his business is striving to "change the world and make it a better place."[3] If this high-flying purpose can be executed in a company's purpose and activities, and it can turn into business (as happens at Whole

Food Market), then the vision works as intended. People need a truly motivating vision. The vision must go further than the business goals and speak to something that helps society and communities function better. People must sense that they are achieving something meaningful through their work.

(2) *The future of the individual as part of the company future.* There needs to be enough opportunities for learning and for advancement in a company. Naturally, money is an important motivator, but certain other factors are even more important. People who are professionally oriented want to know if the employer is interested in developing their skills. These days it is common that this question receives low scores in employee surveys. In other words, companies are often poorly able to respond to this need. It would seem that this is one of the key motivating factors for an employee, and thus its connection to performance is easy to see.

We are not just talking about what each party has to offer, but how sincerely employees are appreciated as human capital that can be fostered and developed, just like any other capital. How eager is the company to really cultivate strengths and to help people develop in the areas that they themselves consider important?

Nowadays, owners and company boards want to find many ways to commit their top managers to staying with the company. To that end, companies have bonus structures and other perks in place, such as extra pensions. They also often have terrific leadership education programs. However, if middle management is left outside these perks, then they feel exploited, and dissatisfaction starts to spread. Commitment by middle managers and line employees can only truly be strengthened if there is a real effort to show concern for the future of each individual. This results in a vision by the employee of his or her individual development within the company. The path can also include career opportunities in other countries or in other business locations.

(3) *Attitude in the company towards work-life balance.* Workers enjoy a much higher degree of flexibility nowadays in comparison to 30 years ago. Simultaneously, the barrier between working life

and the rest of life has been lowered. More and more people feel threatened as their working life encroaches on their private lives. In knowledge work, the border between work and leisure time easily gets blurry. So it comes as no surprise that on the list by Kenexa, work-life balance comes in third as a factor affecting commitment.

In his classic 1957 study *Organization Man*, sociologist William H. Whyte describes a person who dedicates often his entire career to the same company.[4] According to Whyte, this attitude was founded on a social ethic that prioritizes the needs of the organization above the wants and needs of the individual. In return the employee receives stability and energy for other things in his life.

The "organization man" is dying along with his generation. Lifelong working relationships are giving way to a new, more mobile breed of employees. They mirror their own values with those of the company.

According to sociologists, this aspect of progress towards more individualized values has a key impact on society.[5] A company must do quite a bit in order to show that it cares about its employees. Healthy food, sports and culture need to be seen as enticements, just like the opportunity to spend more time with family. It is only then that an employee can be expected to make a good contribution to the company.

It seems that adequate freedom can result in continuous commitment.

The three aforementioned aspects are fundamental to the spiritual well-being and success of any organization. It is quite possible that investing in human capital is the best way to increase productivity in a modern expert organization. Even in the manufacturing industry, it is no longer a matter of how factories can produce goods more efficiently but rather how well work can be organized and employees motivated to perform the work. At the end of the day, increasing productivity is the primary task of company leadership. Thus, it's important to understand the factors affecting commitment.

An entirely new kind of concept of leadership is forming, and one that is not founded on old management ideals. The old theories about hierarchical leadership structures have been refuted. Enterprises that represent the new kind of thinking tend to operate in digital technology markets but not necessarily so. This new self-organizing approach to management has been applied in radical ways by the Dutch nursing company Buurtzorg, United States-based clothing company Patagonia, and Finnish software companies Supercell and Reaktor.[6]

What they have in common is minimal hierarchy: Responsibility and power has been granted to the employees as much as possible. Teams carry the responsibility in practice, and they make decisions jointly within the team. Top leadership has the tasks of making sure that power and responsibility is used correctly, acting as the external "ambassadors" of the company and finding the best employees for the company — employees who share its values.

In the research covering organizational and knowledge leadership, self-organization is recognized as the highest form of organization. Self-organization teeters on the edge of order and chaos. This must be permitted in order to preserve the ideal internal dynamics of the organization.

However, humans love order. Even modern bureaucracy grew from our need to organize and optimize performance. Order and organizational structures ensure that everyone knows their place and the limits of their circle of power. We are conditioned to believe that this is how organizational performance is optimized and substantial quality is created.

When hierarchy is increased, it can easily smother creativity within the organization. It also shrivels enthusiasm and diminishes employees' motivation. Striving to avoid errors prevents learning and growth. From a systemic perspective, learning from mistakes is the best guarantee for organizational sustainability.

Self-expression is becoming more and more important for individuals. People don't thrive if they cannot find sufficient ways for self-expression. Sociologist Ronald Inglehart has studied the evolution of values around the world and has noticed that the desire to self-express has become the major motivation for human activity.[7]

Self-expression takes the person to new dimensions, whereas repeating the same old routine flattens a person's sense of being.

What does this mean at the organizational level? It means that the task at hand is to transform organizations into *dynamic systems*, or systems that are constantly in motion and function organically. According to Ilkka Paananen, founder of Finnish gaming company Supercell (considered to be the world's fastest growing gaming company ever),[8] it is of utmost importance that the enterprise functions like a living organism. The parts that are not viable die off quickly, and the ones that are viable have room to grow. Initiatives live and die with a quick pulse, and quick learning comes from mistakes. This is possible if the decision-making power lies with the functional units and not with central leadership.

Dutch nursing organization Buurtzorg is another excellent example. Over the past 10 years, it has grown from scratch to one of the fastest growing organizations in the Netherlands with over 10,000 employees and has been voted best employer in the Netherlands for several years.[9] Buurtzorg aims to support the independendent life of its customers in all its operations. This principle guides the autonomous life of its teams, consisting of 10–12 nurses. Nursing itself is organized utilizing an easy-to-use web-based intranet system that provides sufficient support for nurses to do their job well. All teams have full authority to decide how they organize their work provided it fulfills the standards of efficiency. Since nurses have no bosses to overlook their performance, they assume a collective leadership. According to our interviews with staff members, it takes around one year for a nurse to learn how to switch from a normal hierarchical organization to this autonomous team-based structure.[10] The most important common denominator making Buurtzorg so unique, was, according to many of our respondents, high trust created through collegial work.[11]

There are three principles at work in dynamic and self-organized structures, as Professor Pirjo Ståhle and researcher Tuomo Kuosa have noted:

(1) *Dynamic systems strive to obtain maximum benefit from new opportunities.* In other words, self-organized structures maintain the ability to recognize changes in the outside world. They are

better able to find the (changing) needs of their customers and if needed can change direction with agility.

(2) *Dynamic systems have the best chance for success when they exist in a complex, spontaneous and mutually interactive network.* In organizational language, this means that the best conditions for success exist in teamwork, networking across organizations and in the freedom to function without interference from upper echelons of the hierarchy. This kind of organizational model, especially along the outer fringes that are full of activity and movement, puts the entire organization in motion. It also helps enterprises, for example, to differentiate themselves in the market.

(3) *The aim of the system to actualize its self-interest is the key to autonomous renewal.* Decentralized power in an organization leads to improved self-direction. For example, the employees in direct contact with customers often become familiar with the problems with current products. If decision-making power lies elsewhere, communication problems and obstacles occur.[12]

We are quite far from the organizational models described above, both in private enterprises and in the public sector. Most currently used models date back to the time of industrialization and are founded on hierarchical organization. At the same time, the public sector is very slowly transforming from a managing role to an enabling and consulting role, thanks partly to pressures in the operating environment but also partly because of its proper initiative. Yet, this role can only be realized if the principle of self-actualization and its resultant renewal are first embraced and implemented.

In traditional companies, there is usually a desperate need for renewed thinking. A director of innovation in the forestry industry stated to me once: "If our people operated with a fraction of the efficiency of our world-class paper mills, we'd have no problems." In other words, his company is better at making a papermaking machine than it is at coming up with a functioning organization.

Leadership and Societal Interaction

The relationship between enterprises and society will intensify during the sixth wave, which has started and which will continue through the middle of this century. There will be more and more alliances and cooperation between the corporate world and the public sector. Those alliances will meet human needs and social problems better than the current system. This requires deep societal understanding on the part of companies. It also requires deep consideration of what best motivates employees to do their best. Human capital will become increasingly important to companies and, thus, ever-greater attention must be paid to managing it.

Human capital and the fostering of it has not traditionally been the main focus of enterprises. In typical companies, the central idea is to manage the product and the service — or the business. The old saying "the business of business is the business" still invites this thought: The success of a company depends on managing the business well. This, however, is not the whole truth, especially not for a company with ambitious goals. Instead of simply concentrating on the business, the manner in which the company operates should be placed under a loupe. Otherwise, they will *never* reach the expert-level knowhow that leads to the best results. And who wouldn't want to achieve the best results?

Human Capital as Key Focus in an Enterprise

An American legend in enterprise research, Jim Collins has studied how good companies become excellent. One of his conclusions was that a requisite for an excellent company is significant investment in building human capital.[13] It seems that managing leadership and human capital demands more pure know-how, sharp thinking and decisive execution than any other business function. This does not have much to do with traditional human resources management, which focuses on bringing people into — and managing them out of — an organization.

As we step into the sixth era of the global system, three major characteristics of leadership development are surfacing. Organizations that aim for excellence take these traits seriously in order to evolve past mediocrity.

(1) *The organization needs a vision that motivates employees.* The vision must go beyond narrow business goals, such as bringing in profits for the shareholders. The vision needs to be created, processed and communicated in a way that earns the commitment of the entire company. In the unstable operating environment of the sixth wave, companies must have a strong internal perception of its direction. This is only possible if the company has a very clear idea of how to maintain a high level of vitality.

Heike Bruch, a professor at the University of St. Gallen in Switzerland and Berndt Vogel, of Henley Business School in the United Kingdom, have pioneered an analysis of the energy level in global organizations and how it can be elevated.[14] They have created the concept of "organizational energy" by categorizing types of organizational work styles: productive and well-being as positive energy and oppressive and corrosive as negative energy. More often than not, the above-mentioned energy types can be found in an organization. It's probably evident what kind of energy dominates among the top leadership prior to a collapse of the energy level in an organization. The most important proactive actions are to clarify the company vision and purpose and to make sure that the employees have a stake in them.

(2) *The organization must understand its societal nature.* As globalization and changing population structures are forcefully shaking the current welfare state model, the real question centers upon how well these changes are viewed as business opportunities. The relationship between companies and society will further intensify. In the future, we will see more and more alliances and partnerships between public and private sectors, which will meet human needs and answer social problems.

Reflecting changes in global and local operating environments, new enterprise cultures are more socially aware. Enterprise values and activities must adapt to the value systems of the next generation of employees and customers. Sustainably successful companies lean heavily on their values to define how they organize themselves and what kind of products and services they bring to the market.

In the sixth wave, the investment in good leadership will lead to renewed goals, particularly in regards to the company's general role in society. These goals are still reflected in company structures and business models. There are some pioneering companies: General Electric, for example, introduced an energy efficiency program called Ecomagination at the end of the last decade, whose initiative to conceive more environmentally friendly products not only created a sales volume of 18 billion dollars by 2010 but also created tremendous brand value. In response to the growing distrust of giant corporations, companies will increasingly attempt to demonstrate their willingness to help solve societal problems through different initiatives and programs.

Richard Barret, a pioneer in value-based leadership, speaks of *whole system change* as a part of the cultural change in companies.[15] Whole system change is comprised of three important points:

(a) The examples set by leaders are crucial. They must show through their actions that they prioritize the vision, mission, values, principles and agreed-upon codes of conduct. For example, when leadership make cost cuts while increasing their own rewards, it sends employees the wrong message.
(b) The values and goals must be congruent in all situations and in all decision-making — even in recruitment decisions. If sustainability is an important company value, then candidates who personally share the same values must be given priority.
(c) Performance measures must be in place in order to assess and monitor the organizational culture. Values and the behavior of individuals and groups must be assessed in a mutually

agreed-upon manner. One of the biggest reasons companies do not follow their own rules is a lack of tracking.

Whole system change is a framework that helps organizations recognize human values, needs and goals. In this approach, values are all-encompassing, from earning money to helping the entirety of humanity. In the sixth wave, an organizational culture that is evolved, harmonious and dynamic can produce a pivotal competitive advantage.

(3) *Employees must understand how they can apply and develop their skills in the organization.* The company must support their ideal of a good working life. In practice this means providing adequate learning opportunities that provide strong, clear insight into how they can become better in the areas where their professional passion lies. However, people are no longer willing to sacrifice their lives for their work. That is why in many surveys, working life balance is noted as one of the top priorities. One of the plagues of our era is that people spend too much time in the office, which ironically decreases productivity.

What should be expected of the leadership of an organization? First of all, all managers should spend less time managing and more time listening to the members of the organization. According to James Kouzes and Barry Posner, who have studied such matters, the most neglected leadership function is feedback.[16] Because they are often afraid of criticism, most managers are not interested in listening to what the organization's members thinks of them. This is destructive to the organization and especially to the manager's ability to understand his or her weaknesses.

Listening to the organization is nevertheless the most efficient signaling system. It allows the manager to anticipate problems in leadership. A manager who is not afraid to listen to criticism obtains valuable information through dialogue. According to Kouzes, actions by the immediate supervisor are the clearest indications of how the organization functions. This is why the behavior of middle management in a large corporation is even more important than that of top management.

How does a good organization become excellent? An organization can't be transformed by telling people they must change their behavior, nor can it be fixed through training, guidance or by altering its structures. An organization also doesn't heal by avoiding conflict or by imposing seemingly innovative programs. A change process also cannot be started with some pompous cultural transformation program.

The culture of an organization can only begin to change when the organization and its leadership start to behave differently. A behavioral sea change is required, both of leadership and employees. The employees must take on an independent and responsible role. Leadership should focus on its core functions, which are holistic management and support of employees in reaching their goals. Leadership must consider the needs of employees who want to grow in their careers. The management of such employees must include coaching in order to enable and invite further growth.

In an excellent enterprise of the sixth wave, people learn to work across organizational boundaries, structures and hierarchies. They are, in fact, masters of change because they are continuously aware of changes in the operating environment. The desire to change must spring-up from within the organization and not from outside pressure, such as the market situation, for example.

Redefining Strategic Goals

In the sixth wave, enterprises will redefine their strategic goals. According to enterprise strategist Michael Porter, the capitalism of the future needs to focus on *shared value* — meaning values that are as important to society as they are to the enterprise itself — rather than focusing purely on *shareholder value growth.*[17] Capitalist ventures must, in other words, learn to generate profits while simultaneously producing value for society by addressing its woes.

It is no wonder that enterprises feel pressure to prove that they are part of the solution for societal issues, rather than the cause. Even though public trust in enterprises has increased in the last few years, they are often accused of short-term profit seeking, while the most important customer needs and long-term impacts receive less attention. Correspondingly, trust in politicians has diminished.[18] In any case, today's society and its collective values place much more attention to business operations than before. Businesses can't strive to maximize shareholder value without caring about their societal impact. Businesses must prove that they are truly concerned with the societal effects of their activities. Politicians, at their end, seem to be challenged with returning trust to the political system.

Organizational culture is based on synchronizing values and operating models. The task of a leader is not solely to encourage employees to use their creativity but also to use fresh approaches and to help them become aware of the values and choices that guide the organization. Whereas the implicit principles and practices of the organization come to light in organizational documents, individual beliefs and personal preferences are manifested in people's thinking and actions. Values are especially crucial in complex operating environments, because the organization needs guiding principles that can be applied in individual cases and situations.

The companies that have built a strong value-based strategy have created a serious competitive edge. In such companies, values are treated like any other process and are measured, monitored and analyzed along with organizational behavior. An organizational culture is especially valuable as a competitive asset, as it can't be copied.

In summary, the challenges to businesses and society in the sixth wave lie in leadership: Business leaders will need to be open to changing course before there is no other choice. Public sector leaders will need to be capable of taking necessary steps to create structures and business practices better suited to the post-industrial society. Politicians will need an even greater sense of responsibility and vision to guide our society into a new era. And regular citizens and employees will need the courage to demand change.

The sixth wave requires leaders to be prepared to face reality. Candor and the ability to delegate and encourage will be requisites of good leadership in the coming decades.

References

1. *Entrepreneur*. 2016. "The Biggest Lesson from Volkswagen: Culture Dictates Behavior." https://www.entrepreneur.com/article/254178.
2. *Business Week*. 2009. "Jack Welch Elaborates: Shareholder Value." Accessed March 8, 2016. https://www.bloomberg.com/news/articles/2009-03-16/jack-welch-elaborates-shareholder-value
3. Fox, Justin. 2011. "The HBR Interview: 'What Is It That Only I Can Do?"' *Harvard Business Review*. January–February 2011.
4. Whyte, William. 1957. *The Organization Man*. New York: Doubleday Anchor Books.
5. Bauman, Zygmunt. 2000. *The Individualized Society*. Cambridge: Polity Press; Beck, Ulrich & Beck-Gernsheim, Elisabeth. 2002. *Individualization: Institutionalized Individualism and Its Social and Political Consequences*. London: Sage Publications; Giddens, Anthony. 1991. *Modernity and Self-Identity*. Cambridge UK: Polity Press.
6. Laloux, Frederic. 2014. *Reinventing Organizations*. Brussels: Nelson Parker; Kurki, Sofi, Puro, Minna, and Wilenius, Markku. 2016. *Reacting the Future. The New Ways to Work: The Case of Reaktor*. FFRC Publications 6/2016.
7. World Values Survey. 2016. "Data & Documentation." Accessed March 8, 2016. http://www.worldvaluessurvey.org/WVSContents.jsp.
8. *Forbes*. 2013. "Is This The Fastest-Growing Game Company Ever?" Accessed March 8, 2016. http://www.forbes.com/sites/karstenstrauss/2013/04/17/is-this-the-fastest-growing-game-company-ever/#2263d78939ea.
9. The Commonwealth Fund. 2015. "Home Care by Self-Governing Nursing Teams: The Netherlands' Buurtzorg Model." http://www.commonwealthfund.org/publications/case-studies/2015/may/home-care-nursing-teams-netherlands.
10. My research group did interviews with Buurtzorg personnel in May 2016.
11. Nandram, Sharda. 2015. *Organizational Innovation by Integrating Simplification*. Cham, Switzerland: Springer.
12. Ståhle, Pirjo & Kuosa, Tuomo. 2009. Self-renewal of systems — new understanding of the development of collectives. *Aikuiskasvatus* 2009, **2**.
13. Collins, James. 2011. *Good to Great: Why Some Companies Make the Leap... and Others Don't*. New York: Harper Business.
14. Bruch, Heike & Vogel, Bernd. 2011. *Fully Charged: How Great Leaders Boost their Organization's Energy and Ignite High Performance*. Boston: Harvard Business Review Press.

15. Barrett, Richard. 2006. *Value Driven Organisation: A Whole System Approach to Cultural Transformation.* Amsterdam: Butterworth & Heinemann.
16. Kouzes, James & Posner, Barry. 2006. *A Leader's Legacy.* San Francisco: Jossey-Bass.
17. Porter, Michael & Kramer, Mark. 2011. "Creating shared value." *Harvard Business Review.*
18. Edelman Trust Barometer. 2016. "2016 Edelman Trust Barometer." Accessed March 8, 2016. http://www.edelman.com/insights/intellectual-property/2016-edelman-trust-barometer/.

Chapter 9

THE POWER OF EDUCATION AND CULTURE

The founding of the industrial society was based on three factors in the end: (1) increased productivity, which was enabled by machines and automation; (2) innovation, which gave birth to new production and consumption segments as well as entirely new manufacturing sectors; and (3) specialization, which led to more sophisticated division of labor. All of these factors have laid the foundation for the present culture of expertise where people become specialized in certain skills and job functions from early on in their education.

This progress has brought on many advantages, starting with increased prosperity and ending with greater satisfaction for individuals who become specialists in their fields, gaining acceptance for their expertise. However, one might still question if specializing has become somewhat of a burden in today's society. People specialize in one field of study or another early in the beginning of their formative years, and further their specialization in the working world. While working, specialists tend to focus on narrower skill sets, deepening their domain knowledge.

As technologies and other structures become more complex, one would think advancement in a different direction would be necessary. Here, people would be able to see the interconnectedness of phenomena and see the world holistically systemically. In Finland, for instance, the idea of a university to help build a civilized society of Finland was precisely born out of this kind of thinking. The problem with specialization could be that there are more and more information bubbles you can't see out from.

When considering revamping education, I'm of the opinion that more focus should be on generic aptitude or those skills that support learning in any subject. The education of the future could be structured around the following five themes:

(1) *Information analysis and organization: starting from absorbing information to the ability to find, critique and recognize sources of information.* The ability to absorb information is a given requirement. However, we should give higher value to how and with what criteria information is being searched. The digital era has of course brought its set of problems to this. The ability to criticize sources must be given higher importance in a world where information flow has exploded, while the quality of it has largely deteriorated. Google and Facebook algorithms drive users insidiously to people with the same opinions and to topics familiar to us, and thus end up narrowing our world. Being active on the internet requires that you regard the information obtained with a critical eye. This is not necessarily self-evident to people who have grown up in a networked world. The ability to use information, albeit of good quality, with consideration for its limitations also requires critical skills. It is important to be able to go beyond the known and conventional barriers and find information in the margins. For example, producers of art and culture can be good sources about the next economic cycle, but so can taxi drivers.

(2) *Learning to learn: moving from recording individual facts towards a communal understanding about learning processes.* Education at all levels is still fundamentally based on learning passive information. More active communal learning processes are much more difficult, because they require social skills in addition to intellectual skills. My long career in educational institutions has however taught me, that people not only learn better and deeper in social learning situations, but also enjoy the learning process more. The ability to express one's thoughts is also connected, something that is also practiced much

less in Finland than in Anglo-Saxon countries — at least when we consider university-level education.

I do believe that communal learning will become more prevalent in the future. There is an entire school of thought around communal learning, founded by a United States professor, Peter Senge.[1] In the future, social skills will become more and more crucial in working life. No matter how skilled someone is in his or her profession, some of the skills and opportunities will be wasted without social aptitude.

(3) *Solution-centric orientation: the ability to solve problems which surface.* Instead of looking for the right answers, students are taught how to ask the right questions, to move between fields of study and to connect them in a new way. Educational institutions with their defined fields of study do not exactly nurture this approach. However, it will become more prevalent in the future to synthesize matters and to build unconventional alliances with open-mindedness around a certain common interest. As society becomes more complex, these kinds of abilities will be in demand. Could Shell and Greenpeace cooperate in the future, for example? How much could a business leader learn from the way a conductor leads his orchestra?

The value of this point of view increases as you ponder any big societal issue. For instance, the best way to deal with the increasing environmental problems of the Baltic Sea is to erase the causes for the nutrient and pollutant loads, and not to oxygenate the basins. Similarly, unemployment is best managed by laying groundwork for new job creation.

The meteorologists, biologist and social scientists that study climate change could delve into the causes and consequences together, by learning from each others' point of view, rather than examining the problem strictly from the point of view of their own discipline.

Reality does not get shaped by human-created models and structures. Solving increasingly complex societal problems requires observing them at their level, in other words, a systemic, holistic and critical vantage point all at once.

(4) *Harnessing creativity: the ability to produce new points of view in all thinking and doing.* Much of the learning in educational

institutions and work places responds to the needs of industrial society and is therefore based on repetition. Even though these forms of learning can't be dismissed, finding new information or solutions becomes increasingly important. Learning and systemic thinking are needed in order to implement creative solutions for all kinds of situations. In the practical working world, this is highlighted as tolerance for uncertainty: how to live and prosper in a world where employment is rarely for the long term and where more and more flexibility to cross professional boundaries is required? Permanent positions seem to be vanishing with increasing speed.[2]

(5) *Cultural skills: the ability to thrive in a multicultural world.* The cultures of the world are getting mixed thanks to increasing globalization. The influence of eastern cultures on the western cultures will increase in the sixth wave. The western hegemony that has lasted a few centuries will transform into a new kind of cultural mix. There are more and more professions where work requires interaction with people from many foreign cultures. The more young people face foreign cultures early in their education and find that they can manage and flourish in it, the better. This allows youth to gain perspective of global events, which can be pivotal later on, in the working world. The more young people experience studying and living abroad for a while, the better.

Emphasizing the above mentioned five skills has its roots in the transformation of the working world, and of the environment, overall. Unconventional employment relationships are becoming more common and people shift quickly from one project or an organization to another. Flexibility and a keen eye for changes are required. We have to be able to seize the moment, when it comes.

The innate curiosity and creativity in students should be tapped in education. Participative methods add to the motivation of students. Individual natural talents must also be respected and given space. In futures research, many methods have been developed for application in different interactive needs.[3]

In the end, the central question in advancing the educational system is how to make it human centric: human as a spiritual, material and social being. In the sixth wave, the more human centric, open operational models will replace mechanistic, system centric operational models.[4]

Education and learning mean individual sophistication in the end. This is where humanity has made giant leaps. Our celebrated educational system also has to be updated to meet the demands of the new era.

What does sophistication mean in the sixth wave? To answer this question we must examine the role and meaning of culture in the coming era. In industrial societies thus far, success of a nation has required natural resources or capital and often both. Wealth was created through them, which in turn enabled investing in components of the infrastructure, such as educational systems and military power.

The situation is about to change drastically. In the future, it will be increasingly more profitable to invest in culture, as opposed to traditional forms of assets. Whenever there is an increase in societal wealth and in the satisfaction of basic needs, people have a natural tendency to direct their interest towards cultural phenomena. A deeper understanding of different cultures is increasingly more valuable as nations globalize.[5]

Culture is an *intangible* asset whose particular allure draws *tangible* assets, or capital, to it. In the future, people's attention will increasingly be focused on the intangible: learning, experiences, well-being, relationships with nature, leading a balanced life, etc. I believe this has to do with a shift in our values: People are seeking experiences that match their deepest values and which bolster their identity and support individual growth — which in turn brings on both a stronger sense of humanness and of being a part of society. According to researchers, values connected to self-expression are steadily climbing in significance (see Chapter 8).[6]

Culture is not typically thought of as an investment but rather as a service. Industry involves investments and culture means experiences we consume. The industrial base of most European countries stem from their respective past, be it founded on, metal, chemical, forest or electronic industries or something else. This is not enough for the future. In addition to more sophisticated services, countries also need cultural attractions that bring attention, visitors, enterprises and euros from around the world. The Europe in the future is much more multicultural than today. This probably includes most European countries.[7]

It is interesting to note that history shows multiculturalism helps in renewal. The rise of United States, as well as the preceding rise of Europe to world power nexus was empowered by their cultural heterogeneity. Even still, in places like Silicon Valley, we found that immigrants are twice as active to start new ventures as native born Americans.[8] Renewal needs heterogeneity.

There is also a question of what type of culture builds up attraction to any particular case. Maybe the case of Munich, the center of Bavaria in Germany is interesting here. Germans have adopted the slogan "laptop and lederhosen" to explain how the unlikely combination of social conservatism and business acumen that made Bavaria from a backward rural area into a high-tech state. While global companies have their offices in Munich, their employees can enjoy the cultural flair of the region: nature, beer gardens and the Alps. It is a kind of European version of Silicon Valley. And fares very well, much because people like to live there.[9]

The Foundation of Culture

Culture can be defined as all that is manmade, including economy and industry. For instance, ancient wood processing skills are part of our cultural heritage, and thanks to those skills we have a lot of useful and beautiful products whose design derives from past centuries. Exported wood products for more than half a millennium. The predicament that the forest industry particularly faces is digitalization. In the 2000s, many factories in developed countries have been shuttered and workers have been let go. Forest industry seemed to be more or less a thing in the past. More recently, as wood has become a fancy element and there is more search for natural materials, there is suddenly a new interest on "wood culture." For instance, there is a rising trend to build wooden skyscrapers.[10]

Much discussion has arisen about the effect of digitalization on traditional industrial sectors, such as the forest industry, and on the manner in which people read books and newspapers. The cultural effect of the rise of Asian cultures has received less attention, whereas the effects of the economy aren't being overlooked by anyone. Asian exports of wood products increased five-fold from 1990 to 2006. China, India and Malaysia have focused on wood products, and Japan with Korea are strong in the paper industry. In those countries, these sectors are growing at an annual pace of 6%, while Western nations are struggling with diminishing production.

But let's return to culture. Religions lie at the center of our cultures. Western culture was founded on Christianity. In the Gothic-era church, focus was on the image produced by Christian ethics: Humans are small and God is magnificent and unattainable. The earthly home of God must be grand, more in accordance to his proportions than those of humans. This is the message of Christianity: No matter what humans do, God always has the last word.

The East departs in a significant way from the West in this regard. The role of the human in Eastern religions or world-view is much different than in the West — whether we look at Buddhism, Confucianism, Shintoism or Hinduism. God's mercy is not all-important but rather human behavior is. The guiding principle of life is to find one's own path and follow it. The gods support and guide, but it is essential that one directs oneself towards a good life and happiness.

As we turn our attention towards today's organizations, one could claim that no matter the cultural background of the company or its workers, business everywhere is guided by the same principles. This is true only on the surface. Deeper influences and propelling forces are harder to ascertain. Every organization has its own "soul," which can be experienced as an ambience. It is hard to pinpoint, but its consequences are clear. For example, fear changes people's behavior rapidly and in the end the company's results. The atmosphere in the organization makes a crucial difference in choosing actions in difficult times. Success is founded more on the internal resources of the company than on the external circumstances.

As I mentioned, Eastern cultural heritage encourages examination of one's own deeds, rather than believing that things are left to the grace of God. Christian ethics teach many worthy values like goodwill, but in the end it leaves everything up to the will of God.

It is estimated that non-OECD countries' output will account for a 61% share of the global gross domestic product (GDP) by the year 2060.[11] An overwhelmingly big thrust of that share will be propelled by Asia. Even in the first 15 years of this century, the shift has been astounding. The economic power of Asia is already very real and very powerful. It is also the most significant reason behind the unprecedented rise in global commodity prices this century. The cultural effect will be noticed in time. It is, however, no less significant than the economic effect.

With this in mind, we can observe the changing relationship between the East and West as societies move into the sixth wave. The predominate culture of the sixth wave will be much more of a blend of Eastern and Western. The traditional Western values will be upset and also *vice versa*: Eastern cultures, often quite closed off, are starting to open up to Western influence, as we have witnessed in both China and Japan. This new synthesis of cultures is leading to fresh ideas about leadership models in organizations.

My experience with multinational companies has convinced me that the new socio-economic era needs a kind of Copernican revolution with human centricity, appropriate humility and a new kind of leadership at its core. The Western business world ought to learn from Buddhist thinking and shift the attention from "me" and "us" towards "others" — in this case towards co-workers, customers and society. All this requires a completely new way of thinking.

There is nothing "soft" in such a mindset. One simple rule proves the point: The more one invests in working in the interest of the stakeholders, the more fruitful the cooperation. I believe that this kind of life philosophy and attitude can more readily be found in Eastern cultures than in the Western ones, because these are precisely the values that are important in Eastern cultures.

Consider Indian Ashok Khosla, former co-chair of Club of Rome and co-chair of International Resource Panel by UNEP. His life work with the organization called Development Alternatives has created over three million agricultural jobs in India through the founding of so-called "social enterprises" whose purpose is to offer services that support the local community (see Chapter 5).[12] His work and attitude symbolizes everything that is missing in our Western culture. Khosla is unpretentious but full of willpower. He is wise but listens to others. He is a guru but does not assume the airs of one. He makes things happen.

While working at German insurance company Allianz, I had the opportunity to work with Clotaire Rapaille, a French anthropologist and market strategist. Tapping his education as an anthropologist, he has developed a method for finding the "cultural code" of a country or organization.[13] I came to think differently about community behavior when I heard his observations about the multilayered nature of human decision-making and how much intuition plays into it. Even if his methods don't necessarily meet all academic criteria, they offer us much learning.

In his research, Rapaille found that the code of the North American culture is youth. One of its dimensions is acceptance of various behavior models and support of individual decisions. Nowhere in the world is this as evident as in Silicon Valley. Everyone is entitled to pursue their own dreams. People there also interact with one another with youthful ease.

The Roots of Our Culture

Every culture has its roots, but all cultures can be said to have common roots. They originate in the dawn of humanity. Some twenty thousand years ago, in the middle of the ice age, people lived in small groups that moved from place to place according to where they thought food was to be found. Gradually these groups founded villages and then cities. The enormous masses of ice started to melt. About 12,000 years ago, temperatures rose rapidly, and 5,000 later agriculture spread widely. Little by little, people settled.[14]

A prominent travel writer, anthropologist and art connoisseur, Bruce Chatwin developed an interesting theory about the nomadic background of humans, which he labeled "the anatomy of restlessness." His key observation was that humans have a built-in cultural gene (which culture researchers call memes) that forces humans to move around and which has its roots in the long period of human evolution prior to the development of our current culture. Urbanization has reduced this movement.

Chatwin deduced that this genetic inheritance continues to urge people to move from place to place in search of new pastures and prey. Thus, people also want to look upon wide vistas instead of the walls of the nearest building, and people who are cooped up in the same city dwelling and are used to the same routines may feel like they live in a prison. They feel restless without knowing why. Chatwin himself experienced this restlessness as overpowering. He was never able to finish writing his "theory of nomadism," but discussed the topic at length in his essays and novels.[15]

The current decade marks the first one, with more people living in cities than in rural areas.[16] There are bound to be problems if city planning doesn't concern itself with the internal restlessness of people. In designing open spaces, we should take Chatwin's advice and create spaces that allow for roaming. City planning should also take into account logistical factors. Bike paths and pedestrian zones, for example, help people satisfy their need for personal mobility.

When living conditions improve, people have the tendency to invest more money in traveling, which satisfies the need for new experiences. The inner eagerness to invent and innovate may also originate from our nomadic instinct. You can best see it in children's urge to play, which satisfies their needs to move about. It is interesting that children are calm when carried, which likely reminds them of the time in their nomadic background when mothers carried their children with them.

Culture is common to humanity. It unifies and separates. You could say that there are 10,000 cultures in the world but only one civilization. As globalization undoubtedly progresses in the sixth wave, cultures will meet and collide more than ever before. The sprawling urban environments provide the meeting ground. Even if that is a threat, it is also an opportunity. As the internal development of Europe has proven, multiculturalism and the cooperation it involves may be the best assurance for peace.

References

1. infed. Peter Senge and the learning organization. Accessed January 23, 2017. http://www.infed.org/mobi/peter-senge-and-the-learning-organization/.
2. Gartner Press Release. Gartner Says Smart Machines Will Have Widespread and Deep Business Impact through 2020. Accessed January 23, 2017. http://www.gartner.com/newsroom/id/2605015.
3. Heinonen, Sikka & Ruotsalainen, Juho 2013. Futures clinique — method for promoting futures learning and provoking radical futures. *European Journal for Futures Research*, **15** (7), 1–11.
4. Nyman, Göte. 2015. University-business-government collaboration: From Institutes to Platforms and Ecosystems. *Triple Helix*, **2** (2), 1–20. Nyman, Göte & Wilenius, Markku. 2014. *What are we good for? Challenges of education in Finland.* Report to Sitra.
5. Wilenius, Markku. 2006. *Towards a Creative Economy: Cultural Competence as a future resource.* Helsinki: Edita.
6. World Values Survey. 2016. "Data & Documentation." Accessed March 8, 2016. http://www.worldvaluessurvey.org/WVSContents.jsp.
7. Collier, Paul. 2013. *Immigration and Multiculturalism in the 21st Century.* Penguin Books.
8. Inc. 2015. "The Most Entrepreneurial Group in America Wasn't Born in America." http://www.inc.com/magazine/201502/adam-bluestein/the-most-entrepreneurial-group-in-america-wasnt-born-in-america.html.
9. Munich ranks high in many city-indexes, see e.g., Fast-Co-Exist. 2012. "The Top 10 Smartest European Cities." Accessed September 14, 2016. https://www.fastcoexist.com/1680856/the-top-10-smartest-euro pean-cities.
10. WorldBuild365. 2015. "10 of the best wooden skyscrapers." Accessed September 14, 2016. https://www.worldbuild365.com/news/sawxe ob2a/ building-architecture/10-of-the-best-wooden-skyscrapers.
11. OECD. 2014. "Policy challenges for the next 50 years." Accessed March 8, 2016. http://www.oecd.org/economy/lookingto2060.htm.
12. Development Alternatives. 2016. "Eco-solutions for people and the planet." Accessed March 8, 2016. http://www.devalt.org/.

13. Rapaille, Clotaire. 2007. *The Culture Code: An Ingenious Way to Understand Why People Around the World Live and Buy as They Do.* New York: Crown Business.
14. Mithen, Steven. 2003. *After the Ice: A Global Human History* 20,000–5000 BC. London: Orion Books.
15. Chatwin, Bruce. 1982. *What Am I Doing Here?* London: Penguin Books.
16. United Nations. 2014. "World's population increasingly urban with more than half living in urban areas." Accessed March 8, 2016. http://www.un.org/en/development/desa/news/population/world-urbanization-prospects-2014.html.

Chapter 10

A REVOLUTION OF AWARENESS

Daniel Goleman, a psychologist known worldwide for the idea of emotional intelligence, has made an excellent case for why a better ability to concentrate is needed in today's world.[1] There are more and more stimuli interrupting our concentration. The number of devices requiring our attention is growing, and the devices themselves contain more and more channels for interaction. A person's thoughts wander almost half of his or her waking hours.

Our environment is changing, making it increasingly more difficult to concentrate on any one thing. The difference is especially noticeable in the case of children and youth. An American youngster sends and receives over 100 text messages per day. Because the center of our attention is constantly shifting, we appear absent all the time. As a lecturer, I'm familiar with listeners who appear physically present but are absent in their minds, with gazes on a display screen.

The splintered usage of time means that short-term matters overshadow long-term ones. Time seems to pass more rapidly due to increasing amounts of experiences available, and the rapid shifting of trends further intensifies this tendency. Shareholders are increasingly impatient and want to see a return on their investment no later than by the next quarter. Networked business models increase connections multifold and require attention in many directions.

The most interesting part the Goleman thesis is precisely this: due to the above-mentioned reasons, it will be more and more valuable to be able to concentrate on only certain tasks at one time. Concentration simply requires an increased effort. *Mindfulness*, or focusing on one's own awareness, is a new form of *fitness*, and it's spreading like wildfire. Pioneering companies have already hired their own coaches to help people exercise their minds and, thus, improve their performance (and company results, of course).

It is interesting to note that a better understanding of people as fine instruments is now developing. There is awareness of how little is known about the functioning of consciousness. It is nevertheless clear that very little of our performance ability is being used. Richard Davidson, neurologist and professor of psychology at University of Wisconsin, has pioneered research about exercises in concentration and meditation and their effect on our mental abilities.[2]

According to Davidson, exercises in concentration and meditation bring about two benefits: One is the improved ability of the frontal lobes to focus, and the other is an improved ability to concentrate despite distractions. These kinds of exercises increase our ability to handle information and helps us exactly when we most need to focus.

Why do we actually need to concentrate and to increase our performance ability? We of course need it in order to attain a better life, but most of all in order to develop as a person. It is well known that if life seems chaotic, it is hard to reach any goals.

As we've noted before, the well-known philosopher Georg Henrik von Wright described the difference between people and animals like this: Animals are incapable of goal-oriented action and are directed by instinct.[3] There are certain key requirements for reaching goals. *First*, repetition and perseverance to overcome innate laziness or lack of commitment. *Second*, having a clear goal — undefined goals are hard to attain. *Third*, the goal must have a concrete meaning that builds commitment.

In the sixth wave, more and more attention will be placed on how our internal capabilities are utilized. Randel Cardas, a professor at top-ranked French business school INSEAD, starts each one of his lectures with a meditation exercise in order to bring his students into a focused and open-minded state.[4] At Google, Chade-Meng Tan's program *Search Inside Yourself* is being followed.[5] Google allows its engineers to spend a fifth of their working hours on their own personal projects. Tan's program started as a result of this practice. Now it is regarded as the most important internal training program at Google. It has helped employees improve their work flow and their internal balance.

The benefits of concentration in our self-development are also evident in psychological research regarding the role of willpower in human life. Roy Baumeister, a social psychologist at the University of Florida, is the pioneer in this field of study. According to him, self-control is key to well-being and success. People who have internalized their goals and figured out their outlook on the world experience the least amount of stress and are most likely to attain their goals.[6]

One way or the other, it is about the person, him- or herself: how to manage the ever-more complex world through careful choices and through listening to one's internal voice. There is no simple solution, but there are rules that have surfaced in the research. Most important is that the development of mental abilities requires consistency and a will to surpass oneself. This, in fact, is what is required in order to develop any skill.[7]

The splintering of the world and the complexity that are built into the sixth wave are creating unprecedented challenges to people's ability to control their lives. The effects of this are already clear: Mental problems are increasingly the reason for early retirement. Our only chance is to strengthen our internal capacity to buffer the impulses and chaos of the world.

Somehow, this does in fact sound like an exciting adventure. Baumeister tells us that not too long ago, talk about internal energy sounded like complete hogwash and his colleagues did not take him seriously. He could however, empirically prove that human willpower does really exist, and that it can be understood and cultivated.

From Collective to Social Consciousness

At their core, humans are social beings with a built-in genetic propensity to adapt to their environment. This has developed into a safety mechanism that has allowed us to quickly deal with new situations. At the same time, this ability to adapt has become an obstacle for our evolution. This is because the new era requires people to think *socially*, rather than *collectively*. What do I mean?

A collective being acts according to collective rules and impulses and from there finds the building blocks for his worldview. Religious communities function in exactly the same way. Looking at the evolution of the world, religions are alive and well: The majority of the world population believes in one God or another. However, religions are losing ground in Western countries and especially in the Nordic countries. This is no coincidence. The Nordic countries are already moving into a post-collective era.

As the worldwide value mapping by the sociologist Ronald Inglehardt proves to us, self-expression is gaining importance as a life value, specifically in the Nordic countries. This means that traditional collectivism is weakening and individualism is strengthening.[8]

Simultaneously, individuals are becoming more consciously and actively engaged in society, even if it doesn't happen through traditional channels, by adhering to a religion or by voting for political parties.

In the sixth wave, an individual will become a member of a community through his or her individual conscious choices. This is already true of the younger generations. Becoming a social being and being able to take the surrounding world into account happens through individual thinking and not through learning a habit. It is only through gaining personal knowledge and experience that individuals can open up a path for understanding the world through someone else's perspective, whether we're talking about understanding nature or poor people in developing countries. Developing this kind of social awareness is key to humanity's survival into the next century.

The life of a socially aware individual is strongly guided by a motivation founded on understanding the meaning and purpose of life. The meaning of life must be discovered internally, as no outsider can provide it. It is only a person who has found his internal meaning that can give his all for the common good.

At the same time, an individual becomes free to act, not in response to outside duress or compulsions but according to his or her independent thinking. An individual is free for as long as he or she has allowed him- or herself the right to decide his or her own worldview. We will see more people trying to attain this during the sixth wave. The increasing amount of information and changing values together produce humans who are internally compelled to decide on their likes and dislikes on their own.

The private will encounter the public in a new way in the coming decades. How does the evolution of internal values affect external values? How do we create conditions that allow people's internal goals to find positive expression in the external world? How do we create a society that supports initiative in all aspects of life?

Even though many things are on the right track in Europe and even though conditions are fertile, we are still far from the goal. We can observe this in the current economic crisis. We have not cared enough about our ability to leave behind old industrial-era structures and institutions. Hence, we are still living in what I call "an industrial coma," sadly evident in the sluggish economic performance of many European countries.

We have a good chance to succeed, but much is required of us all. Next, we will take a look at the future of Finland.

References

1. Goleman, Daniel. 2013. *The Hidden Driver of Excellence.* New York: Bloomsbury.
2. Davidson, Richard. 2012. *The Emotional Life of Your Brain.* New York: Hudson Street Press.
3. Von Wright, Georg H. 1971. *Explanation and Understanding.* Ithaca: Cornell University Press.
4. INSEAD. 2014. "Why I Brought Meditation into the Classroom." Accessed March 8, 2016. http://knowledge.insead.edu/leadership-organisations/why-i-brought-meditation-into-the-classroom-3132.
5. *Business Insider.* 2014. "Here's What Google Teaches Employees In Its 'Search Inside Yourself' Course." Accessed March 8, 2016. http://www.businessinsider.com/search-inside-yourself-googles-life-changing-mindfulness-course-2014-8.

6. Baumeister, Roy & John Tierney. 2011. *Willpower: Rediscovering the Greatest Human Strength.* London: Penguin Books.
7. Goleman, Daniel. 2013. *The Hidden Driver of Excellence.* New York: Bloomsbury.
8. World Values Survey. 2016. "Data & Documentation." Accessed March 8, 2016. http://www.worldvaluessurvey.org/WVSContents.jsp.

Chapter 11

THE OPPORTUNITY FOR FINLAND

In the previous chapters, I have examined global shifts from various perspectives. It is now time to ask what chances for success Finland will have in the world of the future that I sketched out earlier. Will Finland manage to reformulate its current industrial structure in order to better meet global demands?

I would like to present Finland as a case study here, explaining how an individual country can position itself in the context of the changing waves and as a part of the global system. I need to emphasize here that I do not mean to present the "Finnish Case" as an ideal for others to follow. Rather I see it as a symptom of our times: how daringly difficult it is to keep the pace of change, how dramatic it can be when your strengths turn into your weaknesses. As I know my country quite well, it may be interesting for readers to see how I apply my analytical framework to it.

My point here is that as with any other country, we can present a similar case how past evolves and revolves into future. We can observe larger patterns and trends taking individual shape in each country and yet we can recognize very individual destinies. While the case of Finland has great resemblance with countries like Sweden, Norway, Denmark, Germany, Austria or Netherlands, there are also a lot connections and similarities between Finland and Japan, or Finland and Chile. So by presenting the case of Finland I would like to provide understanding, how challenging the moving from fifth to sixth wave actually is.

In a book published after World War II, then Finnish prime minister and later president for 25 years, Urho Kekkonen asked, "Is our country well-enough composed to prosper?"[1] The advice Kekkonen offered to post-war Finland was to harness national resources for the common good. The great rivers and water systems of the North were to be harnessed for energy production, and the mission of the state was advised to be creating new industries. Economizing was required for new investments, because there was no foreign capital available. By and large, this is what actually occurred.

We now find ourselves in more or less the same situation. The picnic is over and our investments are down (see Figure 1). Only a handful of companies since the early 1990s have been able to grow into major exporters of goods or services. Our exports are now 30 billion euros less than what they should be, according to the indications of trends prior to the global financial crisis. Naturally, this has an important role in the so-called sustainability deficit.

The demise of Nokia's mobile phone business, the slow-down of the forest industry investments, and the shut-down of mills have delivered a rough blow to Finns. The only significant investment

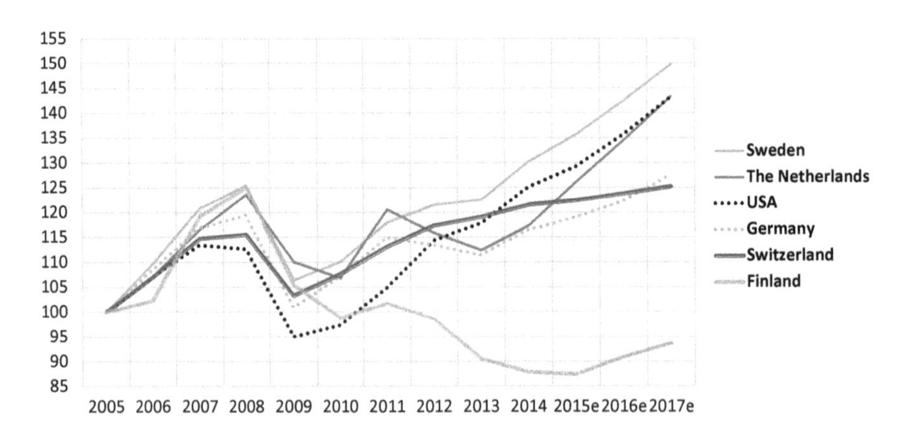

Figure 1. Upswing of investments required in Finland.
Source: The Federation of Finnish Technology Industries.

plans of the last decades have concerned the building of nuclear power plants. This has been met with strong opposition by citizens, and the investments as such appear dubious.[2]

Nevertheless, the forest industry has made some bold moves recently: Metsä Fibre is planning a significant bioproduct/pulp mill in the city of Äänekoski. Finnpulp, held by a group of individual investors, is also developing plans to construct the world's largest pulp mill in Kuopio. Thus, Finland is finally seeing a revival of investment, although other industries and parts of the country are still in an investment slump.

What will Finland look like in 2030? What will its source of prosperity be? Before answering, I must provide a glance into some positive developments.

Nokia held an extraordinary shareholders' meeting in November 2013, during which the sale of the mobile phone business to Microsoft was authorized. The average age of the meeting participants was about 60. Simultaneously, Helsinki hosted Slush, the global technology and startup conference I mentioned in Chapter 7. A wide and international group of entrepreneurs, investors and media representatives participated. The average age of the participants was 30. Slush is the largest and most significant event of its kind in Europe, and thanks to such events, Finland is now recognized as a Silicon Valley of Europe.

A similar phenomenon occurred in the early 1990s, as Finland struggled at the bottom of a recession and was reaching for renewed national growth. Nokia is of course not the whole story but a significant part of it. This is why it's important to remember what took place then and afterwards.

Since the downfall and the ultimate sale of the mobile phones unit to Microsoft, former Nokia employees have invested their capital to start over 500 new companies.[59] The wealth generated through Nokia has been put to work, which can't be necessarily said about "old money."

Since the sale of its mobile phone business, Nokia has been renewed. You could say that it has left behind a business of the fifth wave and is aiming for the sixth. Nokia is building business founded on the growing networking needs and the need for more intelligent information transfer. The emerging world of the Internet of Things (IoT) is the one that Nokia wants to attach its future to.[3]

Current investment targets in Finland are digital technology and the services upon which it's based. There are a rising number of interesting companies in this business field, such as Reaktor, Supercell, Futurice, and Vincit. These companies have not only first-class products but also innovative company cultures and structures. The best of these have created organizational structures based on self-management and a lack of hierarchy. They have satisfied, productive employees.

Reaktor is a shining example of the new kind of entrepreneurship producing excellent results through technological knowhow, a refined service concept and human-centricity.[4] Reaktor was founded at the turn of the millennium by a couple of programmers who simply wished to create the kind of company in which they wanted to work: human- and client-centric and offering the best expertise.

They have since created a company that has grown to over 360 employees. They insist on the principle that power and responsibility lie completely with the operative teams. The work is done cooperatively with the clients, which means that for the most part, the teams work on the clients' premises. This ensures tight communication between the client and the product team and results in quick recovery from mistakes. This is called "agile software development."[5]

Reaktor won the award for best place to work in Finland so many times between the years 2008 and 2011 that it chose to no longer participate in Great Place to Work Institute's annual ranking. In that same period, it was also chosen as one of the three best companies in Europe. Reaktor's reputation in its field is such that all the best people want to work there.

The key to Reaktor's success has likely been its abandonment of industrial practices and the desire to find practices better suited to services, all while carefully considering human needs. It is important to Reaktor that people seek fulfillment in life from things other than just work. Reaktor can be considered part of the international movement towards a systemic and holistic understanding of organizational functions (see more in Chapter 8). This kind of approach has already created plenty of successful companies, examples of which were compiled in *Reinventing Organizations* by consultant and researcher Fredrik Laloux.[6]

Small and medium-sized businesses in Finland are plagued by a lack of growth and internationalization.[7] There seems to be a need for a new generation, which envisions career paths other than toiling away for the conglomerates. Creating one's own success as an entrepreneur is more enjoyable and more rewarding. Even though we can't simulate California's climate in Finland, we are at least capable of creating the kind of entrepreneurial spirit found in Silicon Valley.

When looking at global demand trends in the coming decades, we can note that one of the most significant developments will be that the mobile internet will become available to everyone, across the globe, and serve as everyone's primary means of communication. According to some predictions, the number of mobile internet users will grow from the present 2.2 billion to 3.8 billion by 2020.[8] That represents over half of the population on the planet. This exponential growth has potential to impact the world much more than any other advancement. "Digital inclusion," as it is called, is an enormous growth engine, as it connects people to a common network. Finnish technology can play a major role in building this infrastructure. For example, Finnish company Tecnotree is creating new technology and service models for these markets.

The Future of Industry

Renewable and recyclable options are required to replace the non-renewable materials and energy sources in the building industry, packaging industry and fuel production just as much as the electronics industry. What do Finns have to offer in this development? Are we able to find new solutions that allow us to get rid of wasteful use of plastic and materials like styrofoam, superfluous packaging and clumsy, poor construction materials? Is the Finnish forest industry forward-looking and innovative enough to be able to meet the challenge?

I'm concerned that we'll see the usual wide resistance. If the forest industry can't recognize its part in the coming revolutionary transformation, then it can't make the necessary investments. This is a sector with sizeable 20 billion euros in revenue,[9] but one that has been reluctant to invest in R&D. Investments in the sector received a significant boost with the plans for the next generation Äänekoski bioproduct mill, where the idea is to apply the principles of circular economy into the functioning of a mill.[10] This means in practice that all pulp production side-streams are considered raw material for all kinds of other bioproducts: oil, turpentine, lignin products, firewood and bioelectricity. In recent years, investments made in or planned for the forest industry have risen to several billion euros. The investments are partly in new forest industry territory, such as second-generation biofuel and new biomaterials but also partly in "old" products, such as pulp and carton, which the markets still increasingly demand. In addition, the pulp mill project Finnpulp will require an investment of 1.1 billion euros if it comes into fruition sometime towards the end of the current decade.[11]

Ever since the beginning of financial crisis, the metal and machine industries have had a tough time. The revenues in 2015 were 20 billion euros below 2008 numbers. Yet the traditional industries — forest, metal and chemical — continue to serve as the source of wealth and the basis of exports. It is quite possible that these sectors will shrink in Finland significantly by 2030 as in the last 10 years over 10 billion euros have vanished from their gross-value added.[12]

Within the technology sector, on the other hand, cleantech is growing. Revenues totaled almost 26 billion euros in 2013, whereas only three years prior it was only 18 billion. Energy-efficiency-related technology is the most successful, followed by clean processes, materials and products. Sweden is our primary market, with Germany and Russia just behind. Our handicap is a lack of public funding for sales and marketing, as technology development continues to be the main target of funding. The ambitious goal of Cleantech Finland, the network of Finnish cleantech companies, is to lift revenues to 50 billion by 2020.

Looking beyond the currently stagnated relations with Russia, it seems clear to me that Russia will inevitably grow in importance to our economy. We should seize the opportunity that exists to sell our knowhow in both cleantech and education. Russia must modernize itself, and we can help. However, Russians appreciate quality — and we should wonder if we can offer products and services that meet their requirements since Finns are not exactly known for the quality of their customer service.

The success of the internet gaming industry has delighted many in Finland. Indeed, it has grown 10-fold in only three years, achieving a turnover of 2.4 billion euros in 2015. One reason behind it is the phenomenal success of Supercell, which last year made almost a billion euros in sheer profit.[13] Interestingly, Supercell CEO and founder Ilkka Paananen says it is all about the Finnish "no-nonsense" culture at the center of their way of working.[14] As Paananen stated after releasing their incredible results in February 2016, "These financial results are, of course, great, and we are very proud of them. However, the real highlight for us is how we've been able to get here while staying true to our founding vision that was all about people." He added, "We believed that if we bring together the best people, create the best possible environment for them, then with enough time and some luck, some great games will follow. Games that millions of people around the world will want to play for years and years."[15] As it appears, Paananen has been able to release the creative potential of his employees.

Supercell alone does not possess the leverage to lift the Finnish economy up from its current abyss. It employs only 170 people. However, companies like Supercell are not only successful in their area but also in establishing new business models, ethics and organizational cultures. The owners of Supercell have invested their profits in other new Finnish enterprises. They are paving the way toward a new, healthier kind of capitalism.

Healthcare and healthtech will be part of the big growth sector in the sixth wave. We have a high level of knowhow in healthtech, where companies like Polar and Suunto have already seen tremendous success. A lot of new businesses are springing up, such as those in the Silicon Vallila district in Helsinki, whose campus opened its doors in late 2014.[16] There are plenty of opportunities, from the refining of various types of berries for superfood to creating new diagnostic equipment. I predict that within a decade, enterprises related to healthcare and well-being will grow into the largest business sector in the world.[17]

The Past and the Future of the Forest Industry

The Finnish forest industry faces major issues: The demand of paper and printing materials has been declining for a long time (thanks mainly to digitalization), communication in various forms is moving to the internet at increasing speed and the scarcity of non-renewable resources is creating new challenges. The construction, home décor and packaging industries need to develop new products, services and solutions that are based on wood fibers. As soon as the Finnish forest industry finds a way to respond to this demand, it will become a player in the sixth wave and will carry its wood-industry know-how into the new era.

Let's learn from history. The previous disruption of similar significance occurred during the second Kondratiev wave, between 1830 and 1880. That is when Europe started to quickly become industrialized. Modern communication also began with the increasing dissemination of newspapers and books. The problem back then, as mentioned in Chapter 4, was the use of rags as raw material for paper: Because such material was scarce and expensive, a new solution was needed by the middle of the century.

Engineers and industrialists who believed in new opportunities were a key factor in the success of the industry. A young Finnish mountain engineer, Knut Fredrik Idestam, made a study-journey to Harz in Germany in the 1860s and visited a local groundwood plant, where wood was being mechanically ground up for pulp in order to produce various products. Excited by his discovery, he then founded the first groundwood plant on the shores of Finland's Tammerkoski river in 1865. Thus began the new phase of industrial revolution in Finland.

At the same time, the first laboratories in the United States, England and France started to produce wood pulp with chemical methods. The resulting cellulose was much more like rags than mechanical pulp. The industrialists who understood chemistry, like G.A. Serlachius (originally a pharmacist), were tremendously enthused.

Serlachius was a forest industry pioneer who, together with Ahlström, Gutzeit and others, connected Finland to the global economy in an entirely new way. Finland slowly became an industrialized nation by harnessing the forests, hydropower and railways for raw materials and resources for the paper industry. The transition was not easy, and many — especially those with a lot to lose — were vehemently opposed to the changes. This new industry sector needed a good deal of stick-to-itiveness, stubbornness, courage and capital in order to grow and prosper.

However, the sector succeeded because the need was so obvious: The demand for paper had grown dramatically, due to industrialization and the rising levels of education. The sector did its part in transforming Finland into a sophisticated society.

The same kind of courage and "sisu" (a Finnish word meaning "perseverance" or "guts") must be summoned. It is time for the Finnish forest industry to rise up and meet the needs created by the dramatic growth in the demand for goods and raw materials. The world is in dire need of new solutions based on fiber knowhow. We have a 500-year history in forestry exports. There are numerous opportunities, such as:

- New fiber-based materials for the construction, home décor and packaging industries, which can replace current products based on minerals and synthetics.
- Wood construction, which is experiencing a renaissance and market growth, thanks to health benefits[18] and the proven durability of wood.
- Biofuels, which will to a degree replace fossil fuel and which will create employment in rural areas.
- Xylitol, or birch sugar, which was invented decades ago in Finland but has now become a popular option as a healthy sugar substitute around the globe; berries from gardens and forests could similarly conquer the market thanks to their health benefits.

- Ecologically designed products, which Finnish companies like Aalto and Wirkkala have been exporting for quite some time.
- Promotion and development of tourism by creating tranquil, high-quality experiences in nature.

The opportunities in the bioindustry are not yet clearly understood in Finland, even though there is an excellent bioindustry strategy. In the long run, I foresee tremendous promise in this sector. The actual golden era of the bioindustry will probably occur during the seventh wave, i.e., between 2050 and 2100. Just as advancements in electronics during the fourth Kondratiev wave (1930–1970) laid the groundwork for the information and communications technology revolution (see Chapter 3), advancements in resource-efficient technologies will pave the way for the dominance of biomaterials in the second half of the century.

Our sixth wave research project examined a vast array of opportunities in the forest industry.[19] In 2013 we invited a 100-strong group of forest sector experts, financial sector experts and key innovators to take part in various workshops throughout the year. We worked with them to find answers to our question of what the forest industry should focus on for its developmental activities.

The starting point for the research project is depicted in the below graph (see Figure 2): There is pressure for change in the forestry sector. The digitalization of the key technologies of the fifth wave has led to challenges for the print media markets. Because communication is increasingly digital, the old forestry strongholds, with the paper industry leading the pack, face increasingly serious problems. Demand is dropping, and new competitors are entering the market.

The forest industry is in the middle of a materials revolution that is upsetting the whole of society: Raw materials, products and services based on biomaterials are replacing non-renewable raw materials at an increasing rate. In fact, I strongly believe the this century will show a complete redesign of industrial products as well as consumption patterns. The value for any given artifact will

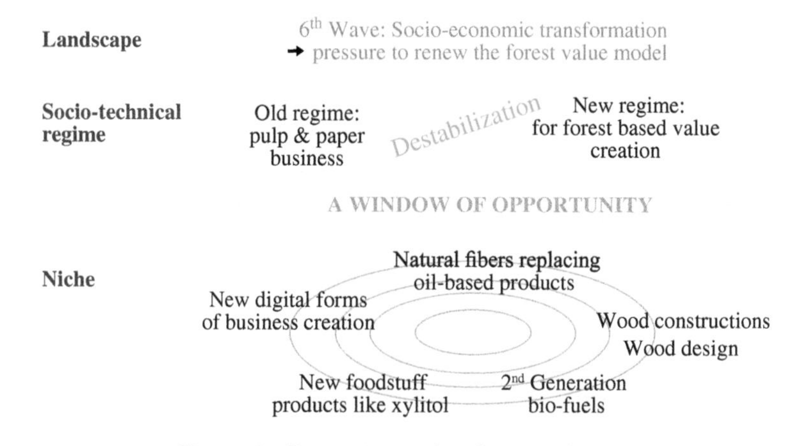

Figure 2. Transition within forest industry.

be determined by its quality to maintain its value. There organic substances will have a central role to play. Moreover, a whole new network of operators and service providers will be generated to further this goal, which is then supported by legislation and taxation. We see now the first signs of this transition.

Naturally, the transition is anything but easy, because we are living in economically tough times and investing in anything new is frowned upon. And yet it is precisely the right time to invest in completely innovative products and services. An example of this is UPM's 200-million-euro investment into a second-generation biodiesel mill project launched in 2014, where logging scraps and sawdust are used as raw materials. There are other projects underway in the forestry sector, mentioned earlier in this chapter.

New projects are indeed called for, as Finland should be rapidly moving towards a bioeconomy, or an economy where refining of natural fibers and recycling have a much more central role. The Finnish Bioindustry Strategy envisions a pioneering role for Finland in bioeconomy. The goal is to increase the revenue in the bio industry sector from 60 billion to 100 billion euros, with 100,000 new jobs being created by 2025.[20] This happens only with new, value-added products and services.

The advancements in bioeconomy have repercussions in other sectors. The chemical industry is especially important, because many of the manufacturing processes of new bioproducts are connected to innovations in chemistry. This, of course, is nothing new. The entire birth and growth of the Finnish forest industry has been dependent on utilizing chemical processes. For example, various "smart paper" materials represent a symbiosis of ICT and the forest industry.

In order for the bioeconomy to advance, the field must also appeal to coming generations. Interest in the forestry field at Aalto University grew when the program was changed from "wood processing" to "bioproduct technology." New investors should be brought into the biotechnology sector, just as has already happened in regular technology. Cleantech Invest and VNT Management are already investing in new energy technologies, but there are no such investors in biotechnology. Risk capital, which is needed for the sector to advance, is missing.

It is important that advancements in the sector are connected with positive changes, such as improved employment, economic growth and sustainable development. The old perception that environmental concerns are a burden to industry should be scrapped. As the economy and employment acquire a new foundation, so too should the advancement of bioeconomy become an example of a more sustainable business model.

Utilizing the forest for recreational experiences is becoming increasingly common. Tourism was one of the few industries that grew in times of financial crisis: Between 2007 and 2013, there was 31% growth, and it continues to grow steadily.[21] There are more and more tourists traveling to Finland who want to experience a genuine, original forest. We should be selling the beauty and diversity of our nature in increasingly varied ways. For instance, appreciation for Finland in Japan is high because the connection with nature is almost as important to the Japanese as it is to Finns. In recent years, the number of Asian tourists has increased, partly thanks to direct flights from Asia to Helsinki, due to Finland's relative proximity to Asia. Also the Germans seem to have increased interest towards nature. For example, there are burial service businesses that offer plots in the woods as opposed to cemeteries. According to some surveys, as many as three in five Germans prefer to be buried in the woods.[22]

Good health is connected to a deep understanding of nature. As I mentioned, Xylitol's beneficial effects on health and in preventing dental decay were being touted in Finland as early as the 1970s. The health benefits of wild berries have also been studied in Finland.[23] Nature tourism has been growing for a long time in Finland. Tourism was one of the few industries that grew in times of financial crisis: Between 2007 and 2013, there was 31% growth, and it continues to grow steadily.[21] Wood-based construction was promoted heavily in Finland in the 1990s, at the same time as in Sweden, but it did not gain ground here as it did in Sweden. The failure has been blamed on the authorities just as much as on the architects. Compared to Central European countries, Finland is actually a developing country in regards to wood construction: Single homes and vacation homes are being built out of wood but no apartment or public buildings are. A wood-based construction boom has started to take hold throughout the world, and Finland should capitalize on the knowhow it has amassed over the centuries.

Something *has* started to happen, in fact. Marco Casagrande, a Finnish architect, has created Paracity, a wood-module construction that is being built in Taiwan.[24] When completed it could be the largest wooden structure in the world. The idea is to be able to easily stack the six-meter modules and connect them to each other. The concept of Paracity as a whole aims to help develop sustainable urban construction, with such features as the recycling of wastewater into drinking water. This is a perfect example of modularity and flexibility, which will be key principles of the world of the sixth wave.

Another principle is to take greenery to "new heights," so to speak. Greens capes, which will be commonly found on the roofs and in the walls of future urban buildings, have multiple benefits: They create comfort, improve air quality and allow for small gardens where one can grow herbs and such. Green thatch-style roofs also collect rain water.[25]

The goal is to bring organic matter to mainly urban environments. Because I happen to also hold a vocational degree as a gardener, I've welcomed this recent, rapid development, as it is part of the holistic understanding of well-being.

It is easy to conclude that through research and development, a lot of information will be gathered in the coming years about the health benefits that result from both nature's bounty and from simply experiencing it. It is already known that hiking and spending time in nature improves one's mood and vitality.[26]

New products and services also require new infrastructure. Nothing sells easily if it is not readily available to the consumer. Moving away from fossil fuel will require a new distribution network for electric vehicles, for example. The distribution of biofuel has to be well organized. Large companies are especially challenged by reaction speed. Being slow to change proved disastrously expensive to the Finnish forest industry behemoths at the beginning of the millennium, when they invested billions in the paper and pulp industry, despite the signs that the days of greatest growth were already far behind and that the markets were beginning to weaken. As a result of faulty investments, the competitive edge of the industry was fully blunted.

Renewal is only possible through investments in product development, refining of services and in increased cooperation. The new Metsä fiber biofactory in Äänekoski is destined to not simply produce pulp but also to create a network of various biomaterials and products, such as bio-oil and bioethanol. There is not much included in the project, however, in regards to new product development.

I'm convinced that something interesting will follow from the rise of the bioeconomy. In looking to the end of the sixth wave in 2050, it's clear that material resources will be utilized in a far smarter and far more efficient way than at the present time. If we were to voyage through time to the end of the century, we would find people looking back with amazement to a time when our kind of wasteful use of resources and destruction of nature was not only possible but permissible. The seventh wave will revolutionize our materials economy, but before that can happen we need the energy revolution and the breakthrough industrial thinking of the sixth wave.

Finland's Future Regarding Energy

Rapid industrialization, corporate interests and energy scarcity have guided Finnish energy politics. These energy politics had one goal: to produce energy as cheaply as possible for energy-intensive industrial corporations. It was justified at the time because of increasing energy use and industrial expansion. This is no longer the case.

The idea that energy politics could serve to develop new Finnish technology by creating attractive domestic markets has been overlooked. Likewise, no focus has been given to the idea of creating lasting job opportunities through renewable and domestic forms of energy. We've stayed on the tried and true path.

In the coming decades, renewable energy use will undoubtedly grow unlike anything else in the industrialized world. The cheapening of renewable energy on one hand, and the increasing cost of nuclear and fossil fuel on the other, have already created a situation in which the resulting risk for locked investments render renewable energy forms much more important than in previous times. The nations that understand the importance of being pioneers in this development will have the best conditions for participating in the creation of the third energy revolution (which follows steam power and fossil fuel). The revolution brought on by renewable energy is going to be one of the most significant changes to come in the sixth wave.

The current situation in Finland is puzzling. Finland has one of the highest energy consumption rates per capita in the world.[27] We consumed 8.5 billion euros worth of fossil fuel based imported energy products in 2012.[28] We are practically the only Western nation that plans to build more nuclear power plants. Meanwhile, total energy consumption has been on the decline since 2006.[29] The economy has problems because the traditional growth sectors — namely the forest, metal and electronic industries — have contracted. The majority of energy required by them could be produced domestically.

Under these conditions, Finland has chosen a path different from other comparable countries, such as Germany, Austria, Denmark, and Sweden, which have persistently worked to bundle energy politics with national growth and labor politics. When considering the figures, things in Finland might look decent: Almost one-third of our energy is produced with renewable resources. Yet, old traditions, more than anything else, have perpetuated this. To a large extent, this is explained by the long-held tradition of tapping the energy available from wood. Traditional Finnish energy sources are industrial waste sludge from forest industry plants, wood burning and hydropower. All other renewable energy sources have not received much attention.

Finland is in a much different position than other countries. Our economy has remained highly dependent on energy. We have a negative trade balance, whereas the other countries mentioned have a positive balance. Even though the share of renewable energy has traditionally been high, it has remained practically unchanged through the 2000s, while other nations have sailed way past us in comparison.[28]

Finland's energy policies have stagnated in the past decades in many aspects: Energy is regarded purely as a cost, and its societal harms or opportunities aren't taken seriously. This is short-sighted, because we are at present at the start of the sixth wave and therefore at the forefront of a major change.

The most important leverage in this change comes from the fact that fossil fuel and nuclear power are not sustainable solutions, whichever way one might measure them. This fact notwithstanding, Finnish energy production is dependent on these sources. The so called "professor task force," to which I myself belong, came out with an energy policy investigation that shows that by the year 2050, as many as 50,000 new jobs could be created in domestic energy production and in growing energy efficiency. One can add to these figures the business activity that would be created as a result.[30]

Denmark, which has roughly the same population as Finland, started years ago to determine the necessary processes for replacing coal with wind energy. Now the industry counts 240 businesses that employ 29,000 people and which produce a quarter of the country's energy. The Danes aim to be independent of coal as soon as by 2030 and completely independent of fossil fuel by 2050. The Danish wind mills are not obtrusive; in fact they are appreciated, because they bring much-needed jobs to rural areas.[31]

Germany is in a league of its own. The German *Energiewende,* or energy turnaround, is one of the most important industry-society initiatives of our time. It has already made Germany into a pioneer in clean energy. It also represents a major investment in significantly increasing the resource productivity of society. For example, the country plans to reduce energy use by 20% in the current decade. The abandonment of nuclear power and creation of conditions for an energy infrastructure based on renewable sources is a long-term investment. However, there are already signs of success: Germany has gained a new sector for exports and 400,000 new jobs. The strategic goal of the *Energiewende* is to reduce national debt by 180 billion euros by the year 2030. A quarter of its electricity is produced with renewable sources, and there is no shortage of energy in Germany. The share of nuclear energy has dropped to much below that: 16%. The price tag on the German energy turnaround is hefty at this stage, to be sure, but I believe that the payback will be multifold in the long term. Finland sorely needs the same kind of pioneering spirit, where even smaller actors can have a major role.

We should quickly shift our energy policies in a new direction. This requires exploitation of renewable natural resources, such as bio-energy, but also wind, solar, geothermal and hydro and wave energy. The sweetest strawberries in the world grow in Finland because the sun shines so long here in the summer. The sunny conditions in southern Finland are as good as those in the middle of Germany. In the summer of 2014, Germany produced as much as half of its electricity through solar sources. In Finland it is negligible: about one tenth of 1%.

In the future, energy independence will also be a matter of national security. To remain dependent on a superpower for energy would be the worst alternative. In addition to increasing our energy independence, we should also increase Nordic cooperation. Norway produces renewable energy much beyond its needs. Finland ought to follow Denmark and buy electricity from Norway. We should also invest in smart electric grids. Regulation and too much bureaucracy should be dismantled, as they turn out to be major bottlenecks for wind power expansion.

Intelligent energy policy in the sixth wave is not driven by direct investments only. Much more significant is how well a country adopts new energy sources as a part of its technology and innovation policies. It requires new kinds of governmental procurement policies, innovative ways to increase cooperation and competition, quotas for renewable energy, auctions and so forth. It is actually much more a question of how we use existing resources than it is about creating new resources.

What Will It Take for Finland to Rise Up?

Ever since the financial crisis, the Finnish economy has regressed at an incredible pace. Finland seems to never have quite recovered from the shock caused by it, unlike comparable countries like Sweden, the Netherlands, Germany and Switzerland. This is still true in early 2017, and can only partly be explained by the increased competition in all sectors throughout the world mostly due to the rapid march of Asia and especially China to the forefront of the world economy.[32] By the end of this decade, Asia will account for at least one-third of the global economy, and somewhere in the late 2020s, the size of China's economy will likely surpass that of the United States.[33] Increasingly, the structure of the Chinese economy will start to resemble that of Western economies, though the strong ownership by the state makes it a very peculiar system. For the Chinese economy to flourish in the long run, two critical conditions have to be met: how to integrate the necessary transparency into the operations of companies and how to release human expression from censorship. Shifting from a centralized model to a more democratic, market-driven dispersed system is for China the ultimate challenge.

However, in Finland, recent history holds the biggest explanations for the distress. Multiple measurements point to Finland's exceptional success in the previous fifth wave (1970–2010). Finland arose from the deep recession in the early 1990's and, with Nokia at the forefront, blossomed by the end of the 1990s. Trouble began at the beginning of the 2000s: First came the massive investment missteps by the forest industry and the telecommunications corporation Sonera. Soon after that, Nokia lost its leading market position, even though the figures pointed toward good profits for many more years. In these two decades, no new industrial flagships emerged, but a few of the old ones like elevator company KONE managed very well. As a whole, things were going pretty well up until the financial crisis. After that Finland's competitive edge was dulled and its exports plunged. In the early 2017, Finland is still strugglening to get its economy out of recession and back on track.

In order for Finland to capitalize on the engines of the sixth wave, a massive shift in industrial structures is required (see Figure 3). Unfortunately, there is absolutely no sign of such a shift. Finland continues to look for solutions from the previous wave, such as planning more nuclear plants, when we should be creating domestic markets for new energy technologies.

	5th Wave Drivers	6th Wave Drivers	
Communication revolution	Forest industry: From pulp & paper...	Bio-industry: ...to new bio-materias and products	Material revolution
	Consumer electronics: From mobile telephones...	Digital services: ...to health, games and IoT	Digital consumption
Industrial infra-structure building	Engineering industry: From industrial ma-chines...	Clean tech industry: ...to smart solutions	Resource efficiency/ Sustainability
Creating welfare system for masses	Reactive healthcare: From treating illness...	Proactive healthcare: ...to supporting health	Intelligent health care

Figure 3. The challenge of the changing wave Case Finland.

The chart in Figure 3 crystallizes the situation in Finland. As far as the forest industry is concerned, Finland should be focusing on the development of new materials and solutions in which smart systems meet biomaterials. As a result, new products and services should be invented that contribute to the shift away from non-renewable and scarce raw materials towards renewable resources. Digital consumerism will move from mobile phones to gaming and experiences.

We have to recognize, nevertheless, that the revolution in communication will continue its victorious march in developing nations for the coming decades and thus create opportunities for people to connect with services. Digital services will evolve rapidly here as well, and they will bring efficient and smart solutions to many traditional fields. In healthcare, new and interesting products and services will connect with technologies that proactively support and maintain health. The traditional machinery industry will find itself in crisis, but the best companies will be able to jump onto the sixth wave, where smart and resource-efficient solutions will create competitive advantages.

Finland is at a difficult turning point. Obsolete industrial capacity must get dismantled, while new know-how and technologies must be built for the growing markets. The questions regard whether there are enough businesses looking to invest in the new sectors and whether there is enough political courage to reform our laws and taxation structure — and whether the public sector can be compelled into supporting the transformation. Unwarranted wage hikes and increased expenses weakened our competitive position (when compared to Germany, for example) by a massive 35% between 2007 and 2012.

Clean Technology as Our Hope for the Future

Technologies that bring both energy and materials efficiency and energy solutions based on renewable sources started to gain global foothold during the last decade.[34] Markets for cleantech started to grow starting in 2007 at an annual pace of over 10%. The market is expected to double from the present 2 trillion euros by the year

2025.[35] The European Commission has grandiose plans to build a circular economy encompassing the entire European economic area. Materials would circulate and logistics would be optimized to support sustainable growth.[36] At this time, the Commission is planning an ambitious development program to further the idea.

In the circular economy, much of the waste would get recycled and in some sectors all of it. If this were truly to happen, then Europe would create an internal market in which its businesses develop products for the global market. Jobs would simultaneously be created for all areas of Europe that are in regression.

The big problems of our time — climate change, exhaustion of fresh water in densely populated areas, shrinking of forested area, diminished fish stock and increasing pollution — require radical action. Even though clean technology has advanced most quickly in Asia, Finland has strengths that could be better utilized to create a new success story in Europe.

In 2010, renewable energy accounted for 16.7% of global energy consumption. Half of this came from alternative sources comprised of hydro, geothermal, solar and wind power. The other half was bio-energy. Globally, investments in renewable energy sources grew to 300 billion dollars in 2011. By 2013 that had shrunk to 250 billion dollars, largely due to the decrease in the cost of the technology and because of shrinking demand in European and United States markets. In 2016, 287 billion dollars was poured into clean power systems.[37]

All in all, the market growth looks promising. The prices for renewable energy have dropped for decades and are almost able to compete with traditional energy sources whose prices are more volatile. Competition has also stiffened, and shifting political winds may radically affect market function. The markets are strengthening, especially in developing nations. This is happening because — similar to what happened to wired phone networks with the rise of mobile networks — a diversely structured energy system lowers distribution costs.

The European Union is strongly committed to increasing production from renewable sources so that by 2030 they would account for a quarter of energy consumption.

During the sixth wave, we should move almost entirely away from fossil fuel so that anthropogenic climate change does not advance to an unsupportable level. The majority of the remaining fossil fuel should be left in the ground. If we don't stave off climate change, the planet will be uninhabitable in the long run. According to calculations at Stanford University, median temperatures would be 16°C higher and the poles would be about 30°C warmer. That would render human life in most corners of the world impossible.[38] Because most of the nonrenewable fossil reserves are in the form of coal and non-traditional shale oil and shale gas, we should focus on exploiting these energy sources as little as possible.

The European Renewable Energy Council (EUREC) has created a plan to produce all energy from renewable sources. This would mean an investment of 2.8 trillion euros and would create the much-needed competitive edge and jobs quota for Europe. Even with such a massive investment, it would be paid back through the savings earned by avoiding carbon emissions and fossil fuel use while simultaneously producing an additional 2 trillion euros worth of energy and creating six million more jobs.[39]

The EUREC vision is certainly ambitious and requires quite some courage on behalf of political decision-makers. On the other hand, Germany has already experienced its energy turnaround, the positive consequences of which can be seen today. Technology that focuses on improving energy efficiency has traditionally been Finland's strength. Companies in this field have grown and created new jobs and have thus been the bright spot in an otherwise stagnated economy.[40] Finland should now focus on consumer-oriented services, because they will grow the fastest in the future. Here Finland is badly lagging.

Europe should indeed seize the opportunity to create a competitive edge that would last far beyond this century. When considering the present position of Europe and its tense relationship with Russia, the importance of energy self-sufficiency should be especially noted. Most of the Union member states import more than half of their energy, with especially heavy import dependency in oil (90%), gas (62%) and uranium (90%). The imports of these energy forms are growing, while European production of fossil fuel is waning, due to exhaustion of sources. The growing share of renewable energy forms has, however, brought stability.[41]

It is time for Europe to find itself again. The eroding competitiveness of the zone should be saved by investing in more sustainable and more competitive energy sources, in increasing energy efficiency and in resource efficient technologies. This requires investment in research and development in these fields. The 80 billion euro investment planned by the Horizon 2020[42] research program, along with private investments, could enable this shift.

The starting point for speeding up development in these fields is fairly good: The European Union has already been a leading developer of renewable energy. Even so, almost half (44%) of the wind energy capacity is in China. In recent years, the fastest growing renewable energy source has been solar energy captured with solar panels, and in 2011 it was the energy production field that grew the most. Even if the ambitious goal of making Europe the center of renewable energy is not reached, renowned economic news bureau Bloomberg predicts the market value of renewable energy production capacity to double to 460 billion euros by 2030.[43] These predictions don't even take into account the effect of increased energy efficiency and smart electricity systems.

In addition to energy, another key resource for humanity is water. It is becoming scarce: Fresh water usage has increased six-fold in 100 years. Fresh water now accounts for only three percent of all water on Earth. Based on current usage and remaining reserves, we can predict that by 2030, half of the global population will suffer from lack of water.[44] If the current trends continue, demand will exceed supply by 40%. This means growing markets for water purification technologies and related consumer services (see more in Chapter 4).

All things considered, Finland is well established to thrive in the cleantech markets. As previously stated, cleantech revenues in Finland are now over 25 billion euros — more than the forest industry — and the sector is growing more than 10% annually.[45] The sector employs 50,000 and could employ many of the 100,000 in Finland who have lost their jobs since the year 2000. The change requires strong political will and the ability to address the weaknesses in the current system. Of course, willingness to invest is also a prerequisite.

The Future of the Financial Sector

As mentioned above, several sectors in Finland have potential for growth: the bio sector that springs from forestry know-how, digital business that grew as an add-on to the electronics industry, cleantech, renewable energy sources, the healthcare technology and service sectors. Creating new industry sectors also requires a healthy financial sector. It is especially important for new and growing businesses that are seeking funding.

The financial sector is the circulatory system of the economy and society. Funding has traditionally been handled by banks and banking firms. There are relatively few early-phase investors, such as angel investors and venture capitalists, but their number is growing. This is one of the central trends in the shifting financing structure: There are more actors and it is becoming more splintered.

Looking at societal needs, it is clear that corporations are likely going to be employing fewer people. Statistics in Finland from the previous decade already tell us that the number of people employed by large industrial corporations has been shrinking, whereas the role of small and medium-sized companies as employers has grown: They employed 80,000 more people in the last decade. Most of the new jobs are being created in the service sector, which is mostly comprised of small businesses.

The small- and medium-sized-business sector will grow, while the public sector will need to reduce its number of employees.[46] Large corporations will continue closing down operations in Finland. In order for Finland to succeed in the future, we must create favorable operating conditions for these small and medium-sized businesses. This is not easy, because our structures are created mainly to support large corporations.

A veritable army of small businesses is needed in order to create a network from which new jobs spring up. From construction to the various services, we need an infrastructure that puts small business in a stronger position, especially when compared to the corporations that set up shop in the industrial era.

But can the financial structure in Finland comply in financing a new growing sector? It is, after all, predisposed to favor large and wealthy corporations. It seems that the Finnish financial sector needs to respond to the following scenarios[47]:

(1) As a result of the financial crisis, the sector is over-regulated. Our unstable tax policies have sent wealth abroad — to Luxemburg and other tax havens — because of more predictable returns. Our government and its tax policies are pivotal, and decisions must be strategic and consistent. Our regulations should become simpler and more straight-forward. We have to make sure that we do not create a system that is too complicated. It's of vital importance to foresee societal shifts and needs and through that create policies that support investments. It is extremely important at this time that society, and all its available means, supports smart investing, which in turn serves society as a whole.

(2) Companies need long-term systematic foresight and decision-making that acts upon it. At the same time, companies must be agile enough to grab hold of opportunities. The kinds of initiatives that involve the developer, the end users and the financier are optimal.

The financial sector and society could advance in tandem if they follow a holistic approach that combines the various sectors. How could we get domestic money to circulate in Finland instead of watching it leave the country? How can inventions (Finns have a real knack for inventing) and innovations be brought to the forefront so that they can develop further? I'm chairman of a foundation that focuses on funding inventions, so I've been witness to the manifold ideas and inventions that have been created all across the country.

(3) The financial sector must understand that the operating environment has changed. Entirely new financing structures are evolving through crowdfunding and through the creation of communal structures. These have sprung up outside of existing financial institutions.

How well can the financial system react to the fact that growth and new production methods happen more and more prevalently in small and medium-sized companies? It's clear that without support from the financial sector, new growth can't take flight in Finland. Risk funding is needed even for the small businesses that have created something new and interesting but that can't offer any collateral.

(4) The success of Finland in the future is largely dependent on how the various actors can link up, network and grow together. Financiers who are ready to invest their expertise in developing businesses are also crucial. We need deep cooperation between the public sector, research organizations and companies. So-called "ecosystem thinking," in which companies draw strength from interdependence, is vital. This has been the major factor in the success story of Silicon Valley.[48]

Even though Finnish society is well organized and corruption is not an issue, the present situation seems far from ideal. Entrepreneurs in Finland are increasingly dissatisfied with the ever-growing bureaucracy: it stifles business and makes the threshold high for adding employees.

(5) The most significant bottleneck for Finnish companies seems to be the lack of financing. The real problem rests in the fact that the old industrial core must be discarded before new and innovative products can be created. Nobody is really daring to invest in product development and new things, which means that products are not being developed past the testing phase.

How does Finland travel further along the path toward a renewed economy? The following conclusions can be drawn from research material[49]:

The financial structures in Finland must be systematically brought forward. Financing must be supported through new legislation, while restrictions on other relatively new forms of financing like crowdfunding must be eased.

The transfer of wealth from one generation to another must be promoted. The current high level of inheritance tax makes it especially difficult if an inherited business has debts that can't be covered by selling a part of its inherited assets. The inheritance tax should be abolished, as has been done in Sweden and Norway, in order to allow companies to go on and grow.

We should also encourage large corporations to circulate innovative ideas whenever they aren't themselves developing them further. There are several such idea pools in Silicon Valley, where inventions that have not been developed or commercialized into products can be traded. Companies like Intellectual Ventures are emerging to become traders for innovations.[50] Moreover, experimentation should be encouraged in order to find business models suited for post-industrial Finland. This experimentation needs a framework law to be enacted to support even more radical experimentation.

The basic problem seems to be the conservatism of the financial sector.[51] The financial sector is very product-centric, whereas in other consumer sectors, the customer has much more of a say about the product and customer interaction is regarded as "par for the course." According to a study by the financial sector itself, the biggest challenge is to find more customer-centric business models. Even more so, as a quintessential but very conservative part of the economy, the financial sector faces a grave challenge to revamp its old ways of thinking and behaving and to become a true part of sixth wave world.[52]

It is a Question of Values

In the end, society and the economy must consider people's values: What kinds of values are society based on, and how do they reflect the values of individuals?[53]

The study that charted the values of individual Finns found the phenomenon that most permeates society is bureaucracy. As we examined the results, it became clear that people are frustrated by the growing complexity in society, which stifles civic activity and initiatives. There are more and more regulations, laws, and hierarchy year after year — if not from the government, then from the EU. Growing complexity has become today's reality. History shows that societies crumble when they surpass a certain level of complexity. This happened to the Roman Empire, for example. Could we build our own society based on the optimization of human interaction?

It is not new to create ideas based on utopian societies. As early as the beginning of the 19th century, Henri de Saint-Simon, Charles Fournier, and Robert Owen were building communities based on equality and communality. These movements were the forerunners for cooperatives and created the basis for organized production and consumption.

The ideas of the utopists were carried forth by the same thing that people aspire for today: how to find a way to work and live that meets the age-old important values of respecting others and of equality. Perhaps we can slowly learn to better understand the motivation and needs of people and through that, make entire organizations more productive. The most important task of leadership is to liberate human capacity and help develop their abilities — not simply as employees but as humans.

When we examine post-industrial nations and their business sectors, we find that the most important value appears to be freedom and the responsibility connected to it. Freedom coupled with minimal hierarchy yields ideas and results. When we add responsibility, we obtain the rules for tomorrow's society.

The case of Finland hopefully delivers a picture of a country in transition. As we enter the sixth wave, all countries will meet similar challenges. Many countries in Asia, for example, will find themselves having skipped one of two phases experienced in Europe. They will head straight towards a model that enable them to take full use of new technologies and thinking based on network models instead of centrally led industrial structures. In India, there is a heavy boom of investments — coming often from Chinese investors — for companies that provide, say, mobile wallets. Large solar energy schemes are now being developed in India, under Prime Minister Narendra Modi.[54] South-Korea, announced in the summer 2016 it will invest 36 billion dollars into its renewable energy sector by 2020.[55] Brazil has one of the fastest growing markets in the world for solar energy. Chile is the latest renewable energy hub in South America with focus on public–private partnerships (PPP) resulting in almost 10 billion dollar investment in commitments.[56] In South Africa, the renewable energy scene grew over 300% between 2014 and 2015.[57]

Simultaneously, all those technologies enabling people to be active through the internet without major investments are growing fast. Mobile internet is expected to reach half of the global population by 2020.[58] All this will give incredible boost to resource productivity all around the world. New technology will facilitate people making better use of what they have, regardless of which part of the world they happen to live. Our globe, hopefully, will become much more balanced in terms of opportunities to live a decent life. But before we get there, we should tackle our hardest problems. That is the topic of the next chapter.

References

1. Kekkonen, Urho. 1952. *Does Our Country Have the Patience to Prosper?* Helsinki: Otava.
2. Auffermann, Burkhard, Suomela, Pertti, Kaivo-oja, Jari, Vehmas, Jarmo, and Luukkanen, Jyrki. 2015. A final solution for a big challenge: The governance of nuclear waste disposal in Finland. In: Brunnengräber, A., Nucci, M. R., Isodoro A. Losada, M., Mez, L., and Schreurs, M. (Eds.). *Nuclear Waste Governance. An International Comparison.* Berlin: Springer-Verlag.
3. *Computerworld.* 2016. "Nokia has high hopes for its its new IoT platform." Accessed September 13, 2016. http://www.computerworld.com/article/3083318/internet-of-things/nokia-has-high-hopes-for-its-its-new-iot-platform.html.
4. Reaktor. 2016. Accessed September 13, 2016. https://reaktor.com/.
5. Kurki, Sofi, Puro, Minna, and Wilenius, Markku. 2016. *Re-acting the Future. The New Ways to Work: The Case of Reaktor.* FFRC Publications 6/2016.
6. Laloux, Frederic. 2014. *Reinventing Organizations.* Brussels: Nelson Parker.
7. Global Entrepreneurship Monitor (GEM). 2016. "Country profile: Finland." Accessed March 8, 2016. http://www.gemconsortium.org/country-profile/61.
8. GSM Association (GSMA). 2016. "Half of the World's Population Connected to the Mobile Internet by 2020, According to New GSMA

Figures." Accessed March 8, 2016. http://www.gsma.com/newsroom/press-release/half-worlds-population-connected-mobile-internet-2020-according-gsma/.

9. Finnish Forest Industries. "The Finnish forest industry in figuers." 2016. Accessed September 3, 2016. http://www.forestindustries.fi/statistics/The-Finnish-forest-industry-in-figures-1274.html.
10. Metsä Group. 2016. "The Next generation bioproduct mill." Accessed September 3, 2016. http://bioproductmill.com/.
11. Finnpulp. 2016. "Finnpulp — The most efficient softwood pulp mill to Kuopio, Finland." Accessed September 3, 2016. http://www.finnpulp.fi/index-en.html.
12. *Helsinki Times.* 2015. "Finnish economy is still paralysed." Accessed September 13, 2016. http://www.helsinkitimes.fi/finland/finland-news/domestic/13657-finnish-economy-is-still-paralysed.html.
13. *VentureBeat.* 2016. "With just 3 games, Supercell made $924M in profits on $2.3B in revenue in 2015" Accessed September 13, 2016. http://venturebeat.com/2016/03/09/with-just-3-games-supercell-made-924m-in-profits-on-2-3b-in-revenue-in-2015/.
14. *South China Morning Post.* 2015. "Six reasons for Finland's record start-up success: Clash of Clans maker Supercell reveals all." Accessed March 8, 2016. http://www.scmp.com/tech/start-ups/article/1877779/six-reasons-finlands-record-start-success-clash-clans-maker-supercell.
15. *VentureBeat.* 2016. "With just 3 games, Supercell made $924M in profits on $2.3B in revenue in 2015" Accessed September 13, 2016. http://venturebeat.com/2016/03/09/with-just-3-games-supercell-made-924m-in-profits-on-2-3b-in-revenue-in-2015/.
16. *Brand New Helsinki.* 2015. "Silicon Vallila — a Global Contender in the Field of Health Technology." Accessed March 8, 2016. http://brandnewhelsinki.fi/en/silicon-vallila-a-global-contender-in-the-field-of-health-technology/.
17. Global Wellness Institute. 2016. Global spa & wellness economy monitor. http://www.globalwellnesssummit.com/images/stories/gsws2014/pdf/GWI_Global_Spa_and_Wellness_Economy_Monitor_Full_Report_Final.pdf.
18. Nordic Structures. 2016. "Wood and Human Health." Accessed March 8, 2016. http://www.nordic.ca/data/files/publication/Wood_Human_Health_final-single.pdf
19. *Ibid.*
20. *Ibid.*
21. Ministry of Employment and the Economy (TEM) 2010. "Finland's Tourism Strategy to 2020: Four good reasons to promote tourist

industry development." Accessed March 8, 2016. Available at: https://www.researchgate.net/profile/Aysegul_Ozkan/project/Research-about-national-tourism-strategy-documents-of-various-countries/attachment/579ee98708ae0d8707009d6d/AS:390157745311745@1470032263664/download/Finlands_Tourism_Strategy_to_2020+%281%29.pdf
22. Final Forest. 2016. Accessed March 8, 2016. http://www.finalforest.de.
23. Irjala, Sanni. 2013. "Berries and Berry Culture in Finland." University of Tampere. Accessed March 8, 2016. https://www15.uta.fi/FAST/FIN/A14PAPS/si-berry.pdf; Kallio, Heikki & Yang, Baoru. 2015. "Strategy of the Food Chemistry and Food Development Units at the University of Turku in relation to food production and properties in the Northern Hemisphere." Accessed March 8, 2016. https://www.utu.fi/en/units/arctic/Documents/Strategy_of_the_Food_Chemistry_and_Food_Development_Units_ARC TIC.pdf.
24. ISB — International Society of Biourbanism. 2013. "Paracity." Accessed September 14, 2016. http://www.biourbanism.org/paracity/.
25. LUOMUS –Finnish Museum of Natural History. 2016. "Fifth Dimension — Green Roofs in Urban Areas." Accessed September 14, 2016. https://www.luomus.fi/en/fifth-dimension-green-roofs-urban-areas.
26. *Yle News*. 2015. "Even a short walk in the woods is good for you, researchers claim." Accessed March 8, 2016. http://yle.fi/uutiset/even_a_short_walk_in_the_woods_is_good_for_you_researchers_claim/7746324.
27. IAEA. 2016. "Finland." Accessed September 14, 2016. https://www.iea.org/countries/membercountries/finland/.
28. Halme, Minna, Hukkinen, Janne, Korppi-Tommola, Jouko, Linnanen, Lassi, Liski, Matti, Loivio, Raimo, Lund, Peter, Luukkanen, Jyrki, Nokso-Koivisto, Oskari, Partanen, Jarmo, and Wilenius, Markku. "New Energy Policy for Providing Growth and Employment." Jyväskylä University Digital Archive. Accessed September 14, 2016. https://jyx.jyu.fi/dspace/handle/123456789/43432.
29. Statistics Finland. 2016. "Total energy consumption fell by 3 per cent in 2015." Accessed September 14, 2016. http://www.stat.fi/til/ehk/2015/04/ehk_2015_04_2016-03-23_tie_001_en.html.
30. Halme *et al.* (2015). Maamme energia (The Energy of our Country). Into Kustannus, Helsinki.
31. Danish Wind Industry Association. 2016. Accessed March 8, 2016. http://www.windpower.org/en; Davidson, Richard. 2012. *The Emotional Life of Your Brain.* New York: Hudson Street Press.
32. Charan, Ram. 2013. *Global Tilt: Leading Your Business through the Great Economic Power Shift.* New York: Crown Business.

33. *Bloomberg.* 2016. "China and the United States: Tale of Two Giant Economies." Accessed September 14, 2016. http://www.bloomberg.com/graphics/2016-us-vs-china-economy/.
34. Eco-Innovation Observatory. 2012. "Closing the Eco-Innovation Gap." Accessed March 8, 2016. http://www.eco-innovation.eu/index.php?option=com_content&view=article&id=420&Itemid=210.
35. Clean Technica. 2012. "Global Cleantech Market Expected to Expand to € 4 Trillion by 2020, Germany to Capitalize." Accessed March 8, 2016. http://cleantechnica.com/2012/09/17/global-cleantech-market-expected-to-expand-to-e4-trillion-by-2020s-germany-to-capitalize.
36. European Commission. 2016. "Closing the Loop: An EU Action Plan for the Circular Economy." Accessed March 8, 2016. http://ec.europa.eu/environment/circular-economy.
37. Pew, Trusts. 2014. "Who's Winning the Clean Energy Race? 2013." Accessed March 8, 2016. Http://Www.Pewtrusts.Org/En/Research-And-Analysis/Reports/2014/04Y03/Whos-Winning-The-Clean-Energy-Race-2013.
38. Millennium Alliance for Humanity and Biosphere (MAHB). 2014. "What If We Burn All The Fossil Fuels?" Accessed March 8, 2016. http://mahb.stanford.edu/library-item/what-if-we-burn-all-the-fossil-fuels/.
39. European Renewable Energy Council (EUREC). 2010. "Re-thinking 2015: A 100% Renewable Energy Vision for the European Union." Accessed March 8, 2016. http://ec.europa.eu/clima/consultations/docs/0005/registered/91650013720-46_european_renewable_energy_council_en.pdf.
40. Cleantech Finland. 2014. "Finland's cleantech future looks bright: 90% of companies planning new Finnish jobs." Accessed March 8, 2016. https://storify.com/CleantechFIN/the-weekly-cleantech-story-17-2014.
41. European Renewable Energy Council (EUREC). 2010. "Re-thinking 2015: A 100% Renewable Energy Vision for the European Union." Accessed March 8, 2016. http://ec.europa.eu/clima/consultations/docs/0005/registered/91650013720-46_european_renewable_energy_council_en.pdf.
42. Horizon 2020 is the biggest-ever EU research and innovation program, with nearly € 80 billion in funding available over 7 years (from 2014 to 2020).
43. See https://www.bnef.com/PressReleases/view/173. Accessed September 23, 2016.
44. United Nations Department of Economic and Social Affairs (UNDESA). 2007. "Water scarcity." Accessed March 8, 2016. http://www. un.org/waterforlifedecade/scarcity.shtml.

45. Cleantech Finland. Accessed March 8, 2016. http://www.cleantechfinland.com.
46. Ahokas, Jussi, Honkatukia, Juha, Lehmus, Markku, Niemi, Janne, Simola, Antti, and Tamminen, Saara. 2015. Työvoiman tarve Suomen taloudessa vuosina 2015–2030." Accessed September 14, 2016. https://www.vatt.fi/file/vatt_publication_pdf/t181.pdf.
47. These observations are based on my research "Sixth Wave and Finland", see more https://www.utu.fi/en/units/ffrc/research/project-archive/foresight-nat/Pages/6th-wave.aspx. Accessed September 23, 2016.
48. Piscione Perry, Deborah. 2013. *Secrets of Silicon Valley: What Everyone Else Can Learn from the Innovation Capital of the World.* New York: Palgrave McMillan.
49. FFRC — Finland Futures Research Centre. 2016. "The 6th Wave and Systemic Innovations for Finland: Success Factors for the Years 2010–2050 (6th Wave)." Accessed September 14, 2016. http://www.utu.fi/en/units/ffrc/research/project-archive/foresight-nat/Pages/6th-wave.aspx.
50. Intellectual Ventures. 2016. Accessed March 8, 2016. http://www.intellectualventures.com/.
51. Puustinen, Pekka. 2015. *FinancialServiceLogic: In the Revolution of Exchange in Banking and Insurance.* Helsinki: Helsinki Capital Partners Advisory.
52. Finanssialan kyvykkyydet 2020 (The Key Competencies of Financial Industry). Finance Finland 2012. http://www.finanssiala.fi/materiaalit/Finanssialan_kyvykkyydet.pdf. Accessed September 23, 2016.
53. I conducted a wide survey in 2011 and 2012 with Suomalaisen Työn Liitto (the Association of Finnish Work) to study people's values.
54. The World Bank. 2016."World Bank, India Sign Deal to Boost Solar Globally." Accessed September 14, 2016. http://www.worldbank.org/en/news/press-release/2016/06/30/world-bank-india-sign-deal-to-boost-solar-globally.
55. Think Geoenergy. 2016. "South Korea to invest up to $36.6 billion into renewable energy sector by 2020." Accessed September 14, 2016. http://www.thinkgeoenergy.com/south-korea-to-invest-up-to-36-6-billion- into-renewable-energy-sector-by-2020/.
56. The World Bank. 2016. "Chile rethinks renewables and gets results." Accessed September 14, 2016. http://blogs.worldbank.org/ppps/chile-rethinks-renewables-and-gets-results.
57. UNEP. 2016. "South Africa opts for sun and wind as green energy investments surge in developing world." Accessed September 14,

2016. http://www.unep.org/stories/RenewableEnergy/South-Africa-opts-for-sun-and-wind-as-green-energy.asp.

58. GSMA. 2014. "Digital Inclusion." Accessed September 14, 2016. http://www.gsma.com/mobilefordevelopment/wp-content/uploads/2014/11/GSMA_Digital-Inclusion-Report_Web_Singles_2.pdf.
59. http://www.kauppalehti.fi/uutiset/entiset-nokialaiset-perustaneet-yli-500-yritysta/iZawYrhj.

Chapter 12

WHAT NEEDS TO BE DONE?

In this book, I have chronicled a historical shift. I have tried to describe the complex logic of social change in order to give you an idea why old answers no longer suffice. Traditional technologies pollute too much, traditional political culture is stagnant, the traditional idea of the economy as a source of eternal growth is outmoded and industrial values have robbed us of part of our humanity.

We find ourselves on the edge of an abyss. We cannot afford to wait until the end of the next cycle — the middle of this century — for change to occur. The change needs to start now, in 2017.

Everything I have studied, heard and understood about the state of our global environment points towards one conclusion: we have but 10 years to make this change in order to ensure that the sixth wave I have envisioned (2010–2050) will get on the right track; there is plentiful evidence for this on the pages of this book. After that fateful point in time, it will be too late. I will describe the necessary changes in five concise points.

First, the energy systems of the world need a virtually total overhaul. *Second*, the principles of circular economy must be adopted as a core component in all economic activity and everyday life. *Third*, we must make full use of new technologies that have already revolutionized part of the world. *Fourth*, the system of political decision-making must be made to adopt long-term goals in their operation. This means that we must redirect our systems of governance, taxation and legislation to support these goals. That in turn requires the creation of a true civil society and the dismantling of hierarchic and bureaucratic systems. *Fifth*, businesses must be made to adopt long-term thinking in order to put an end to the goal-setting based on the quarterly economy.

The Change in Climate and Energy Systems

We must begin by revolutionizing the energy production systems of the world, which still rely on fossil fuels for 81% of its primary energy supply.[1] In the space of 10 years, we must reduce the share of fossil fuels to far below 50%. Considering the reality, this is a daunting task: A reduction of just a few percentage points involves a significant reduction in volume. For the change to be possible at all, a great deal of work is required around the globe. Globally, the crucial issue is how China and India will secure their energy supply, but Europe needs to set out on a new course as well. How can this be achieved? Who will be the pioneers who take the initiative? Some of the necessary new technology already exists. The production cost with renewables has already dropped below the costs of using conventional technology.[2] This is a shocking change, compared to the situation as recently as the 2000s.

The mitigation of climate change calls for much more than just new technology. It calls for a change in our mindset. We must learn to see the world as an interconnected system instead of an array of separate parts. With respect to climate change, this means that the carbon cycle needs to be considered holistically. Apart from emission reduction, a key way to prevent a catastrophic climate change is to nurture initiatives that support the sequestration of carbon in the soil and in forests. This is precisely what the recently launched Carbon Underground project suggests.[3] Why not safeguard the sequestration of carbon in the ground so that we *simultaneously* reduce the volume of harmful atmospheric carbon dioxide *and* improve the quality of the soil? This calls for a new understanding of the role and significance of agriculture and a new vision of the technologies for promoting these goals: soil improvement and carbon sequestration. We must broaden our view of agriculture in the modern era.

The second challenge for systemic understanding is how well we understand the emergence of global crises. The outbreak of the war in Syria is a case in point. The internal conflict there was preceded by a prolonged drought, which turned into a serious water crisis in 2006.[4] Instead of addressing the problem, the ruling Alawite minority, led by President Assad, exacerbated it by protecting their own access to water. These injustices fed the discontent that contributed to the popular uprising, which since then has escalated into a full-blown war, where the divisions have in part run along ethnic and religious demarcation lines.

It has become abundantly clear by now that peaceful management of environmental problems is possible only in countries that have a functioning political system in place, and one that responds to human needs in an adequate manner. As mentioned in Chapter 5, if such a system is not in place, the likelihood of escalation grows exponentially, because new forms of communication (social media in particular) create conditions that allow rapid collective civil action.

Towards a Circular Economy

Increasingly, we must understand and implement the basic tenets of circular economy (or "spiral" economy, to be more precise): matter, energy and human capital all need to circulate. As argued elsewhere in this volume, we must learn to see all activities of nature and humanity in terms of systems and flows instead of separate atomistic entities. How many more polluting gas guzzlers do we need on the roads? When will we begin in earnest to follow the principles of sharing in everything we do and likewise create an infrastructure that makes it possible? Some of the most successful and fastest-growing companies, from Airbnb to Uber, already apply this principle in their operations.

The latest studies show that the benefits of circular economy are incontrovertible. According to a report by the Club of Rome, we have reached the end of the path in how we produce and consume products and services.[5] The old industrial model of "take, make and dispose" has been shown to be unimaginably inefficient. It is now being replaced by an entirely different approach to designing industrial operations and the associated consumption: one that is based on recycling, reuse, disassembly and remanufacturing.

The circular economy is a new conception of society and the economy in which matter, energy and human activity do not simply register as inputs and reemerge as outputs. Its efficiency can't be measured with traditional parameters as an input-output ratio. Its fundamental principle arises from an entirely new conception of the metabolism of society and economy, and a realization of where added value is in actual fact created. What if we were not only to produce things but also maintain and reuse commodities whenever possible?

The by-now classic study from the Ellen Macarthur Foundation shows that on a global scale, the adoption of the principles of circular economy would create new savings based on the circulation of materials and commodities, which in turn would create massive new markets worth up to 700 billion euros.[6] In other words, it would create a massive number of new jobs and added value. It has also been calculated that increasing resource productivity in the European Union by 30% would generate 2–3 million new jobs.

While numbers show that circularity would indeed give a considerable boost to our economies and help create jobs, the most important thing is nevertheless the change it involves in the thought processes and actions that we apply to all sectors of society.[7] It is a truly Copernican revolution in our understanding of how materials, energy and human capital flow through our society. The current problems of our national economies — excessive debt, loss of jobs, the accumulation of wealth in the hands of the few and insupportable environmental deterioration — are all logical consequences of a wrong conception of the economy and its purpose.

The basic underlying principle of the economy should be collaboration instead of monopoly or heavy competition. The very idea of circular economy is to foster collaboration: the supplier cooperating with the manufacturer, the manufacturer with the consumer, the consumer with other consumers and so on down the line. And all this is of course enabled by a society where legislation and taxation are geared towards promoting true resource efficiency and cooperation.

A report by the Club of Rome on the societal benefits of circular economy in five countries (Sweden, Finland, Spain, the Netherlands, and France) clearly shows the massive potentiality of the benefits.[8] The report focuses especially on the impacts of circular economy on carbon emissions and employment. More broadly, the report's purpose was to gain insight into how circularity might help societies decouple a link that is as old as the industrial society itself.

As discussed in previous chapters, industrial societies developed in stages, with each innovation in technology from steam power onwards leading to the creation of production systems that have given us the ability to produce ever-more things with ever-greater efficiency. Over the centuries, steam power, steel, railroads, electricity, chemicals, cars, petrochemicals and, finally, (in the last 40 years) digital technologies and countless other facilitating systems, have all served as extensions of our hands. They have increased the productivity of work and have led to a massive rise in material consumption — all while resulting in serious environmental impacts. This has been the Faustian pact of the industrial age,[9] a connection that has inextricably bound the escalating use of natural resources to economic growth.

We are now in a situation where we can no longer ignore the stark reality that this historical expansion also has its downside. Meanwhile, the new increasingly resource-efficient technologies, such as those based on renewable energy, are slowly gaining ground. The agenda of "sustainability" has crept into political processes. There is increasing concern over how to decouple consumption and its increasing use of natural resources from economic growth.[10] This disquieting development has led to a situation where in just six months we use up all of the replenishing resources the planet can produce in a year. Or to put this in another way: It takes 18 months for the planet to regenerate what we use in a year.[11] We are still on the destructive path that the Club of Rome warned us about in its classic report *Limits to Growth*.[12]

The circular economy report of the Club of Rome proves that in order to create a sufficient response to the challenge of decoupling, we must wholly adopt the concept of circular economy in all our policies.[13] This gives rise to many challenges: How to revise taxation so as to punish the use of non-renewables and material waste and promote the use of human labor. How to create incentives for investments that promote the development of new bio-based products that will replace the products based on non-renewable materials in the construction and packaging industries. How to promote lower energy consumption in construction and transport. How to promote new business models in which people loan their property for a fee, such as a car or an apartment, for collective use. How to steer education in a direction that will enable students to realize the potential of circularity and thus become experts in the key functions of circular economy, such as the recycling and reuse of materials or the adoption of new energy technologies.

The key is in product design: Are products designed to last as long as possible, or are the goals something else? The latter is true for the most part. While the recycling of plastic bottles is admittedly smarter than dumping or incinerating them, the recycling process also requires energy — when plastic bottles are melted and turned into new bottles, natural resources are still consumed. The only sustainable solution is to not have any recyclable plastic bottles at all, but to instead manufacture and sell reusable ones.

If this seems challenging, consider the matter from a longer perspective. The issue here is planetary eschatology.[14] At the end of the sixth wave — around the middle of this century — we will in all likelihood have put an end to a massive part of the chemical reaction that began with the burning of fossil fuels. A wave or two further into the future, we may find ourselves in a situation where there are no longer any mines in the sense that we today understand them. One hundred to 150 years from now, this age will be seen as very strange indeed: a cultural phase that, despite of its relative brevity, had massive impacts on the planet. Future generations will undoubtedly marvel how such irresponsible behavior was possible. How, in just a couple of 100 years, were we able to squander natural resources that had taken billions of years to develop inside the earth?

Professors Harald Sverdrup and Vala Ragnarsdottir are the world's leading experts in the study and modeling of the cycles of minerals and other natural resources. According to them, every year we are using 3,700 million tons of cement; 1,300 million tons of wood, 2,200 million tons of iron and steel, of which 1,500 million tons comes from mines; and we produce 110 million tons of aluminum, 50 million of it from mines. The annual global output of copper, zinc and lead is 35 million tons, of which 16 million comes from within the earth. The other metals account for 50 million tons, 35 million of which are extracted from mines.[15]

After examining the circulation of raw materials and assessing the use of natural resources in the future, they have arrived at the following conclusions:

First, there will not be any serious shortage of copper, aluminum or iron for a long time. Iron production will peak around 2030, with serious scarcity emerging around 2080, which will in turn lead to a serious economic crisis, as iron is such a vital part of all infrastructure.[16]

Second, there will be a serious crisis with respect to phosphorus — a crucial ingredient in modern fertilizers — but it will be due to erosion. In Sverdrup and Ragnarsdottir's estimation, soil erosion due to phosphorus overuse will probably be the greatest threat to civilization in the long run. Without healthy soil, we have no hope of feeding the growing population on Earth. According to FAO, we already saw the peak of arable soil around the year 2000.

Third, problems will escalate and eventually blow up in our faces with regard to the use of fossil fuels, the inefficiency and cost of our systems of production, and the scarcity of nickel and other metals needed for high-tech products. The vision is an apt image of the reasons why the shift to circular economy must take place within the next 10 years.

Making the Most of Technology

There are ways out of this dilemma, however. Karl Schwab, the founder of World Economic Forum, talks about the fourth industrial revolution,[17] by which he refers to the recent avalanche of new technologies that he distinguishes from the previous, third industrial revolution.[18] In the fourth revolution physical, digital and biological levels will converge in ever-changing formats.

The defining characteristics of the fourth industrial revolution — those that distinguish it from previous revolutions — include, *first*, the exponential speed of change facilitated by technological advances and the ever-more-densely networked world. *Second*, changes are broader as well as deeper, which means that the revolution will alter not only operational paradigms but humanity itself. *Third*, the impacts of the revolution are systemic: It is no longer about individual, discrete phenomena but interrelations of phenomena that transcend national and regional boundaries.

I personally see Schwab's fourth industrial revolution as an integral part of the sixth wave. Artificial intelligence and the Internet of Things (IoT) will dramatically alter the way we behave, especially at work. According to one expert assessment, 90% of all news will be produced by artificial intelligence by 2025, and the only human touch will be in the formulation of the algorithms.[19]

Since technology is ultimately just an extension of humanity, what are its effects on society at large and on ourselves as individuals? Perhaps the most significant body of evidence that we have is the impact of the internet. As Manuel Castells, arguably the most important social scientist of our age, once remarked, the effects of the internet in the Information Age have been on a par with the effects of electrical engines in the Industrial Age.[20]

The internet has revolutionized human interaction. The paradox is that virtual reality today is more of a social than physical reality. As of March 2016, there are 3.3 billion internet users in the world, which is roughly 40% of the world population.[21] The number of mobile subscriptions is currently the same as the world population, 7.7 billion. Moreover, 95% of all information produced in the world is in digital format, and most of it is accessible online.[22]

Studies incontrovertibly show that internet use increases social activity, although the media like to claim otherwise. As Manuel

Castells has remarked, the internet is a technology for freedom, although it was originally developed at the behest of the Pentagon.[23] Study after study shows that, thanks to the internet, people today live in the kind of networked society that first began to emerge when three key events created the preconditions for modern communication: the invention of the World Wide Web by Tim Berners-Lee, the global but relatively loose system of internet governance and the development of a networked society. On the cultural front, this was paralleled by the development of a greater emphasis on individuality and autonomy.

In short, the crucial impact of the internet on society is that we have left the age of mass communication and entered an era of mass self-communication. The shift, which emerged in the course of the fifth wave (1970–2010), has had profound impacts on our society and has created the potential for solving the key political issue of the sixth wave: how to build a true democracy in a world where power tends to accumulate in the hands of the few. The history of the 21st century has already shown that the internet and social media have created a new level of communication that serves as a channel for the views of the masses and gives them power. Countries where the free exchange of information is curtailed, such as China, have become anomalies that are facing increasing opposition. Such centrally governed societies that restrict the freedom of speech will not be able to survive in the sixth wave. Just as the open-ended architecture of the internet has shown its superiority over the past two decades, so, too, in the next phase must the social architecture be open ended in order to ensure that the right of the individual for self-expression finally becomes a norm.

Revamping the Political System

In their brilliant book *Why Nations Fail*, Daron Acemoglu and James Robinson study how old power structures paralyze societies and make them fail heavily in their task of securing the well-being of citizens. A case in point is when in January 2000 a partly government-owned bank in Zimbabwe organized a lottery among its customers who had deposited more than 5,000 Zimbabwean dollars in their account. The master of ceremonies of the lottery drew the name of the winner. It was His Excellency R.G. Mugabe.[24] This method for "winning" a lottery in Zimbabwe is the illustration of how old power structures hold sway and prevent the new from emerging.

Corruption and institutional malaise are among the great scourges of contemporary societies. Ask anybody almost anywhere in the world what is the greatest problem in their society, and more likely than not the answer will be corruption. Even the Nordic countries, generally ranked as some of the least corrupt,[25] suffer from rigid and centralized corporatism that hides power and poisons progress and sustainable development in the worst way. The crux of corporatism is that decisions are made in tight circles and without transparent arguments: In modern societies in particular, interest groups play an excessively dominant role in societal decision-making.

The general good of society is a concept that one would like to see gain prominence in the sixth wave. Suboptimization, or sharing perks among a small clique, undermines the ability of any system to produce sustainable solutions. Perhaps the greatest paradox of modern Western societies is that in spite of progress and an average economic growth rate of 3% that has lasted over a century, nearly all Western societies find themselves overburdened with debt and patently unable to focus their resources correctly. Another major issue is rising inequality: in most OECD countries, economic inequality has increased since the mid-1980s. We've reached the point where the ratio between the incomes of the richest and the poorest 10% of the population — which in the 1980s stood at 7-to-1 — is today 10-to-1 and growing. In that same period, the disposable income of 40% of the population has increased only minimally.[26]

I believe this development has been possible only because we have created structures that are too expensive and ineffective. We bolster unhealthy features of society and economy in every way we can, distributing the benefits to the same "nomenklatura" that already possesses power and wealth. Our skewed tax policies discourage work when they should discourage the exploitation of non-renewable raw materials and dirty energy. The European Union pays ludicrous subsidies (40% of its budget) for mostly outdated and resource-exploitative agriculture when we should be encouraging forms of agriculture that protect the environment while producing food. Or to take as an example my own country, Finland: we want to distinguish ourselves as a Western nation that is establishing nuclear energy. This not only is irresponsible in view of future generations, it is also pointless economically, because existing safety standards make nuclear energy simply too expensive. We refuse to face facts and continue to behave as if we were still living 50 years ago.

It seems obvious to me that in the next 10 years, we must ensure that political agendas worldwide all have the right priorities. We must put a stop to the idiotic mantra of economic growth being the panacea for all ills. It is but snake oil peddled by politicians and economists, with no proven positive effects whatsoever.

Over the last few decades, amazing leaps in information technology have given us an unprecedented opportunity to adopt decentralized technologies and models. Regardless of whether we need to find solutions to social problems, to develop our energy systems, to renew education or to reorganize the regulation of work, we need to look at decentralized solutions, because when coupled with intelligence and technology, they are vastly superior. However, such reforms can easily remain unimplemented, even when we know, for example, how to turn the outmoded energy system of a country into a modern one that supports employment and environmental perspectives. In the incipient sixth wave, we no longer can afford not to do it.

Change of Direction in the Corporate Sector

In January 2016, Larry Fink, CEO of BlackRock, the world's largest asset management company, sent a letter to the leaders of S&P 500 companies. He warned them of the short-sightedness of the prevalent economic atmosphere and asked the CEOs to focus instead on "long-termism" — on strategic issues and their articulation. According to Fink, focusing only on quarterly results and dishing out huge dividends to shareholders undermined long-term investments. He also reminded them that environmental and social challenges will only gain in importance as factors affecting the operative environment in the future.[27]

Fink's letter (he had sent similar letters before) was a cry of emergency. The points he made in the letter were not targeted solely at corporate executives but also at investors who demand that companies focus on short-term profits — that is, Wall Street bankers and others whose only motive is to make money hand-over-fist and who ultimately stood behind the present financial crisis.

The ability to think long-term is an imperative that will emerge in the sixth wave. The best corporate leaders have already set an example in the fifth wave. Three of them can be singled out as being in a class by themselves: Steve Jobs, the founder of Apple; Bill Gates, the founder of Microsoft; and Andy Grove, the founder of Intel. In a highly interesting analysis, professors David Yoffie from Harvard and Michael Cusumano from the MIT Sloan School of Management have looked at the similarities between how these three extraordinarily successful corporate leaders built and implemented their strategies.[28]

Possibly the most important common feature uniting these three pioneers was their ability to envision a future that was radically different. Because their visions were so radically different from the reality of the day, they made sure that no other players were in the same ballpark, at least initially.

For example, Bill Gates understood two things: that PCs could eventually be in every home and that software expertise was crucially more valuable than hardware expertise. In the mid-1970s, these ideas were revolutionary.

Andy Grove's insight in the late 1980s was that the old vertical business model in computing, with one company providing everything, could not last — Gordon Moore's famous law that the number of transistors on an integrated circuit will double every 18–24 months would make scaling the business impossible. He therefore narrowed down the strategy of Intel exclusively to microprocessor manufacturing, resulting in the company becoming a world leader in that area.

Steve Jobs created his revolutionary vision in the late 1990s when he understood that the computer would escape from its cage and metamorphose into "insanely great" products: The computer would become a digital hub capable of doing all kinds of things other than computing that people wanted to do, such as listening to music, taking photos and so on. The goal of Apple would be to provide a superior experience in this world of new opportunity. Eventually his vision changed when the computer hub was replaced by the iPad and iPhone.

These three leaders shared a vision that was much earlier formulated by none other than Albert Einstein: "The important thing in visionary thinking is to learn from the past, yet not be bound by it." They did not look into the past to draw conclusions about the future but rather would "look forward and reason back."[29] It was essentially about envisioning a certain future and seeing the company as part of that future.

But just as important as it is to see the future and how it differs from the present was their ability to adapt to changing circumstances — if the operating environment changed, so did their strategy. Another crucial factor was cooperation, which implied an understanding of the needs of the ecosystem. Apple had had the iPad ready a few years before it was released. The problem was that Wi-Fi networks at the time were not sophisticated enough to allow the device to show its full potential. Apple therefore waited until the necessary infrastructure was in place before launching the iPad.[30]

Jobs, Grove and Gates were all visionaries of their age. From the perspective of the sixth wave, however, their thinking was hopelessly narrow. None of them was particularly interested in either accountability or the social or environmental impacts of their company. None of them said anything worthwhile about any of these issues. Quite the contrary: Jobs was famous for ignoring the conditions of workers in Apple's Chinese factories, and he showed no interest in philanthropy or the environmental impacts of Apple products. Admittedly, Bill Gates did later: After giving up his operative position in Microsoft, he become the most important philanthropist in the world, contributing to finding solutions for some of our greatest problems.

The sixth wave will instead breed entrepreneurs like Elon Musk, who seriously want to steer humanity towards a sustainable future.

Musk's crazy dream that runs as the connecting thread through all his companies, from SpaceX to Tesla, is to make space travel possible for all while also saving humanity. Or businessmen like Patagonia founder Yvon Chouinard, who once confessed, "I've never respected [my] profession. It's business that has to take the majority of the blame for being the enemy of nature, for destroying native cultures, for taking from the poor and giving to the rich, and poisoning the earth with effluent from its factories."[31]

In the future, we will also see the rise of businesses that deliberately abandon industrial patterns of thinking and behavior and lay the foundation for a more humane organizational culture. In the past few years, such companies have begun to crop up in various sectors around the world.[32]

When organizations learn to operate like a group of adult peers, instead of a hierarchic kindergarten in which a few "adults" watch over "children," we will witness the rise of a new kind of dynamic within organizations.

The secret reason for this lies in the real history of innovation: Most innovations are made by ordinary people, not by geniuses.[33] The democratization of innovation is the only way that we can steer the course of humanity in the sixth wave so that it will ensure the continued existence of preconditions for good life on our planet. Mark the words of Jos de Blok, founder of the revolutionary and successful Dutch company Buurzorg:

"We are living in a change of eras. Our current models of energy, finance and health care are not sustainable for the future. We need new solutions based on ecological, human-friendly relationships. We need new organizational structures focused on meaningfulness and new economic principles. With a new consciousness, we can improve quality of life for vulnerable citizens at a lower cost".[34]

De Blok's ideas represent a crystallization of the challenges of the sixth wave. Only by changing the way we think and act in society will we be able to safeguard the future of our environment and ourselves. We must do whatever we can to ensure that leaders everywhere will come to realize the truth of this fact.

References

1. International Energy Agency (IEA). 2015. *Key World Energy Statistics.* Accessed September 15, 2016. www.iea.org/publications/freepublications/publication/KeyWorld_Statistics_2015.pdf.
2. Energy Innovation. 2015. "Comparing the Costs of Renewable and Conventional Energy Sources." Accessed March 8, 2016. http://energyinnovation.org/2015/02/07/levelized-cost-of-energy/.
3. The Carbon Underground. 2016. "Why just reduce climate change when we can reverse it?" Accessed March 8, 2016. https://www.thecarbonunderground.org/.
4. *Smithsonian.* 2015. "Is a Lack of Water to Blame for the Conflict in Syria?" Accessed March 8, 2016. http://www.smithsonianmag.com/innovation/is-a-lack-of-water-to-blame-for-the-conflict-in-syria-72513729/?no-ist.
5. Wijkman, Anders & Skånberg, Kristian. 2014. *The Circular Economy and Benefits for Society. Jobs and Climate Clear Winners in an Economy based on Renewable Energy and Resource Efficiency.* Club of Rome.
6. Ellen Macarthur Foundation. 2013. "Towards the Circular Economy." Accessed March 8, 2016. http://www.ellenmacarthurfoundation.org/assets/downloads/publications/TCE_Report-2013.pdf.
7. *Ibid.*
8. Wijkman, Anders & Skånberg, Kristian. 2014. *The Circular Economy and Benefits for Society. Jobs and Climate Clear Winners in an Economy based on Renewable Energy and Resource Efficiency.* Club of Rome.
9. Wilenius, Markku. 1997. *Faust on Wheels. Conceptualizing Modernization and Global Climate Change.* The Finnish Society of Sciences and Letters and The Finnish Academy of Science and Letters. Helsinki. Doctoral Dissertation.
10. Von Weizsäcker, Ernst U. 2009. *Factor Five: Transforming the Global Economy through 80% Improvements in Resource Productivity.* London: Routledge.
11. Global Footprint Network, 2015. "Earth Overshoot Day 2015." Last accessed March 8, 2016. http://www.footprintnetwork.org/en/index.php/GFN/page/earth_overshoot_day/.
12. Meadows, Donella H., Meadows, Dennis L., Randers, Jørgen, and Behrens III, William W. 1972. *The Limits to Growth: A Report of the Club of Rome's Project on the Predicament of Mankind.* New York: Universe Books.

13. Club of Rome. 2015. The Circular Economy and Benefits for Society. Accessed January 24, 2017. http://www.clubofrome.org/wp-content/uploads/2016/03/The-Circular-Economy-and-Benefits-for-Society.pdf.
14. Bardi, Ugo. 2014. *Extracted: How the Quest for Mineral Wealth is Plundering the Planet: A Report to the Club of Rome.* Vermont: Chelsea Green Publishing.
15. Sverdrup, Harald & Ragnarsdottir, Vala. 2014. Natural resources in a planetary perspective. *Geochemical Perspectives*, **3**(2).
16. *Ibid.*
17. World Economic Forum. 2016. "The Fourth Industrial Revolution, by Klaus Schwab." Accessed March 8, 2016. http://www.weforum.org/pages/the-fourth-industrial-revolution-by-klaus-schwab.
18. Rifkin, Jeremy. 2011. *The Third Industrial Revolution: How Lateral Power is Changing, The Economy and the World.* New York: St Martin's Press.
19. Podolny, Shelley. 2015. "If an Algorithm Wrote This, How Would you Even Know?" The New York Times. Accessed 7 March 2015. http://www.nytimes.com/2015/03/08/opinion/sunday/if-an-algorithm-wrote-this-how-would-you-even-know.html.
20. Castells, Manuel. 2014. "The Impact of the Internet on Society: A Global Perspective." MIT Technology Review. Accessed March 8, 2016. https://www.technologyreview.com/s/530566/the-impact-of-the-internet- on-society-a-global-perspective/.
21. Internet Live Stats. 2016. "Internet Users." Accessed March 8, 2016. http://www.internetlivestats.com/internet-users/.
22. Hilbert, Martin & Lopez, Priscila. 2011. "The World's Technological Capacity to Store, Communicate, and Compute Information in Science." Accessed March 8, 2016. http://science.sciencemag.org/content/332/6025/60.
23. Castells, Manuel. 2014. "The Impact of the Internet on Society: A Global Perspective." MIT Technology Review. Accessed March 8, 2016. https://www.technologyreview.com/s/530566/the-impact-of-the-internet-on-society-a-global-perspective/.
24. Acemoglu, Daron & Robinson, James. 2012. *Why Nations Fail. The Origins of Power, Prosperity and Poverty.* London: Profile Books.
25. Transparency International. 2015. "Corruptions Perception Index 2015." Accessed March 8, 2016. http://www.transparency.org/cpi2015#results-table.
26. OECD. 2015. "Divided We Stand: Why Inequality Keeps Rising." Accessed September13, 2016. http://www.oecd.org/els/soc/dividedwestandwhyinequalitykeepsrising.htm.

27. *Business Insider.* 2016. "Here is the letter the world's largest investor, BlackRock CEO Larry Fink, just sent to CEOs everywhere." Accessed March 8, 2016. http://uk.businessinsider.com/blackrock-ceo-larry-fink-letter-to-sp-500-ceos-2016-2.
28. Yoffie, David & Cusumano, Michael. 2015. *Strategy Rules.* New York: Harper Business.
29. *Ibid.*
30. *Ibid.*
31. See this quotation https://www.outsideonline.com/1910236/let-my-people-go-surfing, accessed September 25, 2016. Read more of his thoughts in Chouinard, Yvon. 2005. *Let My People Go Surfing: The Education of a Reluctant Businessman.* London: Penguin Books.
32. Laloux, Frederic. 2014. *Reinventing Organizations.* Brussels: Nelson Parker.
33. Ashton, Kevin. 2015. *How to Fly a Horse: The Secret History of Creation, Invention and Discovery.* New York: Doubleday.
34. Jos de Blok, Interview. https://www.thersa.org/discover/videos/event-videos/2014/11/Jos-de-Blok-on-Organizational-Structures.

EPILOGUE: TOWARDS A COOPERATIVE SOCIETY

If we look at the history of the world, it is hard to miss that all true societal progress involves cooperation. The European Union is a great invention just because it has compelled European countries to cooperate in unprecedented ways. In the future, we shall see new cooperative forms that again enhance our chances to survive as species.

All this happens while the future is being formed by a perpetual motion of dynamic changes, which makes it so hard to predict. As described in this book, we do have the patterns that link past, present and future. But recognizing discontinuations is another major challenge of the academic discipline of futures studies.[1]

Let us look at a particular case here.[2] A group of 160 experts and influencers were gathered for a project at the beginning of the millennium, whose task was to contemplate and report on what the world and Finland would look like in 2015. What did they predict correctly and where were they dead wrong?

Though they highlighted the growing effect of globalization, they did not predict the immense effect of the growth in China. They also did not foresee the direction Russia would take but were unrealistically optimistic about its future development. The group also could not predict the radicalization of Islam, nor the spread of religious conservatism.

Even if they were able to foresee the growing role of information networks, they were completely blind to the growth of social media. The risks in global warming were ignored, even though its effects are now palpable. They were not able to foresee the risks in the European monetary union or the vast growth of the importance of the European Union in our politics in general.

Strategist George Friedman has made an interesting point regarding our perspective of change in the course of history: Even if we take only a 20-year forward-perspective, it is hard to understand the future if we allow ourselves to think it is just more of the same. History shows that things change more than what we can possibly imagine, even in only 20 years.[3]

In 1900, Europe pretty much ruled the world and there was great prosperity around, due to a long period of peace. People tended to think that the wars were over and Europe would continue to rule the world. Only 20 years later Europe was drained by wars, most of the empires such as the Austro-Hungarian, German, Russian, and Ottoman were pushed into history. United States had with its troops put end to a war, showing its great power. In the 1940s, Germany was again strongman in Europe and it was only Britain which could prevent it (or the Soviet army) from ruling over other European countries. Twenty years later, while Germany was defeated, the Cold War was full on with two superblocks that overruled Europe. In the 1980s, the United States had just lost the war with communist North Vietnam and the Soviet Union's power was in its height. The communist movement was still doing well in China. Stepping to 2000, the Soviet Union was ousted from the map, China had turned into a great economic power and the European Union was still without its massive deficit problems.

In 2020 we may again have quite a different situation, based on current events. What is the state of Russia at that time? Where is Europe then, now that we are about to experience Brexit? What has happened with China, which is now showing heavy signs of slowing down? Brazil, too, shaken by economic recession and political turmoil, is undergoing tremendous change.

What do we learn from the past?

First, it is hard to foresee the dynamics of change. It is easy to underestimate longer-range changes. We also don't readily understand how much of the old gets destroyed in the process of creating the new. The arrival of the digital era is a good example of this, and how it cornered the forest and media industries and destroyed the growth of their businesses. The crux of such occurrences are lifestyle changes, which often get ignored or simply left in the background.

Second, it is difficult to understand the decelerators that make change difficult. The staunch institutions of society defend their own benefits: the employers theirs, the employees their own and so on. Institutions don't typically seek change, but rather they seek to preserve the status quo and fortify their positions. They are not willing to give up anything. That is why we are unable to quickly react to changes.

Third, we never seem able to sustain exponential growth or to survive quick downshifts, because we always expect a linear progression. Fast growth almost always includes factors with systemic, holistic consequences. The growth of the Chinese economy has irrevocably affected the world economy in a way that can't solely be traced back to the growth of China. The rapid melting of the polar icecaps is also a systemic change and therefore was once hard to predict.

Finally, changes in deep cultural structures are the most difficult to achieve. They are foreign territory for us. Even though we can perhaps explain, post-fact, the birth of radical Islamic terrorist organization ISIS, to predict it one would have had to delve extremely deeply into all the possibilities that existed before the organization even saw daylight.

I believe that it is possible to predict fundamental shifts and even catastrophic events. Another matter altogether is that if one offers opinions that differ radically from those held by the powers that be, hardly anyone will believe you. As described in Chapter 2, the economist Nouriel Roubini had a complex awareness of the factors leading to the crash of the housing market and to the financial crisis. When he was the only influential economist to (accurately) predict the start of the crisis in 2006, he was laughed at.[4] Being the harbinger is not necessarily a meritorious job.

His prediction was accurate, because he observed the developments systemically or "holistically," as he has himself described. For an economist, he has an exceptionally multifaceted and multicultural background. He understands analogies: He saw that the same patterns that took some of the Asian developing nations into a crisis in the end of the 1990s repeated in the United States Economy of the 2000s. He estimated the joint effect of the developments and was able to predict, with an accuracy of the exact month, the fall of the two financial houses — Lehmann Brothers and Bear Stearns.

The Kondratiev cycles are a similar formula by which one can understand future events through the past. For the formula to work, one has to adapt a holistic approach, which is what I have done in this book. The formula seeks to understand discontinuations while taking advantage of historical analogies. The same multi-dimensional and holistic change that took place as information and communication technology developed — coupled with the ever-growing need of individuals to communicate — is about to occur again.

This time it will happen through new energy and material technology, combined with the human need to use resources more intelligently and with more awareness. This progress requires deeper interaction in all areas of life, and it requires developing *a human-centric culture.*

What do I mean? If one seeks to concretely bring it to the level of an organization, three principles can be deduced, which I predict will grow in importance in the coming decades. I call these the principles of a cooperative society.

(1) Proper organizational functioning is founded on co-creation and quality. The customer is not at the end of the chain but rather a partner in the development of products and services. This requires mutual trust.
(2) The input of all employees is appreciated holistically. It's critical that individuals are socially adept and mature, in addition to being masters within their profession. Each employee is also empowered to make decisions and carry responsibility.

Hierarchical structures are minimized; there are simply various positions.

(3) There is no need for separate workplace and private identities in the new working society. Everyone has the right to be themselves and enjoy their work as their authentic selves. Honoring the uniqueness of each individual lays the foundation for the well-being of a sustainable work organization.

The era that is developing will not only be intelligent but also conscious. Its true engine is the human need to be whole. All human needs — intellectual, emotional and physical — must be recognized and respected. The end result is a human who understands him- or herself ever better.

Thus, because systemic thinking helps us to understand nature through co-creation rather than through competition, the actual sixth-wave society can only come about through increased awareness and a better quality of human interaction.[5]

What kind of democracy do we need in the future? Is it possible to create a political system where citizens can directly participate in political decision-making? Baby steps in this direction have been taken in many countries though Switzerland stands out as an example, where direct democracy has been at work almost for 200 years. There it works as follows: after a new law is being published, any citizen can try to gather a minimum of 50,000 signatures within 100 days of its publication to bring the new law to a general vote. Morever, with 100,000 signatures, you may propose any constitutional amendment which then will be voted upon.[6] Other countries are now following suit, at least on local levels. Local direct democracy is strengthening in many parts of Europe.[7] In Finland citizens can now undertake any initiative that can be enacted by law, and once 50,000 signatures have been obtained in support of the initiative, parliament must then review and discuss the initiative. The first initiative approved by the parliament was the law on equal marriage in the fall of 2014.

The sixth wave will undoubtedly bring about a transition to different kinds of expressions of direct popular power. Even politics can't function analogically in a society based on digital communication. Estonia, as a first country in the world, has bravely embraced electronic voting in their elections,[8] medical records travel smoothly through digital channels and every citizen has an electronic ID that allows them to review their own information on any computer. Many other countries are behind the curve in this regard, but in the next decennium it will be markedly simpler to search for information and to exert influence. The sixth wave is marked by speed, transparency and increasing opportunities to influence.

But above all, the sixth wave must end the destruction of natural resources and the biosphere of our planet. Avoiding the destruction of nature requires increased critical awareness and deeper cooperation for the common good.

My faith in the future of humanity rests upon this.

References

1. Rohrbeck, René. 2011. *Corporate Foresight: Towards a Maturity Model for the Future Orientation of a Firm.* Berlin: Springer Verlag; Casti, John & Wilenius, Markku. 2015. Seizing the X-Events: The Sixth Wave and the Shocks that May Upend It. *Technological Forecasting and Social Change*, **94**, 335–349.
2. Valjakka, Ari. "What Should We See When We Look Into the Year 2040?" Turun Sanomat 24.2.2015.
3. Friedman, George. 2009. *The Next 100 Years. A Forecast for 21st Century.* London: Allison & Busby.
4. *The Guardian.* 2009. "He Told Us So." Accessed March 8, 2016. http://www.theguardian.com/business/2009/jan/24/nouriel-roubini-credit-crunch.
5. *Ibid.*
6. *The Telegraph.* 2007 "How direct democracy makes Switzerland a better place." Accessed September 9, 2016. http://www.telegraph.co.uk/news/1435383/How-direct-democracy-makes-Switzerland-a-better-place.html.
7. Schiller, Theo. 2011. Local direct democracy in Europe — a comparative overview. In: Schiller, Theo (Ed.). *Local direct democracy in Europe*, Wiesbaden: Springer.
8. E-Estonia.com. 2016. "I-voting." Accessed September 9, 2016. https://e-estonia.com/component/i-voting/.

FURTHER READING

Acemoglu, Daron & Robinson, James. 2012. *Why Nations Fail. The Origins of Power, Prosperity and Poverty.* London: Profile Books.

Ackermann, Tjitske, de Lange, Sarah L. and Rooduijn, Matthis (Eds.) 2016. *Radical Right-Win Populist Parties in Europe. Into the Mainstream?* New York: Routledge.

Ahokas, Jussi, Honkatukia, Juha, Lehmus, Markku, Niemi, Janne, Simola, Antti and Tamminen, Saara. 2015. *Työvoiman tarve Suomen taloudessa vuosina 2015–2030.* VATT Research 181. Helsinki: VATT Institute for Economic Research.

Ashton, Kevin. 2015. *How to Fly a Horse: The Secret History of Creation, Invention and Discovery.* New York: Doubleday.

Auffermann, Burkhard, Suomela, Pertti, Kaivo-oja, Jari, Vehmas, Jarmo and Luukkanen, Jyrki. 2015. A final solution for a big challenge: The governance of nuclear waste disposal in Finland. In: Brunnengräber, Achim; Nucci, Maria Rosaria; Isidoro Losada, Ana Maria; Mez, Lutz and Schreurs, Miranda (Eds.) *Nuclear Waste Governance. An International Comparison.* Wiesbaden: Springer-Verlag.

Bardi, Ugo. 2014. *Extracted: How the Quest for Mineral Wealth is Plundering the Planet: A Report to the Club of Rome.* Vermont: Chelsea Green Publishing.

Barrett, Richard. 2006. *Value Driven Organisation: A Whole System Approach to Cultural Transformation.* Amsterdam: Butterworth & Heinemann.

Bauman, Zygmunt. 2000. *The Individualized Society.* Cambridge: Polity Press.

Baumeister, Roy & Tierney, John. 2011. *Willpower: Rediscovering the Greatest Human Strength.* London: Penguin Books.

Beck, Ulrich & Beck-Gernsheim, Elisabeth. 2002. *Individualization: Institutionalized Individualism and its Social and Political Consequences.* London: Sage Publications.

Bruch, Heike & Vogel, Bernd. 2011. *Fully Charged: How Great Leaders Boost their Organization's Energy and Ignite High Performance.* Boston: Harvard Business Review Press.

Casti, John. 2010. *Mood Matters: From Rising Skirt Lengths to the Collapse of World Powers.* New York: Harper Collins.

Casti, John & Wilenius, Markku. 2015. Seizing the X-events: the sixth K-wave and the shocks that may upend it. *Technological Forecasting and Social Change.* 94, 335–349.

Charan, Ram. 2013. *Global Tilt: Leading Your Business through the Great Economic Power Shift.* New York: Crown Business.

Chatwin, Bruce. 1982. *What Am I Doing Here?* London: Penguin Books.

Chouinard, Yvon. 2005. *Let My People Go Surfing: The Education of a Reluctant Businessman.* London: Penguin Books.

Collier, Paul. 2013. *Immigration and Multiculturalism in the 21st Century.* Penguin Books.

Collins, James. 2001. *Good to Great: Why Some Companies Make the Leap... and Others Don't.* New York: Harper Business.

Coyle, Diane. 2011. *The Economics of Enough: How to Run the Economy as if the Future Matters.* New Jersey: Princeton University Press.

Costa, Rebecca. 2010. *The Watchman's Rattle: A Radical New Theory of Collapse.* Philadelphia: Vanguard Press.

Dai, Aiguo. 2011. Drought Under Global Warming. A Review. *WIREs Climate Change*, 2, 45–65.

Davidson, Richard. 2012. *The Emotional Life of Your Brain.* New York: Hudson Street Press.

Devezas, Tessaleno. 2006. *Kondratieff Waves, Warfare and World Security.* Amsterdam: IOS Press.

Diamandis, Peter & Kotler, Steven. 2012. *Abundance: The Future Is Better Than You Think.* New York: Free Press.

Diamond, Jared. 2005. *Collapse: How Societies Choose to Fail or Succeed.* Penguin Books.

Fisher, E. M. & Knutti, R. 2015. Anthropogenic contribution to global occurrence of heavy-precipitation and high-temperature extremes. *Nature Climate Change*, 5, 560–564.

Flannery, Tim. 2010. *Here on Earth: A Twin Biography of the Planet and the Human Race.* London: Penguin Books.

Friedman, George. 2009. *The Next 100 Years. A Forecast for 21st Century.* London: Allison & Busby.

Giddens, Anthony. 1991. *Modernity and Self-Identity.* Cambridge, UK: Polity Press.

Glaser, Charles. 2010. *Rational Theory of International Politics: The Logic of Competition and Cooperation.* New Jersey: Princeton University Press.

Goleman, Daniel. 2013. *The Hidden Driver of Excellence.* New York: Bloomsbury.

Gorbis, Marina. 2013. *The Nature of the Future. Dispatches from the Social-Structured World.* New York: Free Press.

Halme, Minna, Hukkinen, Janne, Korppi-Tommola, Jouko, Linnanen, Lassi, Liski, Matti, Loivio, Raimo, Lund, Peter, Luukkanen, Jyrki, Nokso-Koivisto, Oskari, Partanen, Jarmo and Wilenius, Markku. 2014. *New Energy Policy for Providing Growth and Employment.* Jyväskylä University Digital Archive.

Halme *et al.* (2015). Maamme energia (The Energy of our Country). Into Kustannus, Helsinki.

Heinonen, Srikka. & Ruotsalainen, Juho 2013. Futures clinique — method for promoting futures learning and provoking radical futures. *European Journal for Futures Research*, 15(7).

Isaacson, Walter. 2011. *Steve Jobs.* New York: Simon & Schuster.

Jacobs, Michael & Mazzucato, Mariana. 2015. Rethinking capitalism: An introduction. In: Jacobs, Michael & Mazzucato, Mariana (Eds.). *Rethinking Capitalism. Economics and Policy for Sustainable and Inclusive Growth.* New York: Wiley Blackwell.

Keeling, Charles. 1998. Rewards and penalties of monitoring the earth. *Annual Review Energy Environment*, 23, 25–82.

Kekkonen, Urho. 1952. *Does Our Country Have the Patience to Prosper?* Helsinki: Otava.

Klare, Michael. 2013. *The Race for What's Left. The Global Scramble for the World's Last Resources.* New York: Picador.

Klein, Naomi. 2014. *This Changes Everything. Capitalism vs Climate.* New York: Simon & Schuster.

Kondratiev, Nikolai. 1984. *The Long Wave Cycle.* Guy Daniels, trans. New York: Richardson & Snyder.

Kouzes, James & Posner, Barry. 2006. *A Leader's Legacy.* San Francisco: Jossey-Bass.

Krausmann Fridolin, Gingrich, Simone, Eisenmenger, Nina, Erb Karl-Heinz, Haberl, Helmut & Fischer-Kowalski, Marina. 2012. Growth in global materials use, GDP and population during the 20th century. *Ecological Economics*, 68(10), 2696–2705.

Kurki, Sofi & Wilenius, Markku. 2015. Ethics in the sixth wave: How new ethical companies will transform our economies in the coming decades. *Futures*, 71, 146–158.

Kurki, Sofi, Puro, Minna & Wilenius, Markku. 2016. *Re-acting the Future. The New Ways to Work: The Case of Reaktor.* FFRC eBooks 8/2016. Finland Futures Research Centre, University of Turku.

Kurzweil, Ray. 2012. *How to Create a Mind: The Secret of Human Thought Revealed.* London: Viking.

Laloux, Frederic. 2014. *Reinventing Organizations.* Brussels: Nelson Parker.

Lang, Sabine. 2013. *NGO's, Civil Society and the Public Space.* New York: Cambridge University Press.

Laurance, William & Williamson, Bruce. 2001. Positive feedbacks among forest fragmentation, drought, and climate change in the amazon. *Conservation Biology*, 15(6), 1529–1535.

Lewis, Michael. 2009. *The Big Short: Inside the Doomsday Machine.* New York: W.W. Norton & Company.

Louçã, Francisco & Reijnders, Jan (Eds.) 1999. *The Foundations of Long Wave Theory. Volume I: Models and Methodology.* Cheltenham, UK: Edward Elgar.

Luyendijk, Joris. 2015. *Swimming with Sharks: My Journey into the World of the Bankers.* London: Guardian Faber.

Lutz, Wolfgang, Sanderson, Warren & Scherbov, Sergei. 2008. The coming acceleration of global population ageing. *Nature*, 451, 716–719.

Malaska, Pentti. 2010. *Planetary Statistical Service.* Helsinki: Futura.

Marshall, Tim. 2015. *Prisoners of Geography. Ten Maps That Tell You Everything You Need to Know about Global Politics.* London: Elliot & Thompson.

Maxton, Graeme & Randers, Jørgen. 2016. *Reinventing Prosperity. Managing Economic Growth to Reduce Unemployment, Inequality and Climate Change.* Vancouver: Greystone Books.

Mazzucato, Mariana. 2015. *The Entrepreneurial State.* London: Anthem Press.

Mazzucato, Mariana. 2016. Innovation, the state and patient capital. In: Jacobs, Michael & Mazzucato, Mariana (Eds.). *Rethinking Capitalism. Economics and Policy for Sustainable and Inclusive Growth.* New York: Wiley Blackwell.

Meadows Donella H., Meadows, Dennis L. & Randers Jørgen. 2004. *The 30-year update.* White River Junction: Chelsea Green Publishing.

Meadows, Donella H., Meadows, Dennis L., Randers, Jørgen & Behrens III, William W. 1972. *The Limits to Growth: A Report of the Club of Rome's Project on the Predicament of Mankind.* New York: Universe Books.

Mensch, Gerhard, Coutinho, Charles, and Kaasch, Klaus. 1981. Changing capital values and the propensity to innovate. *Futures*, 13(4), 276–292.

Mithen, Steven. 2003. *After the Ice: A Global Human History 20,000–5000 BC.* London: Orion Books.

Moody, James Bradfield & Novgrady, Bianca. 2010. *The Sixth Wave.* Australia: Random House.

Nandram, Sharda. 2015. *Organizational Innovation by Integrating Simplification.* Cham: Springer.

Neckermann, Lukas. 2015. *The Mobility Revolution: Zero Emissions, Zero Accidents, Zero Ownership.* London: Matador.

Norman, Donald. 2010. *Managing the Complexity.* Cambridge, MA: MIT Press.

Nye, Joseph. 2011. *The Future of Power.* New York: Public Affairs.

Nygrén, Nina, Kontio, Panu, Lyytimäki, Jari, Varho, Vilja & Tapio, Petri. 2015. Early adopters boosting the diffusion of sustainable small-scale energy solutions. *Renewable and Sustainable Energy Reviews*, 46, 79–87.

Nykänen, Pekka & Salminen, Merina. 2014. *Operation Elop.* Helsinki: Teos.

Nyman, Göte. 2015. University-business-government collaboration: From institutes to platforms and ecosystems. *Triple Helix*, 2(2), 1–20.

Nyman, Göte & Wilenius, Markku 2014. *What Are We Good for? Challenges of Education in Finland.* Helsinki: Sitra.

Pauli, Gunter. 2010. *Blue Economy. 10 Years, 100 Innovations, 100 Million Jobs.* Taos: Paradigm Publications.

Perez, Carlota. 2016. Capitalism, Technology and Green Global Age: The Role of History in Helping to shape the Future. In: Jacobs, Michael & Mazzucato, Mariana (Eds.). *Rethinking Capitalism. Economics and Policy for Sustainable and Inclusive Growth.* New York: Wiley Blackwell.

Piscione Perry, Deborah. 2013. *Secrets of Silicon Valley: What Everyone Else Can Learn from the Innovation Capital of the World.* New York: Palgrave McMillan.

Puustinen, Pekka. 2015. *FinancialServiceLogic: In the Revolution of Exchange in Banking and Insurance.* Helsinki: Helsinki Capital Partners Advisory.

Randers, Jørgen. 2012. *2052: Global Forecast for the Next 40 Years.* White River Junction: Chelsea Green Publishing.

Rapaille, Clotaire. 2007. *The Culture Code: An Ingenious Way to Understand Why People Around the World Live and Buy as They Do.* New York: Crown Business

Rifkin, Jeremy. 2011. *The Third Industrial Revolution. How Lateral Power Is Changing the Economy and the World.* New York: St Martin's Press.

Rohrbeck, René. 2011. *Corporate Foresight: Towards a Maturity Model for the Future Orientation of a Firm.* Berlin: Springer Verlag.

Saarikoski, Pentti. 1962. *What is Really Happening.* Helsinki: Otava.

Santonen, Teemu, Kaivo-oja, Jari & Suomala, Jyrki. 2014. The next steps in developing the triple helix model: A brief introduction to national open innovation system (NOIS) paradigm. *Journal on Systemics, Cybernetics and Informatics*, 12(7), 74–82.

Schiller, Theo. 2011. Local direct democracy in Europe — a comparative overview. In: Schiller, Theo (Ed.). *Local Direct Democracy in Europe.* Wiesbaden: Springer.

Schumpeter, Joseph. 1939. *Time Series and Their Normal in Business Cycles: A Theoretical, Historical and Statistical Analysis of the Capitalist Process.* Volume I. Chapter V. New York: McGraw-Hill Book Company.

Sharma, Ruchir. 2013. *Breakout Nations: In Pursuit of the Next Economic Miracles.* New York: W.W. Norton & Co.

Smith, Adam. 2007. An inquiry into the nature and causes of the wealth of nations. Metalibri. Originally published in 1776.

Smith, Greg. 2012. *Why I left Goldman Sachs.* New York: Grand Central Publishing.

Sorkin, Andrew Ross. 2009. *Too Big to Fail. The Inside Story of how Wall Street, and Washington, Fought to Save the Financial System — and themselves.* Viking.

Stiglitz, Joseph E. 2016. Inequality and economic growth. In: Jacobs, Michael & Mazzucato, Mariana (Eds.). *Rethinking Capitalism. Economics and Policy for Sustainable and Inclusive Growth.* Wiley Blackwell.

Stuenkel, Oliver. 2015. *The BRICS and the Future of Global Order.* Lanham: Lexington Books.

Sverdrup, Harald & Ragnarsdottir, Vala. 2014. Natural resources in a planetary perspective. *Geochemical perspectives.* 3(2), 129–341.

Tainter, Joseph. 1988. *The Collapse of Complex Societies.* Cambridge: Cambridge University Press.

Taleb, Nassim Nicolas. 2007. *Black Swan. The Impact of the Highly Improbable.* New York: Random House.

Tapscott, Don & Williams, Anothony. 2010. *Macrowikinomics: Rebooting Business and the World.* London: Atlantic Books.

Tuomi, Ilkka. 2012. Foresight in an unpredictable world. *Technology Analysis & Strategic Management*, 24(8), 735–751.

Vance, Ashlee. 2015. *Elon Musk: Tesla, SpaceX, and the Quest for a Fantastic Future.* New York: Ecco Press.

Varis, Olli. 2014. Resources: Curb vast water use in central Asia. *Nature*, 1, 27–29.

Vilen, Merita & Rumpunen, Risto. 2014. *The Impossible Fall of Nokia.* Helsinki Area, Finland: Moimedia.

Von Weizsäcker, Ernst U. 2009. *Factor Five: Transforming the Global Economy through 80% Improvements in Resource Productivity.* London: Routledge.

Von Wright, Georg H. 1971. *Explanation and Understanding.* Ithaca: Cornell University Press.

Wallerstein, Immanuel. 2003. *The Decline of American Power.* New York: The New Press.

Weiner, Jonathan. 1991. *The Next Hundred Years.* London: Bantam Books.

Whyte, William. 1957. *The Organization Man.* New York: Doubleday Anchor Books.

Wijkman, Anders & Skånberg, Kristian. 2014. *The Circular Economy and Benefits for Society. Jobs and Climate Clear Winners in an Economy based on Renewable Energy and Resource Efficiency.* Club of Rome.

Wilenius, Markku. 2014. Leadership in the sixth wave. Excursions into the new paradigm of the Kondratieff cycle 2010–2050. *European Journal of Futures Research*, 2(36), 1–11.

Wilenius, Markku. 2006. *Towards a Creative Economy: Cultural Competence as a Future Resource.* Helsinki: Edita.

Wilenius, Markku. 1997. *Faust on Wheels. Conceptualizing Modernization and Global Climate Change.* The Finnish Society of Sciences and Letters and The Finnish Academy of Science and Letters. Helsinki. Doctoral Dissertation.

Wilenius, Markku & Kurki, Sofi. 2012. Surfing the Sixth Wave. *Exploring the Next Wave of Global Change.* FFRC eBook 10/2012. Finland Futures Research Centre, University of Turku.

Yi, Lo, Lawal, Billab, and Ajit, Singha. 2004. Effect of climate change on seasonal monsoon in Asia and its impact on the variability of monsoon rainfall in southeast Asia. *Geoscience Frontiers*, 6(6), 817–823.

Yoffie, David & Cusumano, Michael. 2015. *Strategy Rules.* New York: Harper Business.

Yunus, Muhammed. 2011. *Building Social Business. The New Kind of Capitalism that Serves Humanity's Most Pressing Needs.* New York: Public Affairs.

Index

P

R

S

T

U

V

W

Y

Things to do

* Thank M.W. for book
* Mail [illegible]: [illegible]
* Send [illegible] article to [illegible]
*

Lightning Source UK Ltd.
Milton Keynes UK
UKHW02f1337120918
328768UK00007B/125/P